TALKING DATA:
TRANSCRIPTION AND CODING
IN DISCOURSE RESEARCH

Edited by

Jane A. Edwards
University of California at Berkeley

and

Martin D. Lampert
Holy Names College &
University of California at Berkeley

LAWRENCE ERLBAUM ASSOCIATES, PUBLISHERS
1993   Hillsdale, New Jersey   Hove and London

Lawrence Erlbaum Associates, Inc., Publishers
365 Broadway
Hillsdale, New Jersey 07642

Library of Congress Cataloging-in-Publication Data

Talking data : transcription and coding in discourse research / edited
by Jane Edwards, Martin D. Lampert.
   p. cm.
Includes bibliographic references and index.
ISBN 0-8058-0348-3 (cloth). -- ISBN 0-8058-0349-1 (paper)
  1. Transcription. 2. Linguistics--Notation. 3. Discourse
analysis. 4. Computational linguistics. I. Edwards, Jane Anne.
II. Lampert, Martin D.
P226.T35 1992
401'.41--dc20
                             92-18274
                             CIP

Printed in the United States of America
10 9 8 7 6 5 4 3 2

Contents

Part III. Resources

PREFACE

This book presents the reader with a set of diverse, carefully developed and clearly specified systems of transcription and coding, arising from contrasting theoretical perspectives, and presented as alternative choices, situated within the theoretical domain most natural to each. The perspectives represented in the book include first and second language acquisition, interethnic and cross-cultural interaction, information structure, and the study of discourse influences on linguistic expression.

In the contributed chapters, the designers of these systems provide a distillation of collective experiences from the past quarter century, telling in their own words their perspectives on language processes, and how these perspectives have shaped their choice of methodology in transcription and coding of natural language, and describing their systems in detail. Overview chapters by the co-editors then provide design principles and guidelines, concerning issues pertinent to all systems, including such things as reliability, validity, ease of learning, computational tractability, and robustness against error. The final chapter is a compendium of existing computerized archives of language data and information sources, together with details concerning data access and use.

This book is intended for use in undergraduate and graduate level courses in a wide range of disciplines including linguistics, psychology, anthropology, sociology, education, and communication studies. It is also intended as a handbook for established researchers who are interested in preparing transcribed and/or coded data or locating and utilizing transcribed and coded data of others.

This volume reflects the effort of a number of people. We are indebted to our individual contributors for their thoughtful chapters. We are also grateful to the staff at the Berkeley Institute of Cognitive Studies, Linda Daetwyler, Michael Robinson, Katherine Turner, and Florence Wong, for their assistance during production, to our colleagues at the Institute for their advice and support, and to the Alfred P. Sloan Foundation for a grant to the Berkeley Cognitive Sciences Program (Grant No. 86-10-3), which made final completion of this project possible. We would also like to extend a special thanks to Judi Amsel at Lawrence Erlbaum Associates for her invaluable guidance and to our families for their consistent support, interest, and encouragement over the years, and for teaching us the rewards of perseverance when exploring new territory, the pleasures of a job well done, and the value of humor to keep it all in perspective.

Jane A. Edwards
Martin D. Lampert

Contributors

Norine Berenz
Institute of Cognitive Studies
University of California
at Berkeley

Lois Bloom
Teachers College
Columbia University

Wallace L. Chafe
Linguistics Program
University of California
at Santa Barbara

Susanna Cumming
Linguistics Program
University of Colorado
at Boulder

John W. Du Bois
Linguistics Program
University of California
at Santa Barbara

Jane A. Edwards
Institute of Cognitive Studies
University of California
at Berkeley

Konrad Ehlich
Institut für deutsche Sprache und
Literatur
Universität Dortmund, Germany

Susan M. Ervin-Tripp
Psychology Department
University of California
at Berkeley

John J. Gumperz
Anthropology Department
University of California
at Berkeley

Martin D. Lampert
Psychology Department
Holy Names College

Danae Paolino
Linguistics Program
University of California
at Santa Barbara

Stephan Schuetze-Coburn
Linguistics Department
University of California
at Los Angeles

Dan I. Slobin
Psychology Department,
University of California
at Berkeley

I TRANSCRIPTION

1

Principles and Contrasting Systems of Discourse Transcription

Jane A. Edwards
University of California at Berkeley

1. INTRODUCTION

The transcript plays a central role in research on spoken discourse, distilling and freezing in time the complex events and aspects of interaction in categories of interest to the researcher. When well-suited to the theoretical orientation and research question, the transcript enables the researcher to focus efficiently on the fleeting events of an interaction with a minimum of irrelevant and distracting detail. However, choices made concerning what types of information to preserve (or to neglect), what categories to use, and how to organize and display the information in a written and spatial medium can all affect the impressions the researcher derives from the data.

For example, arranging speaker turns one above the other gives the impression of symmetry and mutual interdependence between speakers, whereas arranging them in columns, one for each speaker, can give the impression of an asymmetry between them, with the left-most being the most dominant (Ochs, 1979). Whereas vertical arrangement is adequate for adult–adult conversations, it would be misleading for adult conversations with very young children, which are much more asymmetrical, child-centered and child-controlled. In this and similar ways no transcript is completely theory-neutral or without bias.

At issue in some sense is data accountability. While other issues of this type, such as the representativeness of language samples, and the methodology of describing interactional events have been carefully examined (e.g., in Bloom & Lahey, 1978; Garfinkel, 1967; Kucera, 1992; Kucera & Francis,

1967; Labov, 1972; Leech, 1991, 1992; Levinson, 1983; Svartvik, 1990, to name a few), transcription design has received relatively little attention. Typically, the conventions used in a project are listed in a short table without elaborate discussion, appended as supplementary information to the report of the research findings. To the degree that transcription conventions influence perceptions of the data, it seems important to consider them explicitly, and to systematically enumerate their underlying assumptions and implications for research. Such information is of use not only in arriving at the methods best suited for a particular purpose, but also in compensating for unwanted biases when using data transcribed by others.

A major focus of this book is the ways in which theoretical orientation and research methods shape the design of transcription and coding systems for spoken language. The chapters represent concrete alternatives from different academic disciplines (i.e., linguistics, anthropology, psychology, education, sociology) and theoretical orientations or research purposes (e.g., descriptive linguistics, discourse analysis, conversation analysis, psycholinguistics, crosslinguistic comparison, intercultural communication, and first and second language acquisition).

As background for the more detailed and systematic discussions in the chapters which follow, this chapter has two purposes. First, it discusses several general design principles which are involved in creating systems of discourse description, regardless of content domain or theoretical perspective. Second, it surveys a variety of specific alternative conventions from transcription systems represented in this book and from others in the literature at large, to sketch out the general dimensions of variation across systems and some of their underlying assumptions and implications for research.

Concerning general design principles, there have been several taxonomies of properties desireable in transcripts (Du Bois, 1991; Edwards 1989, 1992a, 1992b; Ehlich & Switalla, 1976; Johansson, 1991). These properties can be subsumed under two more general design goals: (1) that the transcript preserve the information needed by the researcher in a manner which is true to the nature of the interaction itself (termed "authenticity" by Johansson, 1991), and (2) that its conventions be practical with respect to the way in which the data are to be managed and analyzed, for example, easy to read, apply to new data sets, and expand if needed for other purposes (related to Johansson's "practicality"). The first half of this chapter concerns three types of principles subserving these goals, namely, principles of *category design*, *readability* and *computational tractability* of transcripts.

Concerning content-related differences between transcription systems, these are of mainly two types: choices of spatial organization of the information, and choices of the descriptive categories used. Tables of contrasting conventions across a variety of different systems are found in Ehlich and Rehbein (1979), Ehlich and Switalla (1976), and Johansson, Burnard, Edwards and Rosta (1992). A number of these are singled out for discussion in the second major section below, with the intent of highlighting major points of polarity and otherwise informative contrasts, together with differences in the theoretical perspectives which underly and motivate them.

We begin with the discussion of the general design properties.

2. PRINCIPLES UNDERLYING TRANSCRIPT DESIGN

The three types of general design principles, which pertain to discourse description regardless of content domain and research focus, are principles of category design, readability, and computational tractability, discussed separately below.

2.1. Principles of Category Design

In designing a category set for describing a dimension of interest, three properties are particularly important. First, the categories must be *systematically discriminable* in the sense that for every case in the data it is clear for every category whether or not it applies. In the classification of pause length, for example, there must be some basis for deciding between "short" or "long" pauses. Second, the categories needs to be *exhaustive*: For each particular case in the data there must be a category which fits (even if only "miscellaneous"). Third, and most importantly, the categories must be *systematically contrastive*. This requires some further discussion.

When categories are treated as mutually exclusive alternatives—that is, if only one can apply to any particular case in the data—the categories partially determine each other's boundaries. For example, the upper boundary of "short" pause depends on the lower boundary of "long" pause in the system. This is a property of language more generally—e.g., the use of one spatial preposition is determined in part by the other prepositions available for use in that language. Just as the number and type of prepositions differ across languages, so too the number and meaning of transcription categories differ across transcription systems. For example, a "short" pause in sociolinguistic research is often .5 seconds, whereas in research concerning idea units or information packaging, it may be only .2 seconds (see Edwards, 1991).

When categories are not mutually exclusive, as with speech act categories (i.e., the utterance "It's cold in here" can be interpreted as either an assertion about temperature or a polite request to close the door, or both), there is an implicit contrast between the presence and the absence of each individual conceptual property (e.g., presence vs. absence of "assertion"; presence vs. absence of "indirect request").

The researcher's task in choosing a set of descriptive categories is to exploit the contrastiveness of categories, that is, to choose categories which contrast in ways which are most likely to reveal the properties of interest in the research. (For more discussion of category properties, see Edwards, 1992a, 1992b; Lampert & Ervin-Tripp, this volume; concerning contrastiveness in language systems more generally, Lyons, 1977.)

2.2. Principles of Readability

If a transcript is to be analyzed mainly by reading through it line by line, it is important that information be preserved in a form which enables the researcher to extract the main information as quickly as possible without overburdening short term memory. In approaching a transcript, readers necessarily bring with them strategies developed in the course of extensive experience with other types of written materials (e.g., books, newspapers, train schedules, advertisements, personal letters). It makes sense for transcript designers to draw upon reader expectations in their choice of conventions, in part because readers are good at extracting information in these ways from other written materials, but also because strategies based on reading habits are not necessarily subject to conscious awareness and may be difficult to suspend when reading a transcript, even if it is desireable to do so.

Two cues used widely in print to channel reader attention and shape perceptions of the relative importance of different types of information and their degree of interrelationship are: *visual prominence* (e.g., bold face, underlining, font size) and *spatial arrangement* (e.g., nearness to other parts of the text, spatial precedence left to right or top to bottom). For example, chapter titles are expected to be printed in large font, centered, and placed above the body of the text at some vertical distance (rather than being embedded in the body of a text and in the same font size and type). Despite great differences in orientation and research purpose, in looking across transcripts of various types, one notices recurring uses of these cues in transcripts, to highlight information and relationships of interest. In what follows, I summarize six of them. (For more detail and additional examples, see Edwards, 1992a, 1992b.) Several of these overlap with properties mentioned by Du Bois (1991) and Johansson (1991).

Proximity of Related Events

Across transcription systems, events or types of information which are more closely related to each other tend to be placed spatially closer to each other than those that are less closely related. For example, prosodic information, such as prominent syllable stress, is often placed immediately beside the relevant syllable. Similarly, the London–Lund Corpus (Svartvik & Quirk, 1980) encodes the direction of nuclear pitch change by means of nonletter characters inserted on the utterance line, immediately before the relevant syllable (i.e., rise /, fall \, and fall–rise \ /):

(1) Svartvik and Quirk (1980), text S1.3
     1 3 7212280 1 1 A   11 and at ^h\ /ome# .
     1 3 7212290 1 1 A   11 she`s not a ^b\it the way she is at c/ollege#

An example of lesser proximity between prosodic and segmental information is the following:

(2) *MAR: ### oh # that was close!
     %int: <1,4> rising falling

in which prosodic information is placed on separate lines following the utterance, with numerical indices to indicate the relevant word or words on the utterance line (e.g., *<1-4> rising falling*, meaning the first four words were contained under a rising–falling intonation contour).

Visual Separability of Unlike Events

Readability is also improved if events or types of information that are qualitatively different (e.g., spoken words and researcher comments, codes and categories) are encoded in distinctly different ways (e.g., upper versus lower case letter, enclosed in parentheses versus not, letters versus nonalphabetic characters, full words versus abbreviations). These can enable the reader to know what kind of information is involved before actually reading it, and in this way greatly speed interpretation of a text and minimize false attributions (such as perceiving a word as having been spoken when it is actually part of the contextual specifications or research comments). An example is the use of parentheses to set off nonverbal events:

(3) Erickson & Shultz (1982, p. 42)

    (b-2) S: (shifts in chair)

                 I wanna go into counseling too, see...you know,
                 to have two way...like equal balance.

    (c)   C: I see. Ah...what do you know about counseling?

    (d)   S: Nothing. (Smiles and averts eyes, then looks up.)

    (e)   C: Okay...

In contrast, the visual separation of utterance and researcher metacomment is much less in the following example, in which they are separated only by a slash:

(4) *FAT: mm/thinking@q # those are good jokes.

Time–Space Iconicity

Typically in transcripts, temporally prior events are encountered earlier on the page (top to bottom or left to right) than temporally later events. This can include utterances, gestures, door slams, laughs, coughs, and so forth. In this way, temporal sequence is represented relatively directly as spatial sequence.

Logical Priority

For readability, logically prerequisite information for interpreting utterances tends to be encountered earlier on the page than the utterance or utterances to which it is relevant. Information concerning the circumstances of data gathering and the relationships among the speakers tends to be given at the top of the transcript, whereas changes in circumstances or activities during the course of the interaction tend to precede the utterances they contextualize or potentially influence.

Mnemonic Marking

Coded categories are encoded either in directly interpretable abbreviations or in symbolically iconic ways in order to expedite recovery of their meaning during rapid reading. An example of this is the use of a slash (/) for rising tone and backslash (\) for a falling tone, rather than vice versa or instead of an arbitrary numerical code (e.g., "1"). Another source of direct interpretability is a high level of familiarity from other written materials. Du Bois (1991) notes that a number of transcription conventions derive from literary conventions found in novels and plays, with which readers have extensive experience independently of transcript data. Some examples are the use of three dots (...) for pauses, or a dash (-) for interrupted thoughts or utterances. In some sense, time–space iconicity and logical priority (above) could be viewed as additional borrowings from familiar literary conventions.

Efficiency and Compactness

Reading speed can also be increased by marking coded distinctions with as few symbols as possible, so long as meaning is easily recoverable (i.e., encoded mnemonically), to minimize nonessential and distracting clutter in the transcript. For example, the use of slash (/) for rising tone is more compact and efficiently read than would be the use of the full word *rising*. The encoding of spoken words and prosodic information on the same line instead of on separate lines is also a type of compactness.

2.3. Principles for Computational Tractability

For computer analysis, the most important properties are *systematicity* and *predictability* of encoding. Computers interpret things literally, as instructed by the researcher or programmer. This can lead to two types of retrieval errors which can affect research results: *underselection*, that is, overlooking of relevant instances in the data; and *overselection*, that is, retrieval of nonrelevant instances along with relevant ones.

Underselection arises from unanticipated variants, which include pronunciation differences (e.g., *cause* for *because*, or the second person pronoun in *y'know, didja, didya,* etc.), spelling errors, and unexpected variation in punctuation, spacing, or code-syntax. It gives rise to nonexhaustive samples from the corpus, which can be unrepresentative of the data in unknown ways. Common ways of guarding against underselection include (1) providing a predictable standardized form alongside the variant in the online text itself (as in Gumperz and Berenz, this volume), (2) providing a conversion table, whose rows consist of all variants for each standard form in the data (e.g., *you—yknow, y'know, did ya, didja*), and (3) scanning an exhaustive listing of all forms in the data to visually detect likely variants prior to specifying the computer search. For further discussion, see Edwards (1992a, 1992b, and in press).

Overselection involves such things as retrieving unrelated words which just happen to contain the target sequence of letters (e.g., *along,* and *one,* when searching for *on*), and retrieving a word of interest from not only utterance lines but also comment lines in the data. Where the retrieved data are evaluated one utterance at a time following the search, the irrelevant items can be eliminated and present merely a nuisance. With the increasing tendency toward automatic analysis and tabulation, however, there is an increasing risk that such errors could harm results. This is commonly minimized by systematically marking things as different which are to be treated differently by search (e.g., setting comments and utterances apart by enclosing comments within brackets, or having them on separate lines prefixed by a different character string).

When systematically and predictably encoded, the data can be more easily reformatted into other visual displays types, as desired for the particular research purpose at hand. In service of this goal, the Text Encoding Initiative (TEI) (Burnard, 1991) has proposed the use of Standard Generalized Markup Language (SGML) to provide a systematic means of encoding distinctions needed across a variety of domains, ranging from music, poetry and historical literature to spoken language encoding. Each TEI workgroup surveyed the most widespread distinctions in use in their domains and proposed an SGML encoding of them to serve as a lingua franca between equivalent expressions in alternative systems. The format, itself verbose, is intended to be reformatted by filter programs (or interface software) into any number of directly readable formats. The TEI proposal for spoken language and coding is found in Johansson, Burnard, Edwards, and Rosta (1992).

3. CONTRASTING SYSTEMS AND THEIR IMPLICATIONS

With the principles in mind, we turn now to substantive differences between transcription systems, focusing first on spatial arrangement of information, and then on type and level of description.

3.1. Spatial Arrangement

Transcription systems differ with respect to: (1) spatial arrangement of turns by different speakers, and (2) spatial arrangement and representation of contextual comments, gestures, prosody, and coding, relative to utterances.

Spatial Arrangement of Speaker's Turns

There are three main arrangements of speaker turns, referred to here as *vertical, column,* and *partiture.*

(5) VERTICAL:
   A: Did you just get [back]?
   B: [Yes], or rather 2 hours ago. It was a great film.
   A: Really?

(6) COLUMN:

Speaker A	Speaker B
Did you just get [back]?	[Yes], or rather 2 hours ago.
	It was a great film.
Really?	

(7) PARTITURE:
   A: Did you just get [back]?   Really?
   B: [Yes], or rather 2 hours ago. It was a great film.

Each of these has its own strengths and weaknesses, depending on research purpose. As already noted, arranging speaker turns one above the other as in Vertical format biases the reader to perceive speakers as equally engaged and influential on the course of the interaction (Ochs 1979). This format is the most widely used.

In contrast, Column format is useful in highlighting asymmetries among interactants, such as those found in conversations between adults and young children, as these tend to be highly child-centered and child-controlled. This format is suggested for such cases by Ochs (1979) and used by Bloom (this volume) in her study of the interplay of infant gestures and vocalizations during language acquisition, and by Brown (1973) for interactions also with older children. Time is preserved in the vertical dimension, and simultaneous talk by two speakers may be marked explicitly (e.g., by brackets as in (6) above) or by being aligned horizontally, depending on the level of resolution of temporal marking desired.

Partiture format is highly efficient for capturing stretches of an interaction that involve many simultaneous utterances or actions. As described by Ehlich (this volume):

Semiotic events arrayed horizontally on a line follow each other in time, while events on the same vertical axis represent simultaneous acoustic events, produced by different musical instruments, such as the violin, the trumpet and the piano. (p. 129)

This format is used in Ehlich (this volume), Ervin-Tripp (1979), and Tannen (1984).   It is similar to Vertical format in implying equal communicative status of participants and emphasizing turn-taking; it is similar to Column format in preserving time consistently, though in this case in the horizontal rather than vertical dimension.   Its greatest strength is that it efficiently highlights the timing and sequencing of turns among conversational equals.   Overlaps are easily seen by drawing a line vertically across the staff. Its disadvantage is its special requirements for alignment of items when the transcript is corrected or modified, which however can be mitigated by specialized computer programs (see Ehlich, this volume).

Placement of Contextual Comments, Nonverbal Events, Prosody, and Coding

There are four choices of where to place these types of information relative to utterances.   These reflect two independent binary choices.   The first is whether nonverbal and contextual events are to be interleaved with utterances according to order of occurrence in time ("Running Text") or viewed as clarificational information to be attached to individual utterances ("Utterance-Plus-Clarification").   The second is whether added layers of specification should be placed on the same line as the general description of the event ("Interspersed"), or placed on separate tiers attached to it ("Segment-Plus-Specification").   These are described in detail below.

The principles of readability summarized earlier are derived from and collectively define the most commonly used style of transcription, which I call *Running Text* (RT) format due to its parallels with the methods used for preserving conversations in literary works (e.g., novels and plays).   In this format, utterances, nonverbal events and changes in context are arranged on the page in the same order as they occur in time (i.e., left to right and top to bottom).   The following examples, from several areas of language research, are typical:

(8)   Tedlock (1983, p. 112):
   In this case they are guided in that vision by the Ahayuuta
   and one of them impersonates a water-strider by stretching out his
      arms (stretch arms out horizontally to the sides)
   in the four directions, two at a time.
   When the priest does this he IS the water-strider and his arms DO
      reach all the way to the oceans:
   that is his experience.

(9) Atkinson & Heritage (1984, p. xiii):
Tom: I used to ((cough)) smoke a lot
Bob: ((sniff)) He thinks he's tough
Ann: ((snorts))

(10) Cook-Gumperz & Gumperz (1984):
A: It's a maze // but there's / .. and there's a drink down there /
    where Sherm told me to go before //
    (laughter)
S: Where have I told you to go // (laughter)
A: You told me that I / ...
J: The heated room //

(11) Bloom (1973, Alison, third data session):
(M and A sitting on chair; A wearing half-zippered jacket;
fingers in her mouth)
M: What did you see? What did you see over there?
(M points to monitor)
(A looking at monitor with fingers in her mouth)
A: Mommy/

With reference to the arrangement of speaker turns, these examples are in
Vertical format, but Partiture and Column versions of RT also exist (see,
respectively, Ehlich, this volume, and Bloom, this volume).

The systematic ordering of events (left to right and top to bottom)
according to their ordering in time, has the advantage of anchoring all events
to an external frame of reference (i.e., the time line). The uniform treatment of
all events with respect to time eases the perception of temporal structuring
(overlap, sequencing, rhythmic and other properties) of utterances with respect
to other potentially relevant contextual or communicative events. The level of
specification of time differs according to research purpose—from simple
ordering of events (in Examples 8 through 11 and many discourse approaches)
to systematic time tags throughout the discourse (see Bloom, this volume),
useful in linking the transcript with videotape or digitized speech records. The
level of specification of time can be increased if needed without the necessity
of reorganizing the system as a whole.

For reasons of its anchoring to an external reference frame, consistent
treatment of utterance and nonutterance events, and flexibility with respect to
level of temporal specificity, RT was also chosen as the basis of the encoding

system for spoken language proposed within the Text Encoding Initiative (Johansson et al., 1992), described earlier, intended for reliable automatic translation between alternative transcription systems, and flexible reformatting of a given data set into multiple visual formats. The focus of the TEI approach is systematic encoding by means of SGML (Standardized General Markup Language), used in combination with interface programs, which preserve the systematicities of the encoding but present the text to the user (for data entry, reading, and modification) in a format of choice to the user.

When the researcher wishes to provide specification for a particular event or segment of an event, two further choices present themselves. When the added information can be concisely and distinctively encoded, *Interspersed* format can be used, that is, the specification can be interleaved with the basic level description without loss of readability. In the following, prosodic information is interspersed with the (more general) orthographic rendering, discussed earlier as Example (1):

(12) Svartvik and Quirk (1980), text S1.3
    1 3 7212280 1 1 A   11 and at ^h\/ome# .
    1 3 7212290 1 1 A   11 she`s not a ^b\it the way she is at c/ollege#

As the level of complexity increases, or when users plan to focus selectively on some layers to the exclusion of others, it is common to place the specification on separate tiers, labeled as to type. For example, in the TOBI ("TOnes and Break Indices") system of prosodic encoding, proposed by Victor Zue (MIT), Kim Silverman (Nynex), and colleagues (Silverman et al., 1992), the orthographic rendering of the utterance is followed by three specification tiers:

1. a tone tier, for specifying the tonal properties of the fundamental frequency contour of the utterance (this tier has a shorthand notation that marks pitch accents with an asterisk but does not label the tonal attributes);
2. a break-index tier, for specifying the degree of disjuncture between words in the orthographic transcription; and
3. a miscellaneous tier, for additional TOBI notations and for individual or local additions.

This format, which can be called *Segment-Plus-Specification* (SPS) format, is also often used in providing syntactic, morphological and pragmatic information about an utterance. In the following, the "A" tier contains the basic level (orthographic) description of clauses or utterances and nonverbal events, the "B" tier, syntactic descriptors or codes, and the "C" and "D" tiers, semantic codes:

(13) from the Berkeley Crosslinguistic Language Acquisition project (Slobin, 1967):

2;0a 002A ALL CLOSE UP Q. {notes back of bus is open} .

2;0a 002B = -NO -V PC -YN QT

2;0a 002C == CPSP {close-up} PERF {all}

2;0a 002D (Q+POT PERF (C (P SP))) #

In the following example, the "S:" tier contains the orthographic rendering of the utterance, the "m:" tier, its morphological rendering, and the "s:" tier, its syntactic word classes, constituent structure and deep semantic case:

(14) from the Individual Differences in Language Learning project
(Fillmore, Peters, Oestman, Larsen, O'Connor & Parker, 1982):

S: He wen' (=went) out./

m: he *went out

s: (n1a PN.3.M) (v *V PT)

In addition to the Vertical arrangements of SPS in examples 13 and 14, Partiture versions (e.g., Figure 5.9 of Ehlich, this volume) and Column versions (e.g., Figure 6.3 of Bloom, this volume) are also possible, as well as the combination of Vertical and Column found in Lampert and Ervin-Tripp (this volume) and Berman and Slobin (1986), which uses a fixed number of fields (Column format) in coded tiers positioned beneath the utterance segment (Vertical format).

In both Interspersed and SPS, it is sometimes necessary to indicate which parts of the event segment are referred to by the descriptor, that is, the descriptor's exact "scope." This is accomplished variously by: (a) repeating the relevant item (as in "close-up" in Example 13) or (b) using numerical indices to refer to words on the utterance line (as in Du Bois and Schuetze-Coburn, this volume) or (c) explicit time tags (Bloom, this volume, and the TOBI system) or (d) bracketing and/or spacing practices, as in the following two examples or (e) a combination of these.

In Example 15, "<WH" and "WH>" delimit a stretch of speech that was whispered:

(15) from Du Bois, Schuetze-Coburn, Cumming & Paolino (this volume):

...<WH But we were scared,

And boy WH>,

did we ever get in trouble

In Example 16, the scope of the syntactic tags (clusters of upper case letters before each utterance segment) is signaled jointly by parentheses and by vertical alignment:

(16) from the Penn Treebank:
        (S (NP (NP Composer
              (NP Marc Marder))

           ,

           (NP (NP a college friend
                 (PP of
                    (NP
                       (NP Mr. Lane)
                       's)))
              (SBARQ
                 (WHNP who)
                 (S (NP T)
                    (VP earns
                       (NP his living)
                       (S (NP *)
                          (VP playing
                             (NP the double bass)
                             (PP in
                                (NP classical music ensembles))))))))

        ,)

The fourth alternative in spatial arrangement of utterance and nonutterance information is what I call *Utterance-Plus-Clarification* (UPC) format. It involves using subordinate tiers not just for the cotemporaneous properties of a particular event (such as prosody, syntax or semantics of an utterance in the above examples, or body parts, type and extent of motion, and conventionalized meaning for gestures) but also for all nonutterance events (such as nonverbal and contextual events). In contrast to RT format, in which nonverbal and contextual events are interleaved with utterances according to order of occurrence in time, in UPC format, temporal ordering is preserved spatially only for utterances; nonverbal and contextual events are treated mainly as clarificational information for individual utterances, and are placed beneath the utterances for which they are relevant and labeled as to the type (e.g., *sit* for *situational*; *gpx* for *gestural-proxemic*) as in the following:

(17) UPC version of Example (11)
    *MOT: what did you see?
    %sit: Mother and Allison sitting on chair; Allison wearing
           half-zippered jacket; fingers in her mouth
    *MOT: what did you see over there?
    %gpx: <aft> points to monitor
    *ALI: Mommy.
    %gpx: looking at monitor with fingers in her mouth

This format (MacWhinney & Snow, 1985; MacWhinney, 1991) is essentially utterance-based in contrast to RT, which is event-based. UPC format seems best suited for examining utterance-level phenomena, such as the presence of particular morphemes at different points in child language acquisition, and in that context has the advantage of focusing attention primarily on the utterance lines in contrast to all other types of information in the transcript. Its utterance-based structure requires different treatment of the flow of events than is found in the event-based RT format, as discussed below.[1]

Where a clarifying event precedes the utterance to which it is relevant, time and space become nonparallel in the UPC transcript, and an explicit sequence label (<bef>, for before) is inserted before the contextual or nonverbal information to indicate the temporal sequence:

(18) *SAR: see my doggie.
    %par: <bef> whispers. <aft> laughs

In this example, the speaker whispered first, then said "see my doggie," and then laughed.

Because its spatial ordering is utterance-based rather than more generally event-based, the occurrence of a gesture without accompanying utterances leads to examples such as the following, in which a "0" (zero) on the utterance line signals the absence of an utterance, and the nonverbal event is described on a separate tier attached to it, as clarificational information for the nonoccurring utterance:

---

[1] Although Examples 17 through 20 are from the online holdings of a transcription archive (CHILDES), that archive's transcription manuals are apparently shifting increasingly toward RT. These examples are intended not to characterize a particular archive, but rather to illustrate differences between utterance-based and event-based systems in capturing the structure of utterance and nonutterance events in a discourse.

(19) UPC encoding of a gesture without accompanying utterance:
    *URS: Adam # can you put the cork in the cup?
    *ADA: 0.
    %act: puts cork in cup
    *URS: again.
    %sit: Adam doesn't put the cork on the cup

This contrasts with RT, in which nonverbal actions are treated as events of potentially equal communicative status, and therefore interleaved with utterances in the flow of events. From the RT perspective, the absence of the utterance is not significant in itself, and is therefore marked only indirectly (i.e., by the absence of an utterance on the same line as the action):

(20) RT encoding of (19):
    U: Adam # can you put the cork in the cup?
    A: ((puts cork in cup))
    U: again.
    A: ((doesn't put the cork in the cup))

A final difference between RT and UPC concerns the assumed duration of influence of context and nonverbal events on utterances. In UPC format, nonverbal and contextual events are attached to specific utterances to which they are believed relevant. When they are believed relevant to multiple utterances, these events are repeated beneath each utterance. In contrast, RT marks only the inception of an event, leaving open the possibility of indirect influence on later events in the discourse. This is analogous in certain ways to the semiactivation and reactivation of concepts discussed in Chafe (1987, this volume).

Since software can retrieve systematically marked lines above an utterance as easily as below it, the choice between RT and UPC is usually based on other considerations. RT is more versatile than UPC for reasons of its greater time-space iconicity, enabling a focus either on utterances alone (by suppressing information in parentheses) or on the interplay of utterances with nonverbal and contextual events in time. UPC is at its best where the focus is on utterance-level or sentence-level phenomena, such as the morphemes found in child utterances at different points in language acquisition. For discourse types in which nonverbal and contextual events are rare, RT and UPC become functionally equivalent. Translation between UPC and RT can be done largely automatically but requires hand editing for ambiguities of scope: in the UPC direction, to indicate all the utterances to which an event is believed to be relevant; in the RT direction, to arrange events in order of occurrence and to disambiguate instances from UPC in which the same nonverbal or contextual event appears beneath several utterances in a row (i.e., continuing relevance of a single occurring event versus repeated events).

Concerning combinations of the four types of spatial organization discussed in this section, either RT and UPC can easily combine with either Interspersed or SPS but not with each other. To illustrate, utterances and nonverbal events could be sequenced on the page in the order in which they occurred in time (i.e., RT format), with detailed prosodics or gestural specification being provided beneath segments (utterances or nonverbal events) of particular interest (SPS). Furthermore, all four combinations (RT with Interspersed, RT with SPS, UPC with Interspersed, UPC with SPS) are compatible with all three arrangements of speaker turns (i.e., Vertical, Partiture and Column formats) described in the preceding section.

3.2. Level and Type of Description

I have saved for last discussion of the choices which most immutably shape the content of the transcript. Whereas systematically encoded transcripts can be reformatted into other spatial configurations, descriptive categories cannot generally be translated so automatically between systems (largely for reasons of the property of contrastiveness described in the section on principles of category design). While most transcripts involve preserving who said what, and under what circumstances, they differ greatly in the level and type of descriptive categories used. This discussion focuses on five main types of choices, outlined in Table 1.1.

TABLE 1.1

Some Content-Related Alternatives

Notation of words: orthography, eye-dialect, phonetic/phonemic
Unit of analysis: defined by intonation, pauses, syntax
Prosodics:
    Intonation: contours vs. levels
    Pauses: physically measured vs. adjusted for speech rate
    Prominence: pitch vs. loudness vs. lengthening
Turn Taking: latching encoded explicitly vs. by default
Kinesics: gesture globally described vs. analyzed into components

I will focus mainly on the first three of these. The conventions selected for discussion are chosen because they either define contrasting poles of descriptive dimensions or highlight otherwise informative contrasts.

Word Forms

Standard orthography is sufficient for many purposes, but in some cases it must be supplemented, such as, when the specific pronunciation or dialect is important, or to encode forms from spoken language which are not part of the written language (e.g., *'cause, gonna*). There are basically two approaches: (a) the use of modified orthography (e.g., *cause, 'cause,* or *cuz* for the often shortened spoken version of *because*) and (b) the use of the International Phonetic Alphabet (IPA), for phonetic or phonological encoding (e.g., [kʰʌz]).

Modified orthography (sometimes called "eye dialect") doesn't require specialized linguistic training, relying instead on extensions of a code which readers of English already know. However, the inconsistency of grapheme-to-sound correspondences in English orthography (e.g., *good* and *food*; *wood* and *would*) can lead to ambiguity (e.g., *cuz* for *'cause, excuz* for *excuse*), and some feel it gives rise to pejorative stereotypes of speakers and may be more difficult for researchers who are non-native English speakers (Gumperz & Berenz, this volume).

For capturing pronunciation variants, IPA is more precise than modified orthography but it requires specialized training, and may be slower to use in practice. The choice of one or the other depends largely on the level of precision required for the research purpose and on the likely users of the data. (For further discussion see Atkinson & Heritage, 1984; Edwards, 1991; Ehlich, this volume; Gumperz and Berenz, this volume; and Preston, 1985).

Units of Analysis

For analytic purposes, it is common to divide a discourse text into units of some type which in the transcript are bounded either by carriage returns or by explicit markers (e.g., punctuation marks, slashes, etc.).

In written language the basic units are clearly set off by punctuation marks or indentation, and are usually defined syntactically: clause, sentence, paragraph. The units most natural to spoken language are of a different type and often shorter (see Chafe, 1987; Svartvik, 1990). In spoken discourse, many utterances lack explicit subjects or verbs and would be considered as incomplete sentences in written language (e.g., "Bob's." in response to the question, "Whose Picasso is that?"). Discourse researchers often employ units based primarily on intonation (e.g., "tone units" or "intonation units") or bounded by pauses (e.g., the "production units" in Gee & Grosjean, 1983) or some combination of these. These units correlate only partially with each other and with written language units (see Chafe, 1987; Cruttenden, 1986; Schuetze-Coburn, Shapley, & Weber, 1991; and Svartvik, 1990). The extent of correlation depends in part on the type of speech involved. For example, pause-based units may correlate more closely with syntactic structure in sentences read aloud than in spontaneous speech in which pauses arise in part from the speaker's online planning of the remainder of the utterance.

An interesting syntactic unit is the "macrosyntagm" of Loman and Jørgensen (1971, p. 9), that is, a grammatically cohesive unit which is not part of any larger grammatical construction (Johansson, Burnard, Edwards & Rosta, 1992; Rosta, 1990). Unlike a sentence unit in writing, a macrosyntagm may vary greatly in length, from a monosyllabic interjection to a multiword sentence expanded by a large number of subordinate clauses (based on Loman & Jørgensen, 1971, p. 10). Some projects segment the text with respect to more than one type of unit (e.g., using both syntactic and intonation units), including units that may cross-cut each other or partially overlap. Finally, some units may involve satisfying two or more criteria simultaneously, such as both intonational and syntactic criteria.

Whichever units are used, they are important in imposing an infrastructure on the interaction, and are often the locus for descriptive categories used in analyses and comparisons in the data.

Prosody

Prosodic features are properties that "extend over stretches of utterances larger than just one sound" (Cruttenden, 1986, p. 1). These are properties that correlate to some degree with physically measureable dimensions: perceived pitch with the fundamental frequency of the voice; perceived loudness with amplitude; and perceived duration (e.g., length of segments, duration of pause, speech rate) with actual time.   But the correlations between acoustically measured values and perceptually and linguistically significant categories are complex and far from perfect.

> ... they are subject to diverse outside influences. For one, *vowel quality* may interfere with fundamental frequency: vowels articulated high in the mouth have an intrinsically higher fundamental frequency than low vowels. Furthermore, vowel quality may affect intensity: high vowels tend to have less intrinsic intensity than low vowels. And vowel quality may influence duration: high vowels are generally shorter than low vowels. Second, the *point of articulation in consonants* may interact with duration: labial consonants, for instance, are intrinsically longer than alveolars and velars.   Third, the

surrounding sounds or the *phonetic environment* may influence the fundamental frequency of a segment: a vowel following a voiceless fricative, for instance, has a higher fundamental frequency on the average than a vowel following a voiced fricative. Phonetic environment may also influence the intrinsic duration of a sound: a vowel followed by a voiced consonant is regularly longer than the same vowel followed by a voiceless consonant in English. And just as the individual acoustic components are influenced by outside factors, so too they influence each other. Pitch, for instance, may affect intensity if fundamental frequency overlaps with formant frequency.... As hearers we make automatic compensation for differences in fundamental frequency, amplitude and duration which are conditioned by factors such as these. (Couper-Kuhlen, 1986, p. 7)

Due to such influences as vowel height and phonetic context, fundamental frequency has more variation than speakers intend as speech melody, and more than listeners interpret as communicatively significant. Even relatively simple features such as the perception of "rising intonation" covers a wide variety of acoustic contours. Contours that are perceived as functionally equivalent can vary greatly acoustically, stretching over different lengths of speech, or having differing numbers of pitch peaks or different speeds of pitch change. For this reason, an important branch of prosody research involves comparing observed acoustic properties (i.e., measured aspects of waveforms) with the auditory perceptions of listeners (i.e., psychological and linguistic categories). This work serves to clarify the acoustic substrates of listener perceptions of prosody (e.g., 't Hart, Collier & Cohen, 1991).

In contrast, discourse researchers often focus on a different problem. They seek to describe interactions in categories which are as similar as possible to those perceived by the interactants themselves. Therefore, rather than acoustic categories, they tend to use perceptual or "interpretive" categories. For example, they may quantify pause length as number of silent beats relative to the speaker's tempo prior to the pause. Such measures are interpretive in taking into account more information than strictly physical measurements but some have been found capable of being consistently assigned by transcribers and useful in shedding light on the structure of interaction (see Gumperz and Berenz, this volume).

Some kinds of interpretive categories incorporate norms or expectations.

As Crystal (1975) has pointed out, we apparently do use norms or standards in auditory perception. For one, we can form a notion of 'natural speaking level' and are able to determine (regardless of individual voice range) whether someone is speaking near the top or the bottom of his/her voice. (Couper-Kuhlen, 1986, p. 9)

With reference to pauses, the same length pause may appear longer within an utterance than between turns by different speakers. An interspeaker pause which is unexpectedly long or short may be highly significant to interactants, perhaps indicating communicative strain or high rapport depending on communicative norms (as discussed by Erickson & Shultz, 1982; Gumperz & Berenz, this volume; and Tannen, 1984). So long as their interpretive status is borne in mind, much can be gained from such measures, both alone and in combination with acoustic measures.

In contrast to the auditory/interpretive and acoustic traditions, a third, increasingly important research approach relevant to the transcription of prosody is computerized speech recognition (e.g., Lea, 1980; Waibel, 1988) and text-to-speech conversion (e.g., Bachenko & Fitzpatrick, 1990; Knowles & Lawrence, 1987; Svartvik, 1990). These systems seek the most reliable correspondences between acoustic and auditory descriptions, often making explicit also contributions of other factors (i.e., syntactic, semantic, pragmatic and other information) in order to correctly convert waveforms into interpretable strings on the one hand or to generate acceptably natural prosodic contours on the other.

These three approaches contribute importantly to the understanding of the role of prosody in discourse and language use and comprehension, and the acoustic substrates of prosodic perception.

In what follows, I will briefly discuss some of the categorization issues which arise with respect to four aspects of prosodic encoding: pauses, prominence, duration and intonation.

Pauses. Although a pause is experienced as a period of nonphonation, its perceived length, as just noted, depends on additional factors, including: the speaker's rate of articulation, the immediate acoustic environment (e.g., whether it follows a stop consonant or a sibilant, whether it follows a reduced vowel or a stressed one), and the position of the pause in the utterance (e.g., the end of a turn vs. in the middle of a noun phrase). (See O'Connell & Kowal, 1983, for additional causes of variation.) A pause may be perceived as shorter or longer depending on such things as the preceding speech rate and expected pause duration at that point in the discourse. Norms vary within and across cultures. For example, British speakers may use and expect longer interturn pauses than many American speakers (Tannen, 1984).

In order to approximate the likely perceptions of interactants, some researchers quantify pauses as the number of beats of silence, based on speaker's preceding speech rate. Others incorporate normative information such as whether the pause was longer or shorter than expected from position in the utterance and other factors which can be of particular significance to interactants' perceptions of the interaction.

While some systems explicitly mark all detectable pauses (e.g., Chafe, this volume; Du Bois, Schuetze-Coburn, Cumming & Paolino, this volume), others mark only pauses that depart strongly from expectation or are otherwise significant for the interaction (e.g., Ehlich, this volume; Gumperz & Berenz, this volume).   In the latter case, to avoid circularity, communicative significance is established independently of the pause.   All of these are motivated and functional choices within the domain in which they are used.

Even if the pause is explicitly quantified, the classification of it as "short" or "medium" varies with research purpose. Researchers concerned with turn-taking smoothness may consider a "short" pause to be .5 seconds, while those interest in information packaging may consider it to be .2 seconds.

Another issue involves placement of interturn pauses, that is, pauses that occur between turns by different speakers. Placing them at the end of the first speaker's turn, or at the beginning of the second speaker's turn implies that one speaker is more responsible for the occurrence or length of the pause than the other. Placing the pause on a separate line between the turns implies the speakers are mutually responsible.

Under some circumstances, a turn may be thought to consist solely of a pause (i.e., a silent turn) as, for example, in a psychotherapeutic interview when a stressful question is asked by one speaker and the second speaker does not respond (see, for example, Labov & Fanshel, 1977). As Tannen (1981) notes, this is a useful way to indicate the communicatively significant fact of the second speaker's reticence in answering the question, but it is important to recognize it as an inference by the analyst and as interpretive in going beyond the physical data.

Lengthening and Shortening. Another prosodic feature that is tied to time is the length of syllables. This is determined to some degree lexically as a function of which syllable is stressed in the word. For example, the second syllable is longer in *subJECT* than in *SUBject*. In addition, speech rate tends to speed up at the beginnings of phrases ("anacrusis") and to slow down at the ends ("phrase-final lengthing"). Those discourse researchers who mark syllable lengthening or shortening tend to mark it only where it deviates from norms or is interactively significant for other reasons; researchers concerned with speech recognition would probably mark it systematically throughout.

Prominence. A common feature of English is that some syllables are perceived as more prominent than others. The location of a prominence is determined in part lexically. In *ELephants* it is the first syllable; in *esCAPED*, the last. When both words occur within an utterance, one of them will typically receive more prominence than the other, depending on such things as information focus or surprisingness of content. For example, in the utterance, "The elephants escaped." the greater prominence might be on *elephants* in response to the question, "What happened today?" ("The ELephants escaped."), but on *escaped* in response to, "Did you feed the elephants today?" ("No, the elephants had esCAPED.").

Other factors affecting location of prominence within utterances are word class and syntactic structure. Concerning word class, for example, nouns tend to be more prominent than prepositions (Lea, 1980). Concerning syntactic structure, it is often the right-most content word of the utterance that has the greatest prominence (e.g., Chomsky & Halle, 1968; Liberman & Prince, 1977). For intransitive event sentences, it tends to be the right-most word within the syntactic subject: "Your TROUsers are on fire." (Cruttenden, 1986, p. 29). Prominences may also be used to draw attention to parallel structures with contrasting components (e.g., "MARy married the DANE, and ANna, the RUSSian.").

Although pitch, loudness and lengthening are all known to influence perceived prominence in English, researchers have disagreed concerning which of these is generally the most important cue. Some believe that prominence is tied most closely to pitch obtrusion, that is, large shifts in pitch up or down compared to surrounding syllables (e.g., Bolinger, 1986, p. 22). Others consider it to be determined mainly by lengthening with respect to normative vowel quality (e.g., Couper-Kuhlen, 1986, p. 23). And loudness can also play a role, though it is not present in all cases of perceived prominence and hence is not a necessary condition (Cruttenden, 1986).

In discourse transcription, while all systems mark unusual prominence (e.g., contrastive stress and "boosters"), some mark all prominences in utterances (e.g., Du Bois et al., this volume; Gumperz & Berenz, this volume; Svartvik & Quirk, 1980). Researchers differ also in the number of levels of prominence they distinguish (i.e., prominent versus nonprominent or multiple levels, as contrasted by Cruttenden, 1986). The choice depends on research purpose and theoretical assumptions concerning the structure of spoken language.

Intonation. As already noted, there is more variation in the fundamental frequency curve than speakers intend to produce or listeners perceive as part of the speech melody. Couper-Kuhlen (1986) observes:

> we do not perceive a change in pitch whenever there is a change in fundamental frequency. Nor do we perceive regular increments in frequency as regular

intervals of pitch. In fact, psycho-acoustic studies have shown that some quite sizeable changes in fundamental frequency are not perceived at all, while other, minimal changes may produce clear differences in perceived pitch. (p. 63)

An interesting instance of adjustment of perceptions is how listeners handle voiceless consonants. Cruttenden (1986) notes that such consonants—which comprise about one fourth of the consonants in connected English text—have no repetitive waveform and no fundamental frequency, yet they are not experienced by listeners as gaps in pitch patterns.

Another interesting adjustment listeners make concerns "declination." Although generally unnoticed by listeners, there seems to be a tendency for fundamental frequency to drift downward from the beginning to the end of an intonation unit.   For this reason, in order for two syllables to be perceived as equally prominent within an intonation contour, the second one must be lower in pitch (Breckenridge, 1977). Researchers concerned with acoustic substrates may represent intonation contours as being superimposed upon a declining baseline (e.g., 't Hart et al., 1991). Other researchers draw the contours as being superimposed on a level baseline, a slightly less acoustic approach.

Another important split found in the literature is that between "levels" and "contours". Where some researchers have assigned a numerical value to individual syllables, others focus on pitch movement within and across multiple syllables (compared in Ladd, 1983). Frequently types of movements include: (a) "nuclear tones," which extend from the main prominence in a stretch of speech to the end of that unit (e.g., high–rising, low–falling, fall–rise); (b) pitch change on the final syllable of the unit (e.g., rising, falling, continuing); and (c) larger patterns such as the rise–fall–rise pattern observed in the so-called "contradiction contour" of Sag and Liberman (1974):

(21) El^{e}phan$_{ti}$ $_a$ $_{sis}$ $_{is}$ $_{n't}$ $_{in}$ $_{cur}$ $_a$ ^{b} ^{l} $^{e.}$

Cruttenden (1986) provides a useful comparison of these contrasting descriptive approaches (see also Du Bois et al., this volume).

Finally, systems differ in grain or level of precision, from "narrow" to "broad" transcription.   One example of narrow transcription is "interlinear tonetic notation," which resembles musical notation.   In it, "the top and bottom lines represent the top and bottom of the speaker's pitch range and each dot corresponds to a syllable, with the larger dots indicating stressed and/or accented syllables" (Cruttenden, 1986, p. xii). Several additional methods of narrow transcription are surveyed by Ehlich and Rehbein (1979). For most discourse researchers, "broad" transcription is the most useful level of analysis, frequently employing a closed set of categories (such as (a) and (b) in the preceding paragraph). An example from the London–Lund corpus is discussed in the section on principles of readability.

Turn-Taking

Some systems focus on rhythmic synchrony between speakers between and across turns. Others emphasize completion or incompletion of utterances, perhaps distinguishing self-interruptions from interruptions by another speaker. Self-interruptions are in some cases further subclassified into various types of speech repair (e.g., restarts with or without correction). Another encoded distinction concerns the length of pause separating turns. Latching, that is, a shorter-than-expected pause between turns by two speakers, is marked by an overt special symbol in some systems (e.g., Du Bois et al., this volume; and Gumperz & Berenz, this volume). In others, the information is implicitly coded, that is by the *absence of* the otherwise pervasive interturn pause (e.g., Chafe, this volume).

Nonverbal Events or Actions

In most discourse transcription, it is sufficient to refer to nonverbal actions globally, without focus on components (e.g., nods). But some purposes require greater detail (e.g., specification of head position, eye gaze, posture and hand position during a nod). More detailed systems include those of Bloom (this volume), Ehlich (this volume), Erickson and Shultz (1982), Heath (1986), Pittenger, Hockett, and Danehy (1960), and Scherer and Ekman (1982). Bloom's system provides for up to 100 additional specifications.

4. FUTURE TRENDS

While automatic transcription may someday be possible, it is elusive at the moment. Even extraction of words from fluent speech is difficult and error-prone (see Klatt, 1989). Concerning identification of prosodic contours from extracted physical dimensions, considerable progress has been made with read sentences (e.g., Waibel, 1988), but spontaneous speech continues to pose problems. Advances of the future may allow researchers increasing precision and widespread application of these approaches to description and perhaps even enable to some degree automatic transcription.

As for already transcribed materials, the increasing availability of CD-ROM recordings of digitized speech and software for accessing them means greatly speeded access to data records. Labs of the future may involve also more routine linking of video- and audio-tape records, such as that outlined in Bloom (this volume) and Ehlich (this volume), which enable more efficient transcription as well as more convenient focus on multiple dimensions of the speech signal and the interaction at once.

5. SUMMARY AND CONCLUSION

Different methods of transcription highlight different types of information, which may be more or less relevant depending on theoretical orientation and purpose underlying the research. After a discussion of some general principles of category design, readability and computational tractability the chapter surveyed a variety of alternatives in spatial arrangement of speech and nonspeech information in transcripts, and contrasting approaches with respect to encoding of words, choice of analytic units, treatment of prosody, turn-taking, and nonverbal events and activity. The focus in this chapter and in the chapters which follow is on the ways in which transcription conventions influence researcher perspectives and facilitate researcher goals in understanding various types of discourse and language use.

ACKNOWLEDGEMENTS

I wish to thank the following people for helpful suggestions and comments concerning previous drafts: Wallace Chafe, Jack Du Bois, Susan Ervin-Tripp, Stig Johansson, Martin Lampert, and Stephan Schuetze-Coburn. Any remaining inaccuracies are my own.

REFERENCES

Atkinson, J. M., & Heritage, J. (Eds.). (1984). *Structures of social action: Studies in conversation analysis*. Cambridge: Cambridge University Press.

Bachenko, J., & Fitzpatrick, E. (1990). A computational grammar of discourse-neutral prosodic phrasing in English. *Computational Linguistics*, 16, 155–170.

Berman, R. & Slobin, D. I. (1986). *Coding manual: Temporality in discourse*. Berkeley: University of California, Institute of Cognitive Studies.

Bloom, L. (1973). *One word at a time: The use of single word utterances before syntax*. The Hague: Mouton.

Bloom, L., & Lahey, M. (1978). A definition of language. In L. Bloom & M. Lahey (Eds.), *Language development and language disorders* (pp. 3–23). New York: John Wiley.

Bolinger, D. (1986). *Intonation and its parts: Melody in spoken English*. Stanford: Stanford University Press.

Breckenridge, J. (1977). The declination effect. *Journal of the Acoustical Society of America, 61*, supplement 1: S90 (abstract).

Brown, R. (1973). *A first language: The early stages*. Cambridge, MA: Harvard University Press.

Burnard, L. (1991). What is SGML and how does it help? (Document No. TEI EDW 25). Chicago: University of Illinois, Computer Center (M/C 135). (TEI listserver: listserv@uicvm.bitnet)

Chafe, W. (1987). Cognitive constraints on information flow. In R. Tomlin (Ed.), *Coherence and grounding in discourse* (pp. 21–51). Amsterdam: John Benjamins.

Chomsky, N., & Halle, M. (1968). *The sound patterns of English*. New York: Harper and Row.

Cook-Gumperz, J., & Gumperz, J. (1984). *The politics of conversation* (Tech. Rep. No. 23). Berkeley: University of California, Institute of Cognitive Studies.

Couper-Kuhlen, E. (1986). *An introduction to English prosody*. London: Edward Arnold.

Cruttenden, A. (1986). *Intonation*. Cambridge: Cambridge University Press.

Crystal, D. (1975). Relative and absolute in intonation analysis. In D. Crystal (Ed.), *The English tone of voice: Essays in intonation, prosody and paralanguage* (pp. 74–83). London: Edward Arnold.

Du Bois, J. W. (1991). Transcription design principles for spoken language research. *Pragmatics, 1*, 71–106.

Edwards, J. A. (1989). *Transcription and the new functionalism: A counterproposal to the CHILDES CHAT conventions* (Tech. Rep. No. 58). Berkeley: University of California, Institute of Cognitive Studies. (ERIC Document Reproduction Service No. ED 341 236)

Edwards, J. A. (1991). Transcription in discourse. In W. Bright (Ed.), *Oxford International Encyclopedia of Linguistics* (Vol. 1, pp. 367–371). Oxford: Oxford University Press.

Edwards, J. A. (1992a). Computer Methods in Child Language Research: Four Principles for the Use of Archived Data. *Journal of Child Language, 19*, 435–458.

Edwards, J. A. (1992b). Design principles in the transcription of spoken discourse. In J. Svartvik (Ed.), *Directions in Corpus Linguistics: Proceedings of the Nobel Symposium 82, Stockholm, August 4–8, 1991*. New York: Mouton de Gruyter.

Edwards, J. A. (in press). Perfecting research techniques in an imperfect world. *Journal of Child Language, 20*.

Ehlich, K., & Rehbein, J. (1979). Erweiterte halbinterpretative Arbeitstranskriptionen (HIAT 2): Intonation. *Linguistische Berichte, 59*, 51–75.

Ehlich, K., & Switalla, B. (1976). Transkriptionssysteme—Eine exemplarische Übersicht. *Studium Linguistik, 2*, 78–105.

Erickson, F., & Shultz, J. (1982). *The counselor as gatekeeper: Social interaction in interviews*. New York: Academic.

Ervin-Tripp, S. M. (1979). Children's verbal turn-taking. In E. Ochs & B. B. Schieffelin (Eds.), *Developmental pragmatics* (pp. 391–414). New York: Academic.

Fillmore, L. W., Peters, A., Oestman, J. O., Larsen, T., O'Connor, M. C., & Parker, L. (1982). *Coding manual for the Individual Differences in Language Learning project.* Berkeley: University of California, School of Education.

Garfinkel, H. (1967). *Studies in Ethnomethodology.* Englewood Cliffs, NJ: Prentice-Hall.

Gee, J. P., & Grosjean, F. (1983). Performance structures: A psycholinguistic and linguistic appraisal. *Cognitive Psychology, 15,* 411–458.

Heath, C. (1986). *Body movement and speech in medical interaction.* Cambridge: Cambridge University Press.

Johansson, S. (1991). *Some thoughts on the encoding of spoken texts in machine-readable form.* Oslo: University of Oslo, Department of English.

Johansson, S., Burnard, L., Edwards, J., & Rosta, A. (1992). *Text Encoding Initiative, spoken text work group, final report.* Oslo: University of Oslo, Department of English.

Klatt, D. H. (1989). Review of selected models of speech perception. In W. Marslen-Wilson (Ed.), *Lexical representation and process* (pp. 169–226). Cambridge, MA: MIT Press.

Knowles, G., & Lawrence, L. (1981). Automatic intonation assignment. In R. Garside, G. Leech, & G. Sampson (Eds.), *The computational analysis of English: A corpus-based approach.* London: Longman.

Kucera, H. (1992). Brown corpus. In S. C. Shapiro (Ed.), *Encyclopedia of Artificial Intelligence* (Vol. 1, pp. 128–130). New York: John Wiley & Sons.

Kucera, H., & Francis, W. N. (1967). *Computational analysis of present-day American English.* Providence, RI: Brown University Press.

Labov, W. (1972). *Sociolinguistic patterns.* Philadelphia: University of Philadelphia Press.

Labov, W., & Fanshel, D. (1977). *Therapeutic discourse: Psychotherapy as conversation.* New York: Academic.

Ladd, D. R., Jr. (1983). Levels vs. configurations, revisited. In F. B. Agard, G. Kelley, A. Makkai & V. B. Makkai (Eds.), *Essays in honor of Charles F. Hockett.* Leiden: E. J. Brill.

Lea, W. A. (1980). Prosodic aids to speech recognition. In W. A. Lea (Ed.), *Trends in speech recognition* (pp. 166–205). Englewood Cliffs, NJ: Prentice-Hall.

Leech, G. (1991). State of the art in corpus linguistics. In K. Aijmer & B. Altenberg (Eds.), *English corpus linguistics: Studies in honour of Jan Svartvik.* London: Longman.

Leech, G. (1992). Corpora and theories of linguistic performance. In J. Svartvik (Ed.), *Directions in corpus linguistics: Proceedings of the Nobel Symposium 82, Stockholm, August 4–8, 1991* (pp. 105–122). New York: Mouton de Gruyter.

Levinson, S. C. (1983). *Pragmatics.* Cambridge: Cambridge University Press.

Liberman, M., & Prince, A. (1977). On stress and linguistic rhythm. *Linguistic Inquiry, 8,* 249–336.

Loman, G., & Jørgensen, N. (1971). *Manual for analys och beskrivning av makrosyntagmer.* Lund: Lund University Press.

Lyons, J. (1977). *Semantics* (Vol. 1). Cambridge: Cambridge University Press.

MacWhinney, B. (1991). *The CHILDES Project: Computational tools for analyzing talk.* Hillsdale, NJ: Lawrence Erlbaum Associates.

MacWhinney, B., & Snow, C. (1985). The child language data exchange system. *Journal of Child Language, 12,* 271–296.

Ochs, E. (1979). Transcription as theory. In E. Ochs & B. B. Schieffelin (Eds.), *Developmental pragmatics* (pp. 43–72). New York: Academic.

O'Connell, D. C., & Kowal, S. (1983). Pausology. In W. A. Sedelow, Jr. & S. Y. Sedelow (Eds.), *Computers in language research 2: Notating the language of music, and the (pause) rhythms of speech* (pp. 221–301). New York: Mouton.

Pittenger, R. E., Hockett, C. F., & Danehy, J. J. (1960). *The first five minutes; a sample of microscopic interview analysis.* Ithaca, NY: P. Martineau.

Preston, D. (1985). The Li'l Abner Syndrome: Written representations of speech. *American Speech, 60,* 328–336.

Rosta, A. (1990). The system of preparation and annotation of I.C.E. texts. In S. Greenbaum (Ed.), *International Corpus of English Newsletter, 9.*

Sag, I., & Liberman, M. (1975). The intonational disambiguation of indirect speech acts. *Proceedings of the Chicago Linguistics Society, 11,* 487–497.

Scherer, K. R., & Ekman, P. (Eds.). (1982). *Handbook of methods in nonverbal behavior research.* Cambridge: Cambridge University Press.

Schuetze-Coburn, S., Shapley, M., & Weber, E. G. (1991). Units of intonation in discourse: A comparison of acoustic and auditory analyses. *Language and Speech, 34,* 207–234.

Silverman, K., Beckman, M., Pitrelli, J., Ostendorf, M., Wightman, C., Price, P., Pierrehumbert, J., & Hirschberg, J. (1992, October). *TOBI: A standard for labeling English prosody.* Paper presented at the International Conference on Spoken Language Processing, Banff, Alberta, Canada.

Slobin, D. I. (Ed.). (1967). *A field manual for cross-cultural study of the acquisition of communicative competence.* Berkeley: University of California, Department of Psychology.

Svartvik, J. (Ed.). (1990). *The London–Lund corpus of spoken English: Description and research.* Lund: Lund University Press.

Svartvik, J., & Quirk, R. (Eds). (1980). *A corpus of English conversation.* Lund: C. W. K. Gleerup.

Tannen, D. (1981). [Review of W. Labov and D. Fanshel, *Therapeutic discourse: Psychotherapy as conversation*]. *Language, 57,* 481–486.

Tannen, D. (1984). *Conversational style.* Norwood, NJ: Ablex.

Tedlock, D. (1983). *The spoken word and the work of interpretation.* Philadelphia: University of Pennsylvania Press.

't Hart, J., Collier, R, & Cohen, A. (1991). *A perceptual study of intonation: An experimental-phonetic approach to speech melody.* Cambridge: Cambridge University Press.

Waibel, A. (1988). *Prosody and speech recognition.* San Mateo, CA: Morgan Kaufmann.

2 Prosodic and Functional Units of Language

Wallace L. Chafe
University of California at Santa Barbara

1. INTRODUCTION

In this chapter, I describe a system for transcribing and analyzing certain aspects of spoken language. It is a system I have been using, with continuing modifications, over a number of years for various purposes. My goal has been to represent not only the segmental but also selected aspects of the prosodic features of a language in ways that lend themselves to analysis in terms of *information flow*. My use of this term includes, but is not restricted to, the movement of ideas into and out of the consciousness of speakers and hearers, changes in clause level and discourse level topics, manifestations of foregrounding and backgrounding, and phenomena involved in the identifiability (or "definiteness") of referents (see Chafe, 1976, for an earlier overview of some of these phenomena).

In this discussion I focus first on certain major features of the transcription system, in particular those features that lead to the segmentation of discourse into units of considerable cognitive significance that I call *intonation units* and *accent units*. I then present some ideas regarding the relevance of these units to certain aspects of information flow, specifically the movement of ideas into and out of active, semi-active, and inactive consciousness. The *activation status* of ideas is basic to thought and memory, and it is a major determinant of the manner in which thought is verbalized. Although neither the transcription nor the interpretation presented in this chapter is intended to be fixed or final, I hope that this discussion provides something of both practical and theoretical usefulness for researchers with similar interests and goals.

2. TRANSCRIPTION

I illustrate the transcription system with a brief segment of speech excerpted from a conversation. The speaker, a woman who was in conversation with a man, had just been talking about how another woman and her two children had moved into a new apartment. My discussion would obviously be more meaningful if the reader had access to the recording from which I worked. Without such access, the reader can only imagine the sound of this selection. By the end of the discussion I hope to have made at least some of its important features accessible. The features I deal with here include words, pauses, lengthenings, terminal pitch contours, and both primary and secondary accents. These features are particularly useful in establishing the boundaries and nuclei of intonation and accent units, on which the subsequent discussion depends. Other prosodic features one might want to record, such as changes in tempo, volume, or pitch range, laughter, whispering, and so forth, are covered in Du Bois, Schuetze-Coburn, Cumming, and Paolino (this volume).

As a first step I will set down just the words of this excerpt, as shown in (1). I include the pause-filler sound written as *uh*. The (A) shows that these words were produced by a person designated as Speaker A:

(1)(A)   and then the man uh her boyfriend whatever was gonna
move in with them

Although transcribing a sequence of words might seem to be a straightforward procedure, even it may raise some questions. My practice, for example, has been to use standard English spellings, but with allowance for widely used colloquial representations such as *uh* and *gonna*. The former is easily recognizable as a conventional spelling for the common pause-filler. Semistandard spellings such as *gonna* and *wanna* are useful supplements to standard spellings of contractions such as *didn't* and *can't*. Standard spellings increase readability and also have the advantage of making it possible to search for all the occurrences of a word or phrase, as could not be done so easily if attempts were made to capture phonetic niceties. I reject such spellings as *wuz* for *was*, or *thuh* for *the*, because they capture nothing beyond what is already known about the usual pronunciations of these words. For my purposes, I am not interested in the fact that the *d* in the *and* in this example was not pronounced, that the pronunciation of *was* was phonetically obscure, or that the sequence *with them* contained only one dental fricative. Such pronunciations are normal for spoken English.

At the beginning and end of this excerpt, and once within it, there are audible pauses (longer than 200 milliseconds), each of which can be represented with a sequence of three dots, as follows:

34

(2)(A) ... and then the man ... uh her boyfriend whatever was gonna
         move in with them ...

When feasible and desirable, and particularly for pauses longer than half a second, pause measurements can be included in parentheses. Such measurements can be made roughly with a stop watch, or they can be determined more accurately by electronic means if the appropriate equipment is available. It may be that the mind differentiates among short, normal, and long pauses, or something of the sort. Pending the discovery of such perceptual distinctions, we can do our best to show absolute pause durations.

Another feature of the timing of this segment is the fact that the syllables *then, man, uh,* and *in* were extended beyond the normal lengths for such syllables. This lengthening can be shown with the symbol "=":

(3)(A) ... and the=n the ma=n ... uh= her boyfriend whatever was gonna
         move in= with them ...

The second and third pauses in this excerpt are preceded by what a listener perceives as a phrase-final pitch contour, a contour that is heard as signaling the end of a phrase, clause, or sentence. The first pause-bounded segment ends with a nonfalling pitch contour, perceived as the end of a phrase but not of a sentence. The second segment ends with a falling pitch contour of the type associated with the end of a sentence. We can also hear the complex pitch perturbation (creaky voice) that is frequently associated with sentence-final prosody. A detailed study of the various terminal pitch contours to be found in English is still badly needed. In my own transcribing practice, I have compromised by transcribing a variety of nonfalling contours with a single symbol, the comma. This compromise is adequate for my immediate purposes, but I look forward to the additional insights that will follow from a detailed breakdown of these "comma intonations." I transcribe a sentence-final falling contour with a period. The excerpt can thus be rewritten as in (4):

(4)(A) ... and the=n the ma=n, ... uh= her boyfriend whatever was
         gonna move in= with them. ...

For reasons that become clearer below, it is useful to identify each segment of speech ending in a terminal contour as an intonation unit (cf. the similar *intonation-groups* in, for example, Cruttenden, 1986). It has proved helpful to format transcriptions with each intonation unit written on a separate line. I follow the convention of writing the pause that may occur between two intonation units at the beginning of the second unit. Thus, (4) can be rewritten as follows:

(5.1)(A) ... and the=n the ma=n,
(5.2)(A) ... uh= her boyfriend whatever was gonna move in= with them.

The last step is to identify those words that have what I call *primary and secondary accents*, contrasting them with words that can be called *unaccented*. In the usual case, the accented words have both heightened amplitude and heightened pitch on their inherently stressed syllables. Primary accent exhibits higher amplitude and/or pitch than secondary. When a word with primary accent is followed by an unaccented word, there is often a steep drop in pitch to a level below that of the unaccented word, as with the words *boy* and *with*. I use the symbols ^^ and ^ to indicate primary and secondary accents, respectively. This symbol is available on a computer keyboard, requires no unusual printing capabilities, and is easy to manipulate during storage and analysis. Adding primary and secondary accents to the transcription we arrive at (6):

(6.1)(A) ... and ^^the=n the ^^ma=n,
(6.2)(A) ... ^uh= ^her ^^boyfriend whatever was gonna ^^move ^in= ^^with them.

This version includes all the audible features that are used in the analysis to be discussed. However, for reasons that will become clear, I have been adding to my transcriptions one more feature that is derived from a conjunction of prosodic and syntactic criteria. Some but not all intonation units lend themselves to a segmentation into subunits. This segmentation is based on the principle that each subunit should contain one and only one primary accent. Subunits of this kind may be called *accent units*. The stream of speech, as represented in a transcription like (6), tells us where the primary accents are located, but it fails to give us the *boundaries* of accent units. Those boundaries can be located in terms of syntactic constituency. An accent unit consists of the word containing the primary accent plus whatever other words belong to the same constituent as that word. I use the symbol "|" to separate accent units, as shown in (7):

(7.1)(A) ... and ^^the=n | the ^^ma=n,
(7.2)(A) ... ^uh= ^her ^^boyfriend whatever | was gonna ^^move ^in= | ^^with them.

Finally, we can observe that the intonation units in ordinary conversation are of several kinds. The broadest distinction is between those that are *substantive* and those that can be labeled *regulatory*. Substantive intonation units are the contentful stretches of speech that include ideas of people, objects, events, and states. They are in a sense what language is about. Both of the intonation units in (7) are of that kind, as are (8.2) and (8.4) in the following example:

(8.1)(A) ... And so in ^^between the--

(8.2)(A) .. okay the ^^first two ^rooms I are at the t .. at the ..

      ^^front ^part of the ^hall,

(8.3)(B) ... Mhm,

(8.4)(A) .. and so .. ^^between those ... the ^entrances to those

      ^rooms and the ^bathroom I there's a ^lo=ng stretch of ^^hallway.

Regulatory intonation units are those whose primary function is, in one way or another, to regulate the flow of information. An example is (8.3) in the above sequence. The regulatory type includes intonation units composed of *discourse markers* as described by Schiffrin (1987). They can be roughly categorized into at least three subtypes that, taking a lead in part from Halliday (e.g., 1985), might be called *interpersonal, textual,* and *cognitive*. The interpersonal type involves interaction between speaker and hearer. For example, Speaker B in this conversation frequently produced the interpersonal intonation units *mhm* and *oh*, signaling thereby his attentiveness to what was being said and his comprehension of it. The textual subtype functions to regulate the linkage between intonation units (Chafe, 1988). Speaker A often produced the textual intonation units *so* and *but*, indicating a particular kind of linkage between what preceded and what followed. The third, cognitive type signals some mental activity on the part of the speaker. Examples that are common in ordinary speech include *let's see* and *I don't know*. The line between these three types is, however, not clear-cut. For example, the regulatory intonation unit *well* may be interpersonal in responding to a question from the interlocutor, textual in showing that the upcoming response will be relevant to the context, and cognitive in buying time for the speaker. In any case, intonation units with these several regulatory functions clearly contrast as a group with intonation units that convey substantive content.

The sequence in (8) also illustrates, in (8.1), a fragmentary intonation unit: one that was begun but not completed, as signaled by the dash. This one was evidently broken off so that speaker A could provide the background information in (8.2). After speaker B's brief contribution in (8.3), speaker A returned in (8.4) to the idea begun in (8.1), this time successfully completing it. Most fragmentary units are fragments of substantive units, but fragments of regulatory units are not unheard of.

It is useful to differentiate substantive, regulatory, and fragmentary intonation units in a transcription. One way is to add annotation S, R, or F after the designation of the speaker:

(7.1)(A)(S) ... and ^^the=n | the ^^ma=n,
(7.2)(A)(S) ... ^uh= ^her ^^boyfriend whatever | was gonna ^^move
           ^in= | ^^with them.

(8.1)(A)(F) ... And so in ^^between the--
(8.2)(A)(S) .. okay the ^^first two ^rooms | are at the t .. at the
           .. ^^front ^part of the ^hall,
(8.3)(B)(R) ... Mhm,
(8.4)(A)(S) .. and so .. ^^between those ... the ^entrances to those
           ^rooms and the ^bathroom | there's a ^lo=ng stretch of
           ^^hallway.

Such indications are useful because, for example, one may wish to ignore fragmentary intonation units in making calculations for which only successfully completed intonation units are of interest, as in determining the mean length of intonation units. One may also want to distinguish substantive from regulatory intonation units in calculations of this sort.

This, then, is the form of transcription that forms the basis for the kind of analysis to be discussed in the next section.

3. ANALYSIS

Transcriptions of this kind can be useful as evidence for cognitive processes that are at work during the production of spoken language. Whereas transcription requires perceptual skill, analysis is more dependent on introspection, insight, and the creation of hypotheses. I describe here certain hypotheses regarding language and information flow for which transcriptions such as that illustrated in (7) can be used as evidence.

This way of formatting a transcription prejudices the observer to view speech as a succession of intonation units. That is all to the good if intonation units can yield insights into the nature of language and thought. As an intuitive starting point, I can observe that I am able to focus my consciousness on only a very small amount of information at one time and that this focus of consciousness changes quite rapidly as thinking proceeds (Chafe, 1980).

Furthermore, it is plausible to suppose that during the production of language a speaker will focus on the information he or she is verbalizing at that moment. Against this background, an intonation unit is plausibly viewed as the verbal representation of just the information that is in the speaker's focus of consciousness at the moment it is uttered. A speaker's intention in uttering an intonation unit must then be to introduce something resembling that particular focus of consciousness into the attentive listener's consciousness. If each intonation unit, indeed, corresponds to a focus of consciousness, intonation units can give us important insights into how much and what kinds of information can be active at one time in a speaker's mind (see Chafe, 1980, 1987, for more detailed discussion).

If one calculates the lengths of intonation units of the two major types in spoken English, one finds the modal length of regulatory units to be one word and that of substantive units to be five words. Evidently, speakers have in focal consciousness the amount of information that is typically verbalized with about five words of English. One finds in addition that most substantive intonation units take the form of clauses. They are built around a predicative verb phrase with an associated subject that is usually a pronoun. A smaller percentage of intonation units are less than clauses, and a few are more. Particularly interesting, however, is the emerging hypothesis that substantive intonation units verbalize no more than one item of new information (e.g., Chafe, 1987). I have found this hypothesis to be productive in illuminating various other facets of language and thought.

What does it mean to be *new* in this sense? I have hypothesized elsewhere (e.g., Chafe, 1987) that at any given moment information may be in one of three possible states of activation in a person's mind. These states I have called *active*, *semi-active*, and *inactive*. Active information is the small amount that can be in the focus of a person's consciousness at a particular moment. Inactive information includes the vast bulk of possibly available information, what might traditionally be said to be in long-term memory. In addition, some information that is not fully active at the moment appears to be more accessible than completely inactive information. Information of this third type I have called semi-active. It is semi-active either because it was fully active not too long before, or because it is inferable from something that was fully active.

All of this raises the interesting question of the domain of activation. Is information activated and deactivated in units of an identifiable kind? Having examined diverse samples of language with this question in mind, I have found it useful to hypothesize that the domain of activation is usually the accent unit, or more properly the information verbalized in an accent unit. Let us consider first what has often been labeled *new* information. In the terms just outlined, we can say that an item of information is new at the point in a discourse when it has changed from being inactive to being active for the speaker, and when the speaker intends, by verbalizing it, to change it from being inactive to being active for the listener. The already familiar intonation unit (7.1) provides an example:

(7.1)(A)(S) ... and ^^the=n I the ^^ma=n,

Sometime before she uttered (7.1), perhaps only during the initial pause symbolized by the three dots, the idea expressed as *the ^^ma=n* became active in speaker A's consciousness. By uttering (7.1), she intended to activate the same idea in her listener's consciousness. It would appear, then, that the accent unit *the ^^ma=n* verbalized this unit of activated information. With this example before us, we might wonder whether anything similar can be said of the other accent unit here: *and ^^the=n*. It appears, in fact, that the distinction made earlier between substantive and regulatory intonation units can be applied to accent units as well. Thus, whereas the accent unit *the ^^ma=n* is substantive, the accent unit *and ^^the=n* is regulatory. Applied to accent units, this distinction approximates the traditional distinction between *content words* and *function words*. A substantive accent unit will contain at least one open-class word such as a noun, verb, or adjective. A regulatory accent unit will verbalize a linkage, as *and ^^the=n* does, or it may be an interpersonal formula such as *you know* or it may be a cognitive formula such as *let's see*. Given this substantive-regulatory distinction for accent units, we can observe that the distinction among active, semi-active, and inactive information (and hence the given-accessible-new distinction that is based on it) applies only to substantive accent units. Regulatory accent units lie outside the domain of activation.

We can now look at the second intonation unit in (7):

(7.2)(A)(S) ... ^uh= ^her ^^boyfriend whatever I was gonna ^^move
     ^in= I ^^with them.

Here, there are three substantive accent units. The first, which we might call (7.2a), *^uh= ^her ^^boyfriend whatever*, has the same referent as *the ^^ma=n* in (7.1). Simultaneously, however, it supplies a new characterization of that referent, not just that it was a man but also that it was her boyfriend or whatever. The referent itself is already active by virtue of its having been activated in (7.1). It is thus *given* information in (7.2). Examples of this kind suggest that when a referent becomes active in a person's mind, various properties of that referent become semi-active. In this example, once the speaker had thought of the man, it was easier for her to activate the idea of him being the woman's boyfriend or whatever. The accent unit (7.2a), then, combining a given referent with an accessible characterization of that referent, can be said to verbalize accessible information.

The idea expressed in (7.2b), *was gonna ^^move ^in=*, can also be identified as accessible information, but for a different reason. The idea of moving in is an idea that was activated earlier. The sequence of intonation units shown in (7) belong to a portion of the conversation that dealt with a complicated move from one apartment to another. A number of the preceding intonation units had been concerned with this move, and the idea of the move had lapsed into the semi-active state only because the immediately preceding intonation units had focused on the woman and her children, the referents of *her* and *them* in (7.2).

We are left with the conclusion that the only accent unit expressing new information in (7.2) is the last one, (7.2c), *^^with them*. The preceding accent units—the characterization of the man in (7.2a) and the idea of the move expressed in (7.2b)—express accessible ideas. Nothing, however, was said previously, and nothing was inferable, with regard to the man's sharing in this activity. That, specifically, is the new information centered in the primary accented word *^^with* in (7.2c). The total intonation unit (7.2) is a verbalization of what lay in the speaker's focus of consciousness at this point. Only one idea within that focus, however—the idea of the man's participation expressed in (7.2c)—was newly activated.

4. CONCLUSION

In summary, accent units verbalize single ideas that are the domain of activation in consciousness. It is accent units that are the loci of new, accessible, and given information. Intonation units, consisting of one or more accent units, verbalize clusters of such ideas. The given and accessible ideas that may be included within an intonation unit provide a context for the one new idea.

These are the kinds of considerations that have motivated and have been motivated by the transcription system described in the early part of this chapter. Considerations of this sort are basic to a fuller understanding of how language interacts with the capacities of the mind. They illuminate important universal characteristics of language, but they can also provide a basis for contrasting the different strategies that different languages use to convey new, accessible, and given information (cf. Chafe, 1985, for a comparison with a polysynthetic language). Their potential for studies of both first and second language acquisition should be apparent, but to date this potential remains untapped.

REFERENCES

Chafe, W. (1976). Givenness, contrastiveness, definiteness, subjects, topics, and point of view. In C. N. Li (Ed.), *Subject and topic* (pp. 25–55). New York: Academic.

Chafe, W. (1980). The deployment of consciousness in the production of a narrative. In W. Chafe (Ed.), *The pear stories: Cognitive, cultural, and linguistic aspects of narrative production* (pp. 9–50). Norwood, NJ: Ablex.

Chafe, W. (1985). Information flow in Seneca and English. *Berkeley Linguistics Society, 11*, 14–24.

Chafe, W. (1987). Cognitive constraints on information flow. In R. Tomlin (Ed.), *Coherence and grounding in discourse* (pp. 21–55). Amsterdam: John Benjamins.

Chafe, W. (1988). Linking intonation units in spoken English. In J. Haiman & S. Thompson (Eds.), *Clause combining in grammar and discourse* (pp. 1–27). Amsterdam: John Benjamins.

Cruttenden, A. (1986). *Intonation.* Cambridge: Cambridge University Press.

Halliday, M. A. K. (1985). *An introduction to functional grammar.* London: Edward Arnold.

Schiffrin, D. (1987). *Discourse markers.* Cambridge: Cambridge University Press.

APPENDIX
SUMMARY OF TRANSCRIPTION CONVENTIONS*

Category marked	Convention
Basic Units	
Words	Separated by space
Intonation units	Preceded by pause and separated by new line
Accent units	Separated by I ("pipe")
Intonation Contours	
Yes–no question intonation	? (question mark)
Intonation suggesting finality	. (period)
Intonation suggesting nonfinality	, (comma)
Noncompleted word	~ (tilde)
Fragmentary intonation contour	**(F)** at beginning and -- (double dash) at end
Markings Within Utterances	
Pauses	.. for short pause
	... for longer pause or (optional) timing
Syllable lengthening	=
Accents	^^ for primary accent
	^ for secondary accent

*For more detail, see Du Bois, Schuetze-Coburn, Cumming, and Paolino (this volume).

3

Outline of Discourse Transcription

John W. Du Bois
University of California at Santa Barbara

Stephan Schuetze-Coburn
University of California at Los Angeles

Susanna Cumming
University of Colorado at Boulder

Danae Paolino
University of California at Santa Barbara

This article presents a set of basic categories, symbols, and conventions for discourse transcription. *Discourse transcription* can be defined as the process of creating a written representation of a speech event so as to make it accessible to discourse research. In the following pages, we present in outline a framework for carrying out such a discourse transcription. (For a discussion of the principles that underlie the design of transcription systems, see Du Bois, 1991, and Edwards, this volume; for an in-depth treatment of the whole process of discourse transcription, see Du Bois, Schuetze-Coburn, Cumming, & Paolino, 1991.)

For each symbol in this discourse transcription system, a brief explanation of usage is given, illustrated with an example drawn from conversational transcriptions. Where appropriate, we comment on why the discourse feature in question should be attended to.

A word about the examples is in order. All examples cited are drawn from actual conversations, which have been transcribed and checked by the authors.[1] The examples are given in a fairly broad transcription, which

---

[1] Most of the examples are from tape recordings made by the authors, but a few have been contributed by other researchers. For each example given, the source is cited immediately preceding the example.

includes the most basic transcription information: the words and who they were spoken by, the division of the stream of speech into turns and intonation units, the truncation of intonation units and words, intonation contours, medium and long pauses, laughter, and uncertain hearings or indecipherable words. In a more detailed, "narrow" transcription, the transcriber would also include notation of, among other things, accent, tone, prosodic lengthening, and breathing and other vocal noises. Such narrow transcription features have been omitted from most of the transcriptions in this chapter, so as not to overload the reader with too many new symbols at once; but for those sections that deal directly with the transcription of these features, the examples will include them. (Narrowly transcribed versions of most of the examples cited here are presented in Du Bois et al., 1991.) For brevity's sake, the examples represent for the most part short stretches of discourse without a great deal of textual context (cotext). Thus the portions cited are not always whole sentences or whole interactions, but each line that is cited is whole—that is, each intonation unit is presented in its entirety—and no omissions have been made within the stretch of transcription that is cited. Whenever a new notational convention is being introduced, the symbol is written in **boldface** letters in the illustrative examples for that section, in order to highlight the feature in question.

1. UNITS

One of the most striking, if elusive, features of conversation is its division into recognizable units at various levels. Any discourse transcription should indicate at least the most fundamental of these. This section presents symbols for boundaries between units of various kinds, including the intonation unit and the word unit, as well as truncated (uncompleted) variants of these units. (The turn, which is a fundamental unit of conversational discourse, is treated later in conjunction with the speaker identification label.)

1.1. Intonation Unit

A carriage return is used to indicate the end of an intonation unit (in effect, the boundary between two intonation units). Thus, each intonation unit appears on a separate line.[2]

---

[2] In general, a speaker's intonation unit should not be broken up into two lines; but for the occasional intonation unit that is so long that it will not fit on one line, see the section on presentation. Also, it may sometimes be necessary to break an intonation unit using the "intonation unit continued" symbol (described in the section on specialized notations).

Roughly speaking, an intonation unit is a stretch of speech uttered under a single coherent intonation contour. It tends to be marked by cues such as a pause and a shift upward in overall pitch level at its beginning, and a lengthening of its final syllable. For a fuller discussion of intonation units, the cues that mark them, and the methods for identifying them, see Du Bois et al. (1991), Chafe (this volume), and Cruttenden (1986, pp. 35–45).

(1) ((Aesthetics))

    S: That's interesting,

       I mean,

       th- that you should pair the word aesthetics,

       ... with advertising.

    J: Yeah.

1.2. Truncated Intonation Unit

A double hyphen (--) indicates that the speaker breaks off the intonation unit before completing its projected contour.

This truncation occurs primarily in cases where a speaker utters the initial portion of a projected intonation unit but abandons it before finishing—that is, a false start. The double hyphen is *not* intended to represent the case of a unit that appears incomplete when measured against the canons of normative grammar. Intonation units that do not constitute complete clauses are commonplace and usually quite normal—and "complete" as intonation units. For example, conjunctions (*and*) and particles (*well*) frequently appear as complete intonation units marked with a comma at the end, which signals "continuing" intonation (see below)—a kind of incompleteness, if you will, but one that is distinct in principle from the truncation signaled by double hyphen. The unit marked with a comma typically constitutes (apparently) all that the speaker projected to say *within the current unit*, whereas in the unit marked with a double hyphen the speaker projected to say more within the current unit but abandoned some portion of the projected utterance. Truncation is thus measured not against normative notions of clause completeness but against the speaker's presumed projection for the current intonation unit.

(2) ((Ranch))

    R: He doesn't have any --

       ... He doesn't know what's going on in this world.

Note that for every intonation unit that *is* complete, the line should end with *some* representation of its intonation contour (see below). If an intonation unit does not so end, it will in general have the double hyphen that marks truncation.

1.3. Word

The space character is used to separate words, as in normal orthographic convention. A space also separates certain other notations, such as those for laughter, pause, inhalation, and so forth.

(3) ((Aesthetics))
    S: Hm.
        Hm.
        ... Okay.

1.4. Truncated Word

A single hyphen (-) indicates where the speaker has truncated a word, leaving the end of the (projected) word unuttered.[3]
    Truncation is often cued overtly via word-final glottal constriction, but not always—either phenomenon may occur independently of the other. Other truncation cues may include segment shortening, slight rhythmic discontinuities, and so on. (Where it is deemed relevant, the precise pronunciation of the truncated word can be written using phonetic notation.)

(4) ((Friends))
    J: ... You know how they do that,
        so you can't s- ha- --
        you don't have any balance.

This symbol is *not* used to mark words that have been pronounced in an abbreviated fashion as part of an informal speech style. Truncation of a word is measured not against canons of "normal" or "standard" pronunciation but

---

[3] The single hyphen is written at the end of the word or word fragment, with no space intervening. Note that for standard orthographies such as English that use a hyphen to write certain compound words, some care needs to be taken to distinguish this orthographic use of the hyphen from its use for truncated words (and also for truncated intonation units). Because in truncated words the hyphen is followed by a space, whereas in compound words it is generally followed by a letter of the alphabet, this should in general be sufficient to allow automatic discrimination between the two. Similar measures will work for the truncated intonation unit notation.

against the speaker's projected pronunciation for the current word. Only when a speaker projects pronunciation of a word and then fails to complete that projected pronunciation is the phenomenon of word truncation involved.

2. SPEAKERS

2.1. Speaker Identification and Turn Beginning

To identify the speaker of a given turn in the conversation, a code or a proper name (written all in capital letters) is inserted at the beginning of the turn, followed immediately by a colon (:).

(5) ((Door))
>   **A:** Now that we have the [side door] fixed,
>   **B:**   [That's kind of] --
>   **A:** he could.
>   **B:** Yeah,
>   **C:** Yeah.
>   **D:** ... Sure.

Although transcribers often assign prosaic codes such as "A" or "B" to their speakers, the reader tends to get a more vivid impression of who the participants are if their utterances are tagged with personal names, which are always more memorable. The name should in general be a pseudonym, since in any transcription destined for public presentation, privacy considerations would ordinarily preclude use of the speakers' actual names. The choice of names becomes especially important if speakers use names to refer to each other during the course of a conversation, in which case, the pseudonym in the speaker identification label should match that in the spoken reference, so that all relevant persons—whether they are speaking or merely spoken about—are clearly distinguished. If possible, pseudonyms should retain some flavor of the actual names.

(6) ((Aesthetics))
>   **JEFF:**   That's all it does.
>   It doesn't [even] reach a conclusion.
>   **SARAH:**   [mhm],
>   **JEFF:**   The conclusion is up to you.
>   **SARAH:** mhm,
>   **JEFF:**   in going out to --
>   ... to buy the thing.

SARAH: Hm.

Hm.

... Okay.

When it is unclear which of several speakers on a tape is responsible for a particular utterance or noise, the letter *X* is used to label the unidentified speaker.

(7) ((Friends))

X: ((BLOWS WHISTLE))

Note that the stretch of speech between two different speaker labels constitutes, roughly speaking, the discourse unit known as a turn. The picture is somewhat complicated, however, by the listener's interjection of continuative backchannel responses (*mhm*, *yeah*, etc.) into a speaker's extended turn. Although a backchannel response must for clarity's sake bear a speaker label, as must the two sections of the turn it occurs within, one does not want to be misled by this practical consideration into overlooking the essential continuity of the extended turn unit across such fleeting interjections.

2.2. Speech Overlap

Square brackets are used to indicate the beginning (left bracket) and the ending (right bracket) of overlap between the utterances of two speakers. One set of brackets is inserted surrounding the first speaker's overlapping utterance portion, and a second set of brackets surrounds the second speaker's overlapping portion. This notation signals that the two bracketed utterance portions were uttered at the same time.

For the sake of reading clarity, the second speaker's left bracket is aligned vertically under the first speaker's left bracket (by inserting as many spaces as needed). This alignment of space on the page helps to give an iconic sense of the temporal alignment of the two overlapping utterances. Note that only the left bracket need be aligned vertically; for reasons of clarity and practicality it is not advisable to force the right bracket to do so.

(8) ((Depression))

B: Clint is still screaming about that,

...

R: [Because he wanted the stamps],

B: [all those stamps],

... Mom let Ted Kenner have.

Wherever several overlaps occur in rapid succession within a short stretch of speech, distinctive combinations of brackets (e.g., single brackets [ ] vs. double brackets [[ ]]) may be needed to make clear what is overlapping with what. This will be necessary whenever two distinct cases of overlap occur without at least one line of nonoverlapped text between them, because if only one kind of bracket were used (e.g., just single brackets) the reader could be misled to think that the first and second bracketed portions (marked with single brackets) were simultaneous with the third and fourth bracketed portions (if also marked with single rather than double brackets). After one full line of speech containing no overlaps—when there is no longer danger of confusion— the use of double brackets can be dropped and single brackets resumed. If distinctive bracketing is needed again later in the same text, the single and double brackets should be used in alternation. Whenever no other overlaps occur nearby, it is best to use just the single brackets alone.

(9) ((Aesthetics))

    J: [Yeah].

    S: [Which] colors ... all of the communication,

       [[after]] that.

    J: [[Yeah]].

When there are many overlaps in very close succession, it may occasionally be necessary to use more than two kinds of distinctive brackets. For example, triple brackets ([[[ ]]]) or brackets indexed with numbers ([3 3]) can be used to create distinctive bracketing.[4]

(10) ((Dinner))

    B: Nobody wants [to leave].

    A: [They don't] move [[out]].

    S: [[Berkeley]] just keeps [3 getting 3] bigger and [4 bigger 4].

    B: [3 Yeah 3],

                          [4 Yeah 4],

    ... Well it's amazing to me.

Occasionally, it may be useful to employ distinctively marked (e.g., doubled) brackets even when no other overlaps occur nearby, in order to help the reader follow a complicated conversational exchange.

---

[4] The numeral *1* is avoided because it is easily mistaken for the lowercase letter *l* or even the capital *I* in many typefaces; numerals *2* through *9* engender no such confusion.

(11) ((Hypochondria))

    G: ... Well,

        the worst [[thing I ever had,

    K: [[He's a medical miracle]].

    G: was brain]] fever,

        when I had proposed to her.

    K: @ @ @ @

        ... From which you haven't recovered.

Often enough, the second speaker in an overlap begins to speak in the middle of a word being uttered by the first speaker. In such cases, it is useful to keep track of precisely where the overlap begins, because this may carry significant information about how the speakers are responding to each other in "real time" (Schegloff, personal communication). To indicate this, the bracket is placed within the word at a point corresponding to the overlap. (When a bracket is written inside a word, no space should be inserted—whether the bracket is indexed or not—since any space would break up the word and cause it to appear as two separate words.)

(12) ((Hypochondria))

    G: ... Then I had,

        uh,

    K: Cytomegalo[virus],

    G: [Don't] forget,

        cytomegalo[[virus]],

    K: [[@]]

    D: [[What is that]].

3. TRANSITIONAL CONTINUITY

In speech, important information is carried in the speaker's intonation, encompassing fluctuations of pitch and other cues. Although a discourse transcription can never capture a complete representation of the infinite variety of possible intonation contours, it can nonetheless provide a useful representation of at least the more critical intonational information by distinguishing broad *classes* of contours. It is useful to distinguish here between *functional* and *phonetic* analyses of intonation, each of which has its place in discourse transcription. The symbols in this section deal with the functional analysis of intonation, whereas a set of symbols that address the phonetic analysis of intonation is introduced in the section on terminal pitch (see also the section on tone).[5]

The system of categories presented in this section seeks to identify in general terms *one aspect* of intonational function, that of marking *transitional continuity*. When a speaker arrives at the end of an intonation unit, poised to continue on to the next—or not continue—the intonation contour usually gives a fairly clear indication of whether the discourse business at hand will be continued or has finished. This is transitional continuity: the marking of the degree of continuity that occurs at the transition point between one intonation unit and the next. The scope of the continuity—the question of what it is that is being continued or finished—is open-ended: A "final" contour may apply to the end of a sentence, the end of a turn, or the end of some other discourse unit. Whereas it may be possible to make finer discriminations in transitional continuity within the broad class of contours covered by each transitional continuity symbol, the distinctions among "final," "continuing," and "appeal" (see below), at least, seem to be basic.

Although the intonation contour classes in this set are defined in terms of their function, each category is more or less consistently realized by a specific form: a specific phonetic contour, or a set of contours (in effect, intonational allomorphs), where each member of the set is determined by its context. The range of phonetic realizations for a given transitional continuity class differs somewhat from one language to the next, which is one reason for using functionally based categories: They help to ensure that similar intonational functions are written similarly across languages, facilitating comparison even where phonetic realizations differ. Preliminary observations in a limited number of languages suggest that, remarkably, all languages are likely to make intonational distinctions between the transitional continuity classes presented in this section, though their phonetic realizations may vary.

The symbols used to represent transitional continuity here are drawn from those employed in written punctuation. Although using commas and periods in ways that are reminiscent of their function in written language does make it easier to remember them, it also means that the transcriber must guard against slipping into habits of thought associated with written punctuation. In discourse transcription as presented here, the punctuation symbols comma, period, and question mark *always* represent intonation classes and never grammatical or semantic structure per se.

---

[5] For researchers who wish to pursue the representation of intonation in discourse further, the work of Couper-Kuhlen (1986), Cruttenden (1986), Crystal (1975), Cutler and Ladd (1983), Gumperz (1982, this volume), McLemore (1991), Svartvik (1990), Svartvik and Quirk (1980), and others should be consulted (see Couper-Kuhlen, 1986, and Cruttenden, 1986, for additional references). For the notion of intonation unit, see Chafe (this volume) and Du Bois et al. (1991).

3.1. Final

The period (.) indicates a class of intonation contours whose transitional continuity is regularly understood as *final* in a given language. For English and many other languages, this means primarily (but not exclusively) a fall to a low pitch at the end of an intonation unit. It is important to recall that, because this symbol represents an intonational category rather than a syntactic one, it can appear in places other than the end of a sentence. Conversely, it need not appear at the end of every (normative) sentence.

(13) ((Depression))

    R: For what.

    B: ... They make rope of it.

3.2. Continuing

The comma (,) indicates a class of intonation contours whose transitional continuity is regularly understood as *continuing,* in a given language. The contour is often realized in English as a slight rise in pitch at the end of an intonation unit (beginning from a low or mid level), but it may have other realizations as well, each of which presumably has slightly different pragmatic implications. One type of continuing contour is realized by a terminal pitch that remains level; another, by a terminal pitch that falls slightly, but not low enough to be considered final.[6]

(14) ((Ranch))

    R: If you think about it,

        yeah,

        if it rains a lot,

        the horse is always wet,

        and it's always moist,

        it's always on something moist,

        ... Sure it's going to be softer.

3.3. Appeal

The question mark (?) indicates a class of intonation contours whose transitional continuity is regularly understood as an *appeal,* in a given language. (For English, this is often realized by a marked *high rise* in pitch at

---

[6] The significance of the end point of pitch movement is well known (Couper-Kuhlen, 1986, pp. 88–90). As one intonation specialist notes, "The lower the end point, the greater the degree of definiteness and conclusiveness" (Trim, 1970, p. 265, cited in Couper-Kuhlen, 1986, p. 88).

the end of the intonation unit.) "Appeal" here refers to when a speaker, in producing an utterance, seeks a validating response from a listener. The most common type of appeal in this sense is a *yes–no* question, but not all *yes–no* questions are said with the appeal contour, and in such cases the question should not be written with a question mark. Conversely, the appeal contour may be used where there is no *yes–no* question; in such cases, the question mark *is* written. For example, a speaker will often check to see if listeners remember a particular person by uttering that person's name with an appeal contour (high rising pitch), where the response sought from this appeal may be nothing more than a slight nod of recognition. In such cases, the proper name will be written with a question mark following it.

It is important to emphasize that the question mark is *not* used for a grammatical question uttered with intonations other than the appeal contour, such as a final contour. Thus, there will occur grammatical questions (including some *yes–no* questions) that do not carry this type of contour; conversely, the question mark will appear in units that lack the morphosyntactic structure of a (normative) question.

(15) ((Friends))

    J: ... Should we waste him?
        or should we stop him,
        and ... then waste him.

4. TERMINAL PITCH DIRECTION

Whereas analysis according to functional classes (i.e., in terms of transitional continuity and/or other functional classification) captures one kind of information about an intonation contour, there is another kind of intonational information that is worth recording, involving the phonetics of the pitch movement. The symbols in this section iconically represent the movement of pitch at a critical location in the intonation unit: at the end of the unit (i.e., the transition point from one intonation unit to the next). In contrast to the symbols in the last section, which represent a certain aspect of intonational function, these symbols are designed to represent the auditory shape of the pitch movement. Naturally, no finite set of symbols can provide more than a general classification of pitch phonetics, since a complete representation would require an infinitely variable analog display. But when symbols for terminal pitch direction are supplemented with symbols for transitional continuity and tone, the combination is an effective means of capturing key features of intonation at the most reasonable cost in time and effort.

Inevitably, different researchers will wish to take different approaches to representing intonation in discourse. Among the minimalist alternatives available are to use exclusively the categories for transitional continuity, to use some other functional classification, to use just the phonetic categories for terminal pitch direction presented in this section, or to use just the categories for tone. Or the transcriber can use some combination of these, such as the transitional continuity and terminal pitch classifications—a combination that is particularly useful for those primarily interested in how extended discourse is chunked into units, rather than in the subtle and often elusive meanings distinguished by the various intonational tones. (Many other approaches to intonation are represented in the literature; see Cruttenden, 1986 and Couper-Kuhlen, 1986.) The decision about what intonational categories to use will be influenced by one's research goals and theory of intonation, and the degree of delicacy sought for a particular transcription.

4.1. Fall

A backslash (\) indicates that the direction of the terminal pitch movement is falling. This downward-sloping line iconically represents downward movement and is reminiscent of the International Phonetic Association (1989) arrow symbol (↓) for a "global fall" in pitch.

Depending on how low the endpoint of the fall reaches (relative to neighboring pitch levels), such pitch movements may be functionally assigned to the continuing or final contour classes.

    (16) ((Aesthetics))

          J: ... You're not saying something, \
              you're doing something to people. \

4.2. Rise

A slash (/) indicates that the direction of the terminal pitch movement is rising. This upward-sloping line iconically represents upward movement and is reminiscent of the International Phonetic Association (1989) arrow symbol (↑) for a "global rise" in pitch.

Depending on the specific shape and pitch level of the rising movement, the contour may be functionally analyzed as pertaining to the continuing class (often a low or mid rise) or the appeal class (a high rise).

    (17) ((Ranch))

          R: ... And then, /
              they videotape us, /
              as we go. \

4.3. Level

Underscore (_) indicates that the direction of terminal pitch movement is level. This pitch movement is most commonly associated with the continuing contour class.

    (18) ((Cars))

        D: You know, _

           call them on the phone, /

           and uh, _

           ... take a lunch, /

5. ACCENT AND LENGTHENING

It is important for a discourse transcription to indicate which words are characterized by accent and length.

5.1. Primary Accent

A caret (^) indicates a word that bears a primary accent. The primary accent is characterized by its prominent pitch movement carrying intonational meaning; it is where the significant intonational "action" is focused, within the intonation unit. Primary accent is broadly comparable to the "nuclear accent" category of Crystal (1975), Cruttenden (1986), and others, which is characterized as "the most prominent syllable in a tone-unit," whose prominence is generally due to the "presence of noticeable pitch movement" (Couper-Kuhlen, 1986, p. 79).

Although there is some tendency for an intonation unit to contain exactly one primary accent, cases of two primary accents within one intonation unit are common enough. It is for this reason that we avoid the term *nuclear accent*, with its apparent presumption that each unit will contain no more than one nucleus. Also, intonation units containing no primary accent are fairly common, especially among minor intonation units (e.g., one-word intonation units) and truncated intonation units.

In English and many other languages, the particular syllable within the word on which prominence is realized is lexically predictable and thus need not be indicated in a *discourse-level* transcription.[7] Hence the primary accent mark is written immediately before the first letter of the accented word. (For the occasional utterance of a word token in which a prominence is realized on

---

[7] However, for those who prefer to write the accent mark immediately before the actual stressed syllable, there is no harm in doing this.

a syllable other than the expected one, this fact can be captured by using the notation provided for phonetic transcription [see below].) But for languages in which a word's stressed syllable is *not* lexically predictable, the primary accent notation should be written immediately before the stressed syllable (which hence may place the symbol within the word).

    (19) ((Forces))

        B: ^I met `him,
           and I `thought he was a `ni=ce ^kid.
        S: He ^is a nice `kid,
           but he's ^wei=rd.

5.2. Secondary Accent

A raised vertical stroke or grave accent (`) indicates a word that bears a secondary accent, relative to nearby primary accented and unaccented words.

    (20) ((Hypochondria))

        G: ...(2.2) `a=nd of course,
           a `lot of herb ^tea,
           when I'd `rather be drinking ^whiskey.

   Because it can be difficult to distinguish reliably among three degrees of accent—primary, secondary, and (implicitly) nonaccent—some researchers may prefer to mark only two degrees of accent, corresponding to "accented" (to be written with the raised stroke, i.e., the grave accent character) versus "unaccented" (unmarked).

5.3. Booster

The exclamation point (!) can be used optionally to mark a high "booster"— very roughly, a higher than expected pitch on a word.[8] Low booster can optionally be written with a semicolon (;). For a fuller discussion of the concept of booster, see Crystal (1975) and Cruttenden (1986). The booster symbol is written immediately before the word in question and any symbols for accent.

---

[8] An extrahigh booster can optionally be written with two exclamation points (!!).

5.4. Lengthening

An equal sign (=) indicates that the preceding segment is lengthened prosodically, to a degree greater than what is expected on the basis of accent and lexical stress patterns. The slight lengthening that is to be expected when a syllable is accented is not marked with the equal sign, being implicit in the accent marking. Similarly, segments that are *phonemically* long (in a language with a contrast between long and short vowels, or long and short consonants) do not on that account receive the equal sign notation: Phonemic length should be written with a different notation (e.g., doubled letters). For sounds that are represented in standard orthography by a digraph (e.g., in English, *ee*, *ea*, *oo*, *ph*, *ch*, *tt*, etc.), the convention is that the equal sign is written after the final letter of the digraph.

Prosodic lengthening is especially important to indicate because of its role as a potential cue for intonation unit boundaries (Cruttenden, 1986, pp. 35–45): It frequently occurs at the end of an intonation unit.

(21) ((Hypochondria))

K: ... ^Greg's never had a a ^co=ld,
or the ^flu=,

6. TONE

Each major intonation unit is in general characterized by some kind of prominent pitch movement, which carries the most significant intonational information about that unit. The locus of this prominent pitch movement is generally centered on the word which bears the primary accent: either the sole primary accent, or if there is more than one in a particular intonation unit, the last one. The various distinctive intonational shapes that are possible in this position are commonly called tones. A tone's pitch contour is often realized across a spread of several words, frequently extending from the last primary accent until the end of the unit. Because the shape of this pitch contour carries the most distinctive intonational meaning in the unit, it is useful to have symbols that can at least partly capture the differences. The classification of tones remains a substantial challenge for intonation specialists, as is attested by the existence of several competing classificatory systems, each with its adherents (see, for example, the various systems described in Couper-Kuhlen, 1986, and Cruttenden, 1986, and in the many references they cite).

This section presents notations for rising, falling, rising–falling, falling–rising, and level tones. The symbol for tone is written immediately before the accented word, with no intervening space. (Alternatively, the marks can be placed immediately before the *syllable*, rather than the word, that bears the accent.)   When tone is written, it may be possible to dispense with as redundant the primary accent mark, at least on one analysis.

6.1. Fall

A backslash (\) before a primary accented word indicates that the contour associated with the accent is falling.

(22) ((Forces))

A: he can't \spell.

6.2. Rise

A slash (/) before a primary accented word indicates that the contour associated with the accent is rising.

(23) ((Hypochondria))

D: Is he going to make her become a /Catholic?

6.3. Fall–Rise

The combination backslash–slash (\ /) before a primary accented word indicates that the contour associated with the accent is first falling, then rising. This pitch movement can cooccur with any of the transitional continuity classes, though it is more common with continuing and final than with appeal.

(24) ((Ranch))

R: If you \ /think about it,

   yeah,

   if it /rains a lot,

    the horse is always \ /wet,

   and it's always /moist,

   it's always on something \ /moist,

   ... \Sure it's going to be softer.

6.4. Rise–Fall

The combination slash–backslash (/ \) before a primary accented word indicates that the intonation contour associated with the accent is first rising, then falling. This pitch movement often cooccurs with a widened pitch range, which may be interpreted as expressing "high involvement". The transitional continuity class it is most often associated with is final.

   (25) ((Aesthetics))

       S: ... A lot of it's really / \bad.

6.5. Level

An underscore (_) before a primary accented word indicates that the contour associated with the accent is level.

   (26) ((Hypochondria))

       K: ...(1.2) They just _represent,

          each of the _days,

7. PAUSE

The placement and timing of pauses in spoken discourse conveys significant information about the speaker's discourse production process (Chafe, 1980b) and orientation toward the ongoing conversational interaction (e.g., Goodwin, 1981). Each pause should be indicated explicitly using one of the three notations presented in this section. As the intonational symbols (e.g., comma and single period) do not of themselves denote pause, any pause—even a slight one—that occurs in conjunction with an intonation contour must be specifically indicated using one of the pause notations.

7.1. Long

A sequence of three dots (...) immediately followed by a number in single parentheses is used to represent relatively long pauses (.7 seconds or longer). The approximate duration is indicated within parentheses to the nearest 10th of a second. That is, the duration is indicated as (.7), (.8), (1.6), and so on.

   (27) ((Ranch))

       R: ... This .. is a type of person,

         ...(.9) that ...(.7) is like ...(1.0) a hermit.

Ordinarily, a pause between two intonation units is written together with the unit that follows it (never with the one that precedes it). However, if a pause is attributable to more than one speaker (as when, during a long pause, it is unclear who is going to speak next), it is often preferable to place the pause notation on a separate line by itself. In some cases, the questions of who a pause belongs to, how long it lasts, and even whether it has occurred in a specific place, become subtly and inextricably linked to the interpretation of turn-taking and overlapping between speakers.

> (28) ((Depression))
>> B: ... I remember,
>> ...(.8) I used to help Billy,
>> and I'd get twenty-five cents a week,
>> ...(1.2)
>> R: [A week].
>> B: [Twenty] --

Whereas some researchers use subjective judgments of pause duration relativized to each speaker's current tempo (a "second" for a fast speaker is objectively shorter than a "second" for a slow speaker), this is in general not advisable, due to the difficulties in making such judgments consistently and reliably and in interpreting the "time" notations that result. Among other things, if a pause occurs at a turn boundary between the utterances of two speakers with different tempos, it is unclear which speaker should be used as the basis for relativizing the duration. Even a pause within the speech of a single speaker can be problematic if it occurs between a rapid stretch of syllables and a slow stretch—a fairly common configuration in everyday speech. Unless such ambiguities can be addressed, the only reliable practice is to indicate the actual pause duration in clock time (preferably as measured instrumentally).

7.2. Medium

A sequence of three dots (...) indicates a pause of medium length—one that is noticeable but not very long, about half a second in duration (specifically, between 0.3 and 0.6 seconds, inclusive).

> (29) ((Hypochondria))
>> G: ...(1.7) I'd like to have .. my ... lungs,
>> ... my entire respiratory tract,
>> ... replaced,
>> ... with .. asbestos.
>> .. or something.

7.3. Short

A sequence of two dots (..) indicates a brief break in speech rhythm, that is, a very short, barely perceptible pause (about 0.2 seconds or less).

> (30) ((Ranch))
>
> R: .. a reining pattern is,
>
> .. a pattern where you .. do sliding stops,
>
> .. spins,
>
> ... lead changes,
>
> .. I know you probably don't know what that is.

It is important to note that not all brief silences are to be classified as pauses. The moment of silence that necessarily occurs during a lexically or phonologically required voiceless stop should not be classified as a pause, even if it is longer than expected (as in an emphatic or "marcato" pronunciation of a word containing a voiceless stop). The reason for this is that for discourse research what matters is the pause as a functional cue to aspects of discourse production and conversational interaction, not as a raw acoustic fact.

7.4. Latching

A zero within single parentheses (0) indicates that the following utterance "latches" onto the preceding utterance, that is, there is no pause (or "zero" pause) between the two speakers' turns. Because it symbolizes a noticeable lack of pause between actual *turns*, mere continuative backchannel responses (*m=hm*, etc.) are not ordinarily marked with this symbol.

> (31) ((Cars))
>
> G: .. I was using number seven,
>
> .. gun number seven,
>
> D: (0) It broke the [chisel].
>
> G: [and] it broke my chisel,
>
> man.
>
> <X Now X> --
>
> D: (0) So now you have no chisel.
>
> G: (0) <X It's X> my only good chisel.
>
> man,

Since simply not writing in any pause notation—not even a two-dot pause—will already serve to suggest the absence of a pause, the latching notation is to some degree redundant. This plus the fact that determining the presence of latching presupposes a potentially difficult judgment about the turn (or nonturn) status of an utterance leads some researchers to avoid this transcriptional category.

8. VOCAL NOISES

The participants in a conversation do more with their vocal tracts than just utter words: They also cough, yawn, click, inhale, laugh, and produce a variety of other noises. The notations in this section are designed to allow the transcriber to easily notate nonverbal noises produced in the vocal tracts of speech event participants. The reason for distinguishing vocal noises made by speech event participants as a special category is that participants often use this channel to give each other subtle cues about aspects of the ongoing linguistic interaction, as when a speaker takes a sharp in-breath in order to signal the purpose to speak next (Sacks, Schegloff, & Jefferson, 1974). Crickets chirping and microphones rustling do not consistently carry such interpersonal meanings for humans.

8.1. Vocal Noises

Single parentheses surrounding a description written in capital letters **(COUGH)** are used to indicate nonverbal noises produced in the vocal tract of speech event participants. This kind of notation encompasses coughing, throat clearing, tongue clicking, breathing, and so on, but not dish washing, finger drumming, dogs barking, and so forth (for which double parentheses are available; see below).

The capital letters and parentheses help to make it clear that the words so written were not actually uttered by the speaker; that is, rather than *saying* the word *cough*, the speaker *did* cough. (For some high-frequency vocal noises, a special nonalphabetic symbol is used—e.g., @ for laughter—and in such cases the parentheses are unnecessary.)

The notation (THROAT) indicates the sound made by someone clearing their throat. Similarly, (GULP) can be used to represent a gulping sound, and (SWALLOW), (SNIFF), (SNORT), (BURP), and (YAWN) likewise represent the indicated sounds. Additional notations in this format can be generated as needed for indicating other vocal noises.

(32) ((Aesthetics))

    S: (H) **(THROAT)**

       Yeah.

The notation **(TSK)** indicates the utterance of a click of the tongue—in English this is usually an alveolar click—as an isolated vocal sound, for example, what is commonly written *tsk* in newspaper cartoon style.

(33) ((Ranch))

    R: and then,

       ... **(TSK)** our job,

       is to shape the shoe,

       ... to the horse's foot.

8.2. Glottal Stop

The percent sign (%) indicates a *paralinguistically* introduced glottal stop or glottal constriction. This notation is *not* used in positions where glottal stop is phonologically predictable, as at the beginning of vowel-initial words (under certain conditions) in English. Nor is this notation used where glottal stop is lexically required, as in certain words in languages with *phonemic* glottal stop. (For "creaky" or glottalized voice quality extending over whole words or longer stretches of speech, see "Quality" below.)

One reason for taking the trouble to transcribe paralinguistic glottal stop is that speakers often seem to produce it when they abandon a word or utterance. To the extent that glottal stop functions as an objective cue for abandoned utterances, it is useful to have it on record. Glottal stop and glottal constriction may act as cues to other aspects of the discourse production process as well.

(34) ((Ranch))

    R: it's mandatory,

       you have to --

       % to graduate,

       you know,

       % well,

       to ... get the degree,

       you know,

       ... you have to take this class.

8.3. Inhalation

A capital *H* in single parentheses **(H)** indicates audible inhalation.[9]

In conversation, breathing is more than just a bodily necessity; it can be used, for example, as a signal that one is about to take a turn at speaking (Jefferson, 1984, p. 353f.; Sacks et al., 1974).

> (35) ((Hypochondria))
>
> K: ... **(H)** leukemia,
>   ... **(H)** bronchitis,
>   ... **(H)** uh,
>   tuberculosis,
>   @ @ @ @ **(H)**
>   and he's recovered from all of them.

Where a pause and a quiet inhalation occur in immediate succession, it is often difficult to separate the two (e.g., in order to time the pause). In such cases, it may be preferable to write the pause and inhalation together with no intervening space and to assign any indication of duration to the pause-plus-inhalation complex taken as a whole.

8.4. Exhalation

A capital *H* followed by a small *x* within single parentheses **(Hx)** indicates audible exhalation.[10]

> (36) ((Depression))
>
> B: ...(4.3) **(Hx)** ... Kids in the city miss so much.

Sometimes a speaker audibly inhales and exhales several times in immediate succession. All of this can be written within a single set of parentheses: (H Hx H Hx).

Note that neither the inhalation symbol (H) nor the exhalation symbol (Hx) is used within a word (e.g., for breathy voiced segments, laughter, etc.).

---

[9] For some purposes, it may be useful to make use of multiple *H*s to represent iconically the relative duration of a long inhalation: (HHHHHHHHHH). For example, this may be called for if another speaker overlaps with the inhalation and one wishes to show the exact point where overlap begins and ends.

[10] Again, in some circumstances it may be helpful to make use of a series of *H*s to iconically represent the duration of a long exhalation: (HHHHHx). Note that since the lowercase *x* in this notation acts in effect as a sort of "subscript" attached to the string of *H*s, it is written only once.

Because of the serious potential for confusion that an ambiguous use of H would introduce, other notations using discriminable characters (Du Bois, 1991) are preferable (see the next section).

8.5. Laughter

The @ symbol is used to represent laughter. One token of the symbol @ is used for each "syllable," or pulse, of laughter. (The @ symbol bears a certain mnemonic resemblance to the pervasive "smiley face" icon.)

Because the placement of laughter can be of great consequence for a conversational interaction (Jefferson, 1979, 1984), it is important to note it carefully. Although laughter falls in the category of nonverbal vocal tract sounds, and so by present conventions could in principle be written within single parentheses (i.e., as (LAUGH)), it occurs so pervasively that it warrants its own distinctive symbol. The @ symbol has the additional advantages of being easily reiterated in a minimum of space—allowing the duration of the laughter in "syllables" to be represented iconically—and of being readily discriminable when written within a word.

(37) ((Hypochondria))

   K: @@@@

   ... From which you haven't recovered.

For laughter of extended duration, the transcriber may prefer to write just a single laugh symbol followed by an indication of duration—if it is not easy to determine how many syllables of laughter there are (as is often the case when several people are laughing at once) or if the investigator is simply not especially interested in how many laugh syllables have occurred.

(38) ((Miracle))

   ALL: @(**12.7**)

Sometimes it is useful to distinguish between different kinds of laughter. For example, the symbol @N can be used for nasal laughter, a usually voiceless laugh in which the air is emitted through the nose. To the extent that further distinctions among kinds of laughter may be significant (Jefferson, 1979), such distinctions can be indicated by suffixing various characters to the @ symbol as modifiers of it, with the resulting complexes (e.g., @I@I, @A@A) defined by the researcher. (The unmarked symbol for all kinds of laughter, however, is simply @.)

(39) ((Aesthetics))

  J: ... You're not supposed to use these powerful [techniques].
  S: [@N@N@N]
   ... Hm.

9. QUALITY

There are many occasions in conversation where, for a stretch of a few words
or lines, a speaker's voice takes on some special quality, shifts in pitch, or
slows in tempo, and so on. Because this kind of momentary marked quality or
prosody can serve important functions in exposing some perhaps unverbalized
aspect of the speaker's stance or the speech production process, and because it
can have consequences for the ongoing spoken interaction, it is important to
record it. But because the special qualities that can occur are so diverse, the
notation must be flexible enough to meet any demands that may arise in the
discourse material. The notational formula introduced in this section is
designed to accommodate this kind of diversity.

9.1. Types of Quality

Angle brackets **<Y Y>** are used to indicate that the stretch of text which they
enclose has a marked quality or prosody of some sort. The particular quality
(higher pitch, increased loudness, etc.) is specified by a supplementary symbol,
represented here by Y. The text enclosed within these symbols often amounts
to several words and may run across several lines. The marked quality is
judged relative to the surrounding discourse produced by the same speaker.
For example, a sentence would be marked for tempo if it is noticeably quicker
or slower than the speaker's current or usual tempo. This set of symbols
(partly based on Boase, 1990) is in principle open-ended, and new ones can be
developed to suit a particular investigator's needs. For most transcribing
purposes, these notations are used sparingly, to indicate just those phenomena
that are of special interest and consequence for the spoken interaction.
 Listed here are some of the more common types.

  Loudness

    <F   **F>** forte: loud
    <P   **P>** piano: soft
    <CR   **CR>** crescendo: gradually louder
    <DIM **DIM>** diminuendo: gradually softer

Pitch

<HI	**HI>**	higher pitch level
<LO	**LO>**	lowered pitch level
<W	**W>**	widened pitch range
<N	**N>**	narrowed pitch range
<PAR	**PAR>**	parenthetical prosody

Tempo and Rhythm

<A	**A>**	allegro: rapid speech
<L	**L>**	lento: slow speech
<RH	**RH>**	rhythmic: stresses in a beatable rhythm
<MRC	**MRC>**	marcato: each word distinct and emphasized
<ARH	**ARH>**	arrhythmic: halting speech

Voice quality

<WH	**WH>**	whispered
<BR	**BR>**	breathy
<HSK	**HSK>**	husky
<%	**%>**	creaky (or: <CRK CRK>)
<FAL	**FAL>**	falsetto
<TRM	**TRM>**	tremulous
<SOB	**SOB>**	sobbing
<CRY	**CRY>**	crying
<YWN	**YWN>**	yawning
<SGH	**SGH>**	sighing

Following are instances of several of these notations. The angle-bracket pair <F F> is used to enclose a stretch of forte speech (produced with relatively increased loudness).

(40) ((Hypochondria))

  A: <F It's not the end of Chanukah F>,
    in case you're interested.

The angle-bracket pair <P P> is used to enclose a stretch of piano speech.

(41) ((Ranch))

    R: ... But uh,

      ...(3.0) <P What was I going to say P>,

      ...(3.5) X- --

      Oh,

      it's really tiring,

      though.

The angle bracket notation **<W W>** marks widened pitch range. (This is a marked prosody often interpreted as displaying "high involvement" or "surprise.") The increased pitch range is often accompanied by sudden pitch movement and in English is frequently associated with a pronounced rise–fall tone, which may be accompanied by increased loudness.

(42) ((Cars))

    D: ... No basketball.

    G: ... **<W Really W>**.

The angle-bracket pair **<MRC MRC>** is used for a stretch of marcato speech, in which each word is uttered distinctly and with emphasis.

(43) ((Friends))

    J: ... But the goldfish got stuck,

      ... **<MRC** halfway into his mouth **MRC>**.

The angle-bracket pair **<WH WH>** is used to enclose words uttered in a whisper.

(44) ((Africa))

    A: they let us alone.

      ... **<WH** But we were scared,

      And boy **WH>**,

      did we ever get in trouble,

      from Mel and Ervin.

The angle-bracket pair **<% %>** (alternatively **<CRK CRK>**) indicates creakiness or glottalization of the enclosed words.

(45) ((Aesthetics))

> J: <% Tha%- this% --
> I wonder about that though,
> I mean %>,
> when I think of ads,

In cases where it seems useful to specify the precise location of a special quality that begins and/or ends at some point within a word, an underscore can be added to the usual angle bracket notation (e.g., **<WH_ _WH>** or **<%_ _%>**) so as to separate the (capital) letters of the quality notation from the letters of the word they enclose. Thus, if just the fourth through sixth syllables of the word *cytomegalovirus* were whispered, this could be written as "cyto<**WH**_megalo_**WH**>virus." Where one is not so concerned to avoid ambiguity, the underscore symbols could be dispensed with. This works especially well with nonalphabetic notations like those for creaky quality ("cyto<%megalo%>virus") or laugh quality ("cyto<@megalo@>virus"; see next section). This word-internal quality notation is likely to be used but rarely.

9.2. Laugh Quality

The angle bracket pair **<@ @>** indicates a laughing quality over a stretch of speaking, that is, laughter during the words enclosed between the two @ symbols. (The angle brackets can be combined with notations for other kinds of laughter as well, e.g., **<@N @N>**, etc.)

(46) ((Africa))

> A: ... and they stepped out in the road,
> and not only did they have uniforms on,
> but they <@ also had guns @>.
> @ @ @

If a laugh occurs during the utterance of just one word, this can also be indicated simply by prefixing the word with one @ sign and dispensing with the angle brackets.

(47) ((Friends))

> N: You know,
> this was a rented @snake,
> @

For most transcription purposes, it is sufficient to use the laugh quality brackets to frame whole words or groups of words (the convention followed in this work). But some researchers may wish to indicate on which particular syllables within a word laughter occurs. To do this, each pulse (syllable) of laughter receives one @ token, which is written within the word at the appropriate place, before the laugh-tinged sounds.

> (48) ((Lunch))
>
>> R: ...(1.0) When they quit going to Littleton,
>>   every week to see his gra@ndmo@the@r @ @ @,

Sometimes a speaker speaks with a smile rather than a laugh, causing their speech to be tinged with an audible "smile" quality. If desired, this can be written with laugh brackets with the letters *SM* affixed: **<@SM @SM>**.

9.3. Quotation Quality

The angle-bracket pair **<Q Q>** indicates a stretch of speech characterized by a "quotation" quality. Its use is warranted where there is some actual shift in the quality of the stretch of quoted speech, as when the quoting speaker imitates some mannerism of the quoted speaker. Where no such shift is audible, this notation should not be used.[11]

> (49) ((Friends))
>
>> J: This is a literal quote,
>>   he says to me,
>>   ... **<Q** I'm going to restrain you.
>>   to the fence **Q>**.

Note that the quotation symbol is not used for metalanguage, such as the name of a letter or a reference to a word (Du Bois et al., 1991), unless this is accompanied by an audible quotation quality.

9.4. Multiple Quality Features

When a stretch of speech is characterized by two or more coextensive special qualities worth noting, these are indicated with multiple angle brackets **<Y<Z**

---

[11] Some may wish to use plain double quotation marks (" ") for marking quotations that do not carry a special voice quality; but this should be recognized as part of functional coding rather than transcription per se.

Z>Y>. (The several angle-bracket notations are juxtaposed without any space between them.)

(50) ((Friends))

    J: So the guy yells at me,

        ... <Q<F Is that your dog F>Q>?

10. PHONETICS

Although a discourse transcription does not generally seek to represent every variation in pronunciation, there are times when the question of how a word was pronounced takes on immediate significance for the spoken interaction. In such cases, it is useful to have available a way of writing that can unambiguously indicate the actual pronunciation of a particular word or words—without, hopefully, requiring too much in the way of special knowledge or special characters.   This section presents a way of citing phonetic (or phonemic) transcriptions for selected words. (A set of symbols that can be used for making precise phonetic transcriptions without requiring special characters is provided in Du Bois et al., 1991.)

10.1. Phonetic/Phonemic Transcription

A symbol complex composed of slashes surrounded by single parentheses (/ /) is used to enclose a representation of the actual pronunciation of a word. The phonetic (or phonemic) transcription is given *in addition* to the traditional orthographic representation of the same word(s), which it follows.

The transcription itself can be written in several different ways, depending on the degree of precision sought and the enthusiasm of the transcriber. The following example illustrates the option of supplementing standard orthography with selected phonetic symbols—in this case, stress marks—in order to represent just enough of the actual pronunciation to allow the interchange to be understood.

(51) ((Cafe))

    A: Virago_(/ `Virago/).

    C: ... Virago_(/ `Virago/)?

    A: ... I don't know how you pronounce it.

    B: [I thought it was] Virago_(/Vi`rago/),

    A: [<X Does X> this] --

The next example illustrates a more precise, and more ambitious, style of phonemic transcription (Du Bois et al., 1991).

> (52) ((Comparative))
>> G: But this Naiman_(/ `naIm6n/) book,
>> or Naiman_(/ `neIm6n/),
>> I don't know how he says his name,

In general, phonetic transcription is used only where the actual pronunciation of a word is of special significance for the analyst's purposes. Most of the time, standard orthography used alone will be sufficient. A sparing use of phonetic detail notations has the important advantage of making transcriptions easier to read.

11. TRANSCRIBER'S PERSPECTIVE

In addition to symbols for representing speech per se, the transcriber occasionally needs to indicate some aspect of his or her perspective on the transcription—in effect, a metatranscriptional interjection. This section provides several symbols that allow the transcriber to insert useful comments or observations, while keeping such interjections clearly distinct from the actual speech.

11.1. Researcher's Comment

A pair of double parentheses (( )) encloses any comment the transcriber or researcher chooses to make. The comment is written all in capital letters, in order to make it quite clear to the reader that the words in question are not actual speech. Comments interjected into the transcription in this way are best kept short, for the sake of a readable transcription.

This notation is also used for indicating any nonlinguistic events that take place within the spoken interaction, such as ambient noises or other noises (excluding vocal noises). But such sounds and other events are usually noted only if they are relevant to the conversational interaction at hand—as when participants comment on or otherwise react to the noise.

> (53) ((Friends))
>> N: and they're,
>> ... you know,
>> ... ((DOG BARKS EXCITEDLY))
>> ...

J: You know --

You know about this piece?

N: She always does that. ((REFERENCE TO DOG))

If a researcher plans to make fairly extended or pervasive commentary—for example, commenting on every turn—it may be preferable to set up a column format, using one side of the page for transcription and the other side for commentary.

11.2. Uncertain Hearing

A pair of angle brackets <X X> marked with the capital letter *X*—the *X* suggesting an unknown quantity—is used to mark portions of the text that are not clearly audible to the transcriber, to such an extent that there is some doubt as to what words were spoken.   The words so enclosed represent the transcriber's best guess as to what was said, but their accuracy is not assured.[12]

(54) ((Hypochondria))

G: ... Well,

I [don't] normally sound like Lucille Ball.

K: [<X That's X>] --

11.3. Indecipherable Syllable

The capital letter X (again, mnemonically suggesting an unknown quantity) is used to indicate speech that is not audible enough to allow a reasonable guess as to what was said. One X is used for each syllable of indecipherable speech. It is usually possible to make at least a rough estimate of how many syllables were uttered, even when one cannot make out what the words are.

(55) ((Cars))

D: It was basically me,

you know,

X going out.

The problem of going out.

---

[12] If one is unable to decide between two possible hearings of a stretch of speech, one can indicate both alternatives, as follows:

<X words X><X2 other words X2>

This device should be used most sparingly, however. If the words can be made out at all, it is almost always possible to decide which alternative is the more likely.

The methods and conventions presented in the remaining sections in this article deal either with specialized transcriptional categories or with research practices which, while not strictly speaking part of transcription per se, are closely linked to the production and use of discourse transcriptions.

12. DURATION

12.1. Duration of Simple Events

A number in parentheses (N) may be used to indicate the duration in seconds of any inhalation, hesitation, word, laugh, or other event that is of special interest. For instance, if an inhalation or exhalation is significantly long, its duration can be indicated in the same manner as for pauses, that is, with a number in parentheses immediately following it. In the following example, the notation indicates that the inhalation lasts 0.9 seconds.

(56) ((Forces))
    A: ...(1.0) (H)(.9) A=nd,

Similarly, in the following example, the hesitation word *um* (a "filled pause") is held for 0.7 seconds.

(57) ((Aesthetics))
    S: u=m(.7),

Aside from its use for notating pause duration, for most transcribing purposes this degree of delicacy will not often be needed.

12.2. Duration of Complex Events

The duration of a complex event (a sequence of pauses and hesitation words, for instance) can be indicated, when it is of special interest, using angle brackets (cf. Chafe, 1980a, p. 301). The duration of the items to be timed (written in parentheses in the usual way) is affixed to both the left and right brackets <(N) (N)>. Because proliferation of this kind of detail can quickly make a transcription difficult to read, for most purposes it will be used but rarely.

(58) ((Ranch))
    R: <(1.3) % .. (H) %
       ... % .. (1.3)> But .. uh,

13. SPECIALIZED NOTATIONS

This section presents a variety of specialized or miscellaneous notations and conventions. Some of the notations are for phenomena that are but rarely encountered, whereas other notations are of specialized interest or application.

13.1. Intonation Unit Continued

An ampersand (&) is used to mark each of the two halves of an intonation unit that for one reason or another the transcriber has split up and written on two lines. (It is not used when a unit is merely too long to fit on one line; for that, see the section on presentation.)

This is a notation that is needed only rarely. But occasionally, the complex realities of conversational interaction bring two fundamental representational principles of the present transcription system into conflict. First, vertical space on the page iconically represents the sequential order of turns (and the passage of time). Second, each intonation unit appears on a single line. But what is to be done when a speaker starts an intonation unit, pauses, and then finishes it, while a second speaker interjects a whole turn during the pause? In order to preserve (as far as possible) the principle that lines written higher on the page represent earlier turns, it is necessary, on rare occasions such as these, to break up an intonation unit into two lines. When this is done, the ampersands are used to mark the continuity of the unit across the intervening material. In such cases, even though the words appear on two separate lines, they should nevertheless be considered part of a single intonation unit.

(59) ((Lunch))

    R: When he was real little,

       [he] almost died of pneumonia.

    L: [Oh].

    R: when he was &

    L: Oh really?

    M: Hey.

    R: & three.

13.2. Accent Unit Boundary

The "pipe" symbol (I) is used by some researchers to separate one accent unit from the next, where more than one accent unit occurs within one intonation unit (Chafe, this volume). The accent unit boundary represents a juncture that marks the scope of a nuclear accent.[13]

13.3. Embedded Intonation Unit

Angle brackets marked with pipe symbols (<| |>) may be used to enclose an embedded intonation unit.[14] This occurs where a larger intonation unit is temporarily interrupted while a parenthetical utterance—at a different pitch level—is inserted, after which the larger intonation unit is resumed. The impression given is that if the interrupting phrase were suppressed, the remaining material would fit together as a single coherent intonation unit. This potentially controversial category sometimes occurs with utterances of hesitation words such as *uh* or phrases such as *you know*.

13.4. Restart

A capital initial letter can be used to roughly indicate a "restart," that is, the start of a new unit or a restart after a false start. Speakers may signal a restart by shifting to a new baseline intonation level: A higher initial pitch level from which subsequent pitches will gradually tend to drift down over the next stretch of speech (i.e., "declination"; see Schuetze-Coburn, Shapley, & Weber, 1991), until a new restart begins the process all over again. (Capital letters are also used in the standard way for the first letter of a proper noun, the pronoun *I* in English, and so on.)

```
(60)  ((Hypochondria))
        K: But he'll recover,
            He'll --
        D: What is that.
        K: He'll be over his leprosy [soon].
        G:                          [Nothing],
            it's just dry skin.
            ... There isn't --
            It's no disease,
            at all.
```

---

[13] This usage is similar to that of the International Phonetic Association (1989) for marking a "minor (foot) group."

[14] Regarding embedded tone units, a comparable but distinct category, see Boase (1990) and Svartvik and Quirk (1980).

K: Athletic feet.

... foot.

D: foot.

13.5. False Start

Plain angle brackets < > are used to enclose words that are false starts or "editables"—when such indication is desired.

For a widely known language such as English it is probably best to avoid inserting implicit judgments about correctness and repair at the transcription level (Edwards, 1992). (Such interpretations are commonplace, and fully appropriate, at the more interpretive and theory-bound level of *coding*.) But the picture changes when one considers little-known languages. A linguist who publishes a transcription of a language that is known by only a few individuals in the world would do a decided disservice to simply reproduce all the words as spoken, without any indication of which were considered correct and which were not, in the eyes of the native speaker. This is, after all, the kind of knowledge which native speakers of English make use of implicitly whenever they read and understand an English-language transcription that does not explicitly alert them to the dysfluencies it contains. But in a little-known language, such knowledge may well be inaccessible to any but the linguist who published the text and one or more native speakers in a faraway place.

Thus, while for most purposes one would not specially mark false starts in a transcription of English discourse, one should do so in, for example, a language such as Xinca or Sacapultec Maya. (English examples are presented in the following with this notation just to illustrate how it would be used.)

(61) ((Door))

    A: and <they> --

       they poked into <the-> the molding,

       along the [side].

    B: [unhhunh],

13.6. Code Switching

Angle brackets labeled with *L2* (<**L2 L2**>) may be used to mark stretches where the speaker has shifted into a language different from the one he or she has been speaking, or from the one that dominates the current conversation. If several languages are involved, each can be indicated by its own number: <**L3 L3**>, <**L4 L4**>, and so on. Alternatively, more mnemonic (if more cumbersome) codes can be assigned: <L2SP L2SP> for Spanish, <L2XIN

L2XIN> for Xinca, and so on. In either case, a key should be given in the header of the transcription, spelling out the full name of each language so abbreviated. (For example, such a key would indicate that in the transcription from which the following example is taken, L2 equals Spanish.)

(62) ((Dig))

A: So we don't really know if it was the <L2 vice-rector L2>,

Although this notation goes somewhat beyond pure transcription per se, it is useful for making clear to the reader when code switching has taken place and for ensuring that computer searches will not mix up words from two different languages.

13.7. Marginal Words

When listening to ordinary conversation, the transcriber is always confronted with a few words and sounds for which ordinary spelling conventions—designed for written language—offer little or no guidance. The transcriber faced with such a word, rather than simply inventing an ad hoc spelling that may or may not be recognized by other readers, should preferably follow some sort of standard practice.

In this section, we present some suggestions on how to spell various marginal words (or "vocalizations"; see Tottie, 1989)—such as those used in filled pauses, backchannel responses, and so on—so that they can be transcribed consistently, allowing for both ease of reading and automatic identification. For some of these words, spelling can be derived from an already existing informal spelling convention discernable in the practice of playwrights, novelists, and especially cartoonists. The spellings *uh, unh, um* represent hesitation words (filled pauses); *hm, m, huh,* and *hunh* express various nuances of awareness, wonder, or other backchannel response; *mhm, unhhunh,* and *uhuh,* (all with final syllable stressed) are backchannels or affirmative responses; *unh-unh* (with the first syllable stressed) is a negative response; and *uh-oh* is a mild alarm cry. (The last two words are pronounced with a glottal stop between the two syllables.)

(63) ((Aesthetics))

    J: I think of ... aesthetics,
       and,
    S: **mhm,**
    J: **uh,**
       ...

S: **Hm**.

 ... @

 ...

J: ... creation of desire,

 for one thing.

S: **mhm**,

14. NONTRANSCRIPTION LINES

It is useful to include a certain amount of background or "bookkeeping" information about the text being transcribed, within the text file itself. When this is done, the lines containing background information should be carefully distinguished from actual transcription lines. Other kinds of nontranscription information, such as interlinear gloss lines, should be distinguished as well.

14.1. Nontranscription Line

The dollar sign ($) marks any line in a transcription file that is not part of the transcription per se but that encodes other useful information. Examples might include lines indicating the title of a transcribed text, the transcriber's name, the recording date, and so on. In such lines, it is helpful to use the colon to mark the boundary between the information category label and the specific information that falls under that category.

$ TRANSCRIPTION TITLE:	Door Story
$ TAPE TITLE:	Door
$ FILENAME:	door.trn
$ PRINTOUT DATE:	(etc., etc.)
$ RECORDING DATE:	
$ RECORDED BY:	
$ SPEAKER 1:	
$ SPEAKER 2:	
(etc.)	

14.2. Interlinear Gloss Line

For many languages (especially relatively little-known ones), it is advisable to include, along with the transcription itself, an interlinear gloss line and/or free translation, as in the following example from a conversation in Sacapultec Maya:[15]

(64) ((SacPear 2))
     S: ... k-inijel   x-ee-b'eek?
     ... Erg3pl-all Cp-Abs3pl-go
     ... They all left?

Note that including a pause symbol in the second (gloss) line is not merely redundant: It helps to ensure that each word (and morpheme) in the text line is unambiguously aligned with, and can be automatically matched to, its gloss in the line below.

If for computational purposes it becomes necessary to make clear that the gloss and free translation lines do not represent actual speech, they may be marked with a backslash or other distinctive sign plus capital letter at the beginning of the line: \G for the gloss line, \F for the free translation line, \M for morphosyntactic category, and so on.

(65) ((SacPear 2))
    \T I: .. e   re-`en   x-0-inw-il   ta=j.
    \G   .. FOC the-Abs1sg Cp-Abs3-Erg1sg-see not
    \F   .. I didn't see it.

If need be, interlinear lines marked with a distinctive sign can also be used to introduce certain types of specialized transcription information.   For example, for transcribing videotape, a separate line beginning with \EYE could be placed above each transcription line to record the eye gaze of speech event participants, as iconically synchronized to their simultaneous verbal utterances (see Goodwin, 1981). (This notation must be considered "fragile" [Du Bois, 1991], however, because the indication of temporal synchronization depends on maintaining the vertical alignment of the two lines.)

15. RESERVED SYMBOLS

In any transcription system designed for general discourse research, allowance must be made for recording certain kinds of specialized information, which may differ from language to language and from researcher to researcher. This information may include some kinds that are not strictly speaking part of

---

[15] For an explanation of the glosses used in this and the next example, see Du Bois (1987).

discourse transcription per se. Language-specific spelling conventions and phonemic orthography, as well as coding of morphosyntactic categories and structure, may each call for the use of some specialized symbols. Some of the symbols that are not used for discourse transcription need to be reserved for this; this section presents suggested notations for each of these domains. In addition, a few symbols are left undefined, free to accommodate the diverse special needs of users of the system. Naturally, different researchers will have different requirements, and even the symbols spoken about here as "reserved" are available to be exploited for other purposes if they are not needed for the purposes described.

15.1. Phonemic/Orthographic Symbols

Apostrophe (') should be reserved for contractions (*she'll*, *don't*) in English and other similar orthographies. In other languages, it may be needed for representing palatalized consonants, ejective consonants, and so on, according to the orthographic conventions of the language in question.

15.2. Morphosyntactic Coding

Researchers who want to study the morphological and/or syntactic structures in their spoken discourse data need to reserve a certain number of symbols for coding purposes. Probably the most important need is for indicating morpheme boundaries (in languages where this is desirable), for which the plus sign (+) can be reserved.[16] For other, more specialized forms of morphosyntactic coding, the following symbols may be reserved: asterisk (*), number sign (#), and curly brackets ({}) (Du Bois & Schuetze-Coburn, this volume). Of course, if these symbols are not needed for morphosyntactic coding they can be freely used for other purposes.

15.3. User-Definable Symbols

Several symbols have deliberately been left without a specific definition in this system to give researchers room to expand the system to meet their special

---

[16] Alternatively, hyphen (-) can be used for morpheme boundaries. The hyphen is undoubtedly the most widely used symbol for morpheme boundary, but it is also rather widely used for word truncation (as in this system). It is possible to use hyphen for both morpheme boundary and truncation, given their distinct environments—morpheme boundary is generally word-internal and truncation is word-external—as long as the researcher takes care to distinguish the two functions when appropriate (e.g. by using contextual cues). Alternatively, the plus can be used for truncation and the hyphen for morpheme boundary by simply reversing the symbol values proposed here.

needs. The double quotation mark (")[17] or tilde (~) can be combined with numbers, letters, or other symbols to form digraphs (Y", 2", &", ~A, ~B, etc.), and in this way new symbols can be generated as needed. Also, researchers who do not subscribe to a particular transcriptional category (such as the accent unit) can redefine the symbol in question to fit their needs.

Among complex notations, the angle bracket notation discussed earlier allows for constructing an open-ended set of user-defined symbols for features that apply over a stretch of discourse. And the single parenthesis notation allows for creation of an unlimited set of symbols for vocal noises.

16. PRESENTATION

One important use of transcriptions is for illustrating some discourse phenomenon in an article or book, or for presenting some analysis of it. Usually, the attention of the reader is being directed to some particular feature within the discourse extract in question. Thus, in addition to the symbols for transcription per se, certain conventions for the *presentation* of transcriptions are useful, for which we here present some suggestions, based in part on the practice of the Conversation Analysis tradition (Atkinson & Heritage, 1984, p. xvi).

A salient line of text can be indicated by placing a visually prominent symbol, such as an arrow or bullet, in the left margin of the line. To call attention to individual words, they can be boldfaced, underlined, or italicized. To show where some linguistic material (e.g., several lines of nonpertinent text) has been omitted from a discourse example, the number of lines left out can be given within double parentheses ((6 LINES OMITTED)).

Occasionally, an intonation unit is too long to fit on one line. Whenever typographical considerations make it necessary to break a long intonation unit into two successive lines on the page, the remainder (the portion that is shifted down onto the second line) should be set indented five to ten spaces from beneath the first word of the line above.

To allow easy reference to specific places in one's texts, each line can be numbered consecutively in the left or right margin, beginning with the numeral 1 for the first line, 2 for the second, and so on (or, every fifth line can be so marked, etc.).

---

[17] But see a possible use for the double quotation mark (") under "Quotation Quality."

ACKNOWLEDGMENTS

This chapter was based on research supported by the National Science Foundation under grant No. IST85-19924 ("Information Transfer Constraints and Strategies in Natural Language Communication," John W. Du Bois, Principal Investigator), which we gratefully acknowledge. Additional support was received from the University of California, Santa Barbara Office of Instructional Development and from the Center for the Study of Discourse at the Community and Organization Research Institute of the University of California, Santa Barbara.

The discourse transcription system described in this chapter draws substantially from the work of many people. Discourse researchers from a wide variety of orientations have contributed insights, techniques, and perspective to the present formulation, and many will doubtless recognize in this document their own contributions. Among the most direct influences have been those of Wallace Chafe, Norman McQuown, Elinor Ochs, and Emanuel Schegloff (and indirectly, Gail Jefferson). For their many valuable comments on and contributions to this document and to the system it describes, we thank Karin Aijmer, Bengt Altenberg, Roger Anderson, Ingegerd Bäcklund, Maria Luiza Braga, Wallace Chafe, Patricia Clancy, Laurie Crain, Alan Cruttenden, Alessandro Duranti, Jane Edwards, Christine Cox Eriksson, W. Nelson Francis, Christer Geisler, Charles Goodwin, Caroline Henton, John Heritage, Knut Hofland, Marie Iding, Stig Johansson, Geoffrey Leech, Marianne Mithun, Bengt Nordberg, Elinor Ochs, Yoshi Ono, Asa Persson, Janine Scancarelli, Emanuel Schegloff, Emily Sityar, Jan Svartvik, Sandra Thompson, Gunnel Tottie, and Donald Zimmerman. We are also most appreciative of the many comments we have received from the participants in a discourse transcription seminar held at the University of California, Santa Barbara (Summer-Fall 1988), and at presentations given by the first author at the Stockholm Conference on Computers in the Humanities and at the Universities of Lund and Gothenburg (all September 1989). We thank the students in the first author's courses on discourse transcription at the University of California, Santa Barbara (Fall 1988 and Spring 1990) and Uppsala University (Fall 1989). We are especially grateful for the lively representation of diverse viewpoints and the incisive commentary at the conferences on Discourse Transcription (January 1989), Current Issues in Corpus Linguistics (June 1990), and Representing Intonation in Spoken Discourse (July 1990), all held at the University of California, Santa Barbara under the sponsorship of the Linguistics Department and the Center for the Study of Discourse. We are glad to express our thanks to these people and the many others from whom we have gained insights and borrowed ideas—while recognizing that undoubtedly they all would do things at least a little differently. Their contributions to the formulation of the transcription system have been invaluable and are reflected in virtually every page of this chapter. None of our many benefactors should be held accountable for the choices made in arriving at the final form of the transcription system or its description, for which responsibility rests with us.

REFERENCES

Atkinson, J. M., & Heritage, J. (Eds.). (1984). *Structures of social action: Studies in conversation analysis.* Cambridge: Cambridge University Press.

Boase, S. (1990). *London-Lund Corpus: Example text and transcription guides.* Unpublished manuscript, Survey of English Usage, University College, London.

Chafe, W. L. (Ed.). (1980a). The pear stories: Cognitive, cultural, and linguistic aspects of narrative production. Norwood, NJ: Ablex.

Chafe, W. L. (1980b). Some reasons for hesitating. In H. W. Dechert & M. Raupach (Eds.), *Temporal variables in speech* (pp. 169–180). The Hague: Mouton.

Couper-Kuhlen, E. (1986). *An introduction to English prosody.* London: Edward Arnold.

Cruttenden, A. (1986). *Intonation.* Cambridge: Cambridge University Press.

Crystal, D. (1975). *The English tone of voice: Essays in intonation, prosody, and paralanguage.* London: Edward Arnold.

Cutler, A., & Ladd, D. R. (Eds.). (1983). *Prosody: Models and measurements.* Berlin: Springer-Verlag.

Du Bois, J. W. (1987). Absolutive zero: Paradigm adaptivity in Sacapultec Maya. *Lingua,* **71,** 203–222. (Reprinted in R. M. W. Dixon, Ed., *Studies in Ergativity,* pp. 203–222. Amsterdam: North-Holland.)

Du Bois, J. W. (1991). Transcription design principles for spoken discourse research. *Pragmatics,* **1,** 71–106.

Du Bois, J. W., Schuetze-Coburn, S., Cumming, S., & Paolino, D. (1991). *Discourse transcription.* Unpublished manuscript, University of California, Santa Barbara.

Edwards, J. A. (1992). Computer methods in child language research: Four principles for the use of archives data. *Journal of Child Language,* **19,** 435-458.

Goodwin, C. (1981). *Conversational organization: Interaction between speakers and hearers.* New York: Academic Press.

Gumperz, J. (1982). *Discourse strategies.* Cambridge: Cambridge University Press.

International Phonetic Association. (1989). Report on the 1989 Kiel Convention. *Journal of the International Phonetic Association,* **19,** 67–80.

Jefferson, G. (1979). A technique for inviting laughter and its subsequent acceptance declination. In G. Psathas (Ed.), *Everyday language: Studies in ethnomethodology* (pp. 79–96). New York: Irvington Publishers.

Jefferson, G. (1984). On the organization of laughter in talk about troubles. In J. M. Atkinson & J. Heritage (Eds.), *Structures of social action: Studies in conversation analysis* (pp. 346–369). Cambridge: Cambridge University Press.

McLemore, C. (1991). *The pragmatic interpretation of English intonation: Sorority speech.* Unpublished doctoral dissertation, University of Texas, Austin.

Sacks, H., Schegloff, E. A., & Jefferson, G. (1974). A simplest systematics for the organization of turn-taking for conversation. *Language, 50*, 696–735.

Schuetze-Coburn, S., Shapley, M., & Weber, E. G. (1991). Units of intonation in discourse: A comparison of acoustic and auditory analyses. *Language and Speech, 34*, 207–234.

Svartvik, J. (Ed.). (1990). *The London-Lund corpus of spoken English: Description and research.* Lund, Sweden: Lund University Press.

Svartvik, J., & Quirk, R. (Ed.). (1980). *A corpus of English conversation.* Lund, Sweden: C. W. K. Gleerup.

Tottie, G. (1989). What does *uh-(h)uh* mean: American English vocalizations and the Swedish learner. In B. Odenstedt & G. Persson (Eds.), *Instead of flowers: Papers in honor of Mats Rydén.* Stockholm: Almqvist and Wiksell.

Trim, J. (1970). Some continuously variable features in British English intonation. *Proceedings of the 10th International Congress of Linguists IV* (pp. 263–268). Bucharest, Romania: Editions de l'Académie de la République Socialiste de Roumanie.

APPENDIX
SYMBOLS FOR DISCOURSE TRANSCRIPTION

Units
Intonation unit	{carriage return}
Truncated intonation unit	--
Word	{space}
Truncated word	-
Speaker identity/turn start	:
Speech overlap	[ ]

Transitional Continuity
Final	.
Continuing	,
Appeal	?

Terminal Pitch Direction
Fall	\
Rise	/
Level	_

Accent and Lengthening
Primary accent	^
Secondary accent	`
High booster	!
Low booster	;
Lengthening	=

Tone
Fall	\
Rise	/
Fall-rise	\ /
Rise-fall	/ \
Level	_

Pause
Long	...(N)
Medium	...
Short	..
Latching	(0)

(cont.)

Appendix Continued

Vocal Noises
    Vocal noises   ( )
    Inhalation   (H)
    Exhalation   (Hx)
    Glottal stop   %
    Laughter   @

Quality
    Quality   <Y Y>
    Laugh quality   <@ @>
    Quotation quality   <Q Q>

Phonetics
    Phonetic/phonemic transcription (/ /)

Transcriber's Perspective
    Researcher's comment   (( ))
    Uncertain hearing   <X X>
    Indecipherable syllable   X

Specialized Notations
    Duration   (N)
    Intonation unit continued   &
    Accent unit boundary |
    Embedded intonation unit   <| |>
    Restart   {Capital Initial}
    False start   < >
    Code switching   <L2 L2>
    Nontranscription line $

Reserved Symbols
    Phonemic/orthographic symbols '
    Morphosyntactic coding   + * # { }
    User-definable symbols   " ~

4

Transcribing Conversational Exchanges

John J. Gumperz
Norine Berenz
University of California at Berkeley

1. THE THEORETICAL PERSPECTIVE

This chapter presents a way of transcribing and otherwise preparing for systematic analysis audio- and videotaped oral performances of all kinds, ranging from chat to formal discussion and ritual event, from within a sociolinguistic and functional perspective. We include monologues on the assumption that speakers always address themselves to real or imagined listeners, frequently relying on shifts in voice in response to actual or supposed listener reaction, as well as on other rhetorical devices used by participants in multiple party encounters.

We assume, then, that talk is basically interactive in nature, typically involving two or more participants. What we seek to account for is the ongoing, cooperative process of conversing in which all participants, both speakers and listeners, are simultaneously engaged in producing talk, monitoring what is said, and exchanging verbal and nonverbal backchannel signals to indicate how a turn at speaking is developing and how it is being received. Turn-taking or speaker change, the phenomenon that has received so much attention in the work of conversation analysts (Atkinson & Heritage, 1984), is clearly one of the basic strategies on which conversational cooperation depends. But speaker change does not just happen in response to structurally determinable characteristics of an exchange. Rather, it is accomplished interactively as part of the process of conversing. Conversing in turn rests on speakers' and listeners' interpretation of verbal and nonverbal signs or contextualization conventions, that is, systems of cues that guide conversational management (Gumperz, 1982, 1992). Cues marking the transition relevance points where speaker change ordinarily occurs are a subset of contextualization conventions. Other functionally similar signs are used to negotiate such matters as topic change or change in perspective, relative emphasis or salience of information, style shifting, degree of formality and the like, or to achieve the kind of rhythmic integration that often marks smooth interaction (Gumperz, 1982).

Our transcription system attempts to set down on paper all those perceptual cues that past research and ongoing analyses show participants rely on in their online processing of conversational management signs. Many of the phenomena we record—for example, pausing, timing of exchanges, rhythm, prosody, and other paralinguistic signs—are also dealt with in other chapters of this volume (Du Bois, Schuetze-Coburn, Cumming, & Paolino; Ehlich). What is emphasized in our approach is the rhetorical impact these signs have in affecting the *situated interpretations* on which the conduct and outcome of the exchange depends. Transcription, when seen from this basically functional perspective, is an integral part of the analysis of inferential processes. So that, in transcribing a feature such as pausing, for example, we are less interested in *absolute* duration and more in the *interpretive evaluation* relative to other matters of timing and rhythm within the event. In rendering prosodic, intonational, and paralinguistic phenomena, we similarly concentrate on just those features of pitch, tune, and accent that can be shown to affect situated interpretation at the interactive or relational level as well as at the level of content. In other words, we present in this chapter a transcription system that focuses on speakers' and listeners' use of verbal and nonverbal signs both to convey or understand information and to maintain what Goffman calls "conversational involvement." Before turning to the transcription system as such, we will discuss briefly the analytic procedures we employ in transforming raw tapes into analyzable transcripts and the basic interpretive categories in which analysis is grounded.

2. THE INTERPRETIVE LEVEL OF ANALYSIS

The present transcription system was developed in the course of ethnographic fieldwork in urban institutions of various kinds and typically involves the following procedures. After an initial period of interviewing and participant-observation where basic information on the history, social characteristics, everyday practices, and goals of the institution in question are collected, working hypotheses are generated and encounter types most likely to provide the information with which to test these hypotheses are identified. Tape recordings of such encounters, varying in length from a few minutes to several hours, are then collected and compared systematically with a range of other encounters both within and outside the particular institutional context. The source data for these comparisons come in large part from previously collected and partially analyzed recordings that are stored in Disclab, a computerized archive of audio- and videotaped materials located at the University of California, Berkeley. Although our primary focus has been on institutional encounters, at the present stage of its development, the methodology is a general one, applicable to interactions of all kinds.

At the initial stage of analysis, we work with raw recordings that cover everything that transpires within a certain time span. In many cases, the encounters take the form of interactive situations that carry such folk labels as *job interview, medical consultation, parent-teacher conference, management committee meeting, classroom session,* and the like. Labels can tell us a great deal about the nature of the interaction and relationships among participants and about likely topics and expected outcomes. Yet this background information is never sufficient to account for the observable features of an interaction, nor are labels and the folk knowledge associated with them identical with the schematic information, that is, the implicit or taken-for-granted background expectations, that participants rely on to guide their own actions and to interpret what transpires at any one point in the interaction. Everyday encounters, in fact, rarely if ever adhere to pre-set agendas. For example, Classroom sessions consist partly of informal talk in addition to the planned lesson. Similarly, in medical consultations much time may be taken up by the exchange of personal information and informal anecdotes.

The lack of correspondence between labels and interpretive practices raises serious problems for a functional approach. Even relatively simple, that is, perceptually salient or instrumentally measurable and seemingly indexical, signs such as pausing, pitch register shift and the like can be seen to have many functions. Charles Fillmore provides an anecdote concerning his use of pausing in the course of giving expert courtroom testimony. When he took a little more time than usual in answering the opposing attorney's question, the attorney, addressing himself to the court reporter, said, "Let the record show that the witness hesitated before answering." Presumably, the attorney, in accordance with the established California evidence code, interpreted the pause as unwillingness or at least reluctance to cooperate in answering the question. Fillmore reports that in actuality his delayed response was motivated only by his attempt to suppress a cough. Clearly, pauses have as many possible interpretations as possible causes. Aside from those that result from the nonlinguistic demands on the relevant physical mechanisms, pauses can be rhetorically motivated or serve as turn holders to allow for speech planning, among other things. What holds for pauses is also true of other contextualization cues. Conversational interpretation is inherently highly context dependent. We therefore need to sharpen our notion of context to deal with the problems that arise.

A main goal of contextualization analysis is to make explicit the processes by which the presuppositions that affect or channel interpretation at any one point are negotiated and to show how talk at any one point coheres with the preceding and following talk. What the analysis focuses on is the process of signaling that shapes participants' notions of what the context is (see Gumperz, 1992, for more detailed illustrations). We do not seek to assign context-free functions to any one cue in isolation, nor do we seek to be exhaustive in our representation of the characteristics of the talk. Rather, we transcribe all those signs that, on the basis of the analysis as a whole, can be shown to enter into that process. It is in this sense that we can say that transcription is an integral part of an overall process of interpretive analysis that includes both the translation of oral recordings into written symbols and the evaluation or assessment of communicative intent.

2.1. The Event

Analysis begins with the segmentation of the interaction into thematically coherent and empirically boundable portions, that is, *events*, within the encounter as a whole. In the first pass through, it is often difficult to isolate longer, thematically coherent episodes. We discover such episodes through turn-by-turn scanning that focuses on two levels of analysis: content and rhythmic organization (Erickson & Shultz, 1982; Gumperz, 1982). At the level of content, events have several characteristics commonly associated with narrative organization, namely detectable beginnings, middles, and ends. Ends are of particular interest because they provide empirical information on outcomes or on what communicative ends participants intended to achieve, whether successful or not. This outcome information can then be used as evidence on which to base hypotheses concerning (a) what participants might have inferred at any particular point and (b) how such inferences were cued.

The output of this initial phase of the analysis is a segmentation of the tape session into sequences in which the more clearly bounded events alternate with the less clearly bounded or transitional ones. In the second stage of the analysis, the individual events or portions thereof are subjected to more detailed sequential examination and transcribed using the system described herein. Analysis begins with clearly bounded events. Once these are analyzed, the other less clearly bounded events are also more readily understood. Comparative analyses are based mainly on such events (Gumperz & Roberts, 1991). In what follows, we present our transcription system in such a way as to roughly reflect the stages of the transcription process.

2.2. Speaking Turns and Informational Phrases

We use the term *sequential analysis* to refer to the detailed examination of the local moves and countermoves that constitute a speech exchange. The basic unit of sequencing is the speaking turn—that string of utterances produced by a single speaker and bounded by other participants' turns. Yet speaker change units are not the fundamental units of speech production. Phoneticians of all persuasions agree that speech production in everyday interaction is best described not in terms of lexical items or mere strings thereof but in terms of phraselike units variously called breath groups (Couper-Kuhlen, 1986), idea units (Chafe, this volume), intonational phrases, or, as we—maintaining of our functional perspective—would prefer to say, informational phrases.

The best way to characterize an informational phrase is as a rhythmically bounded, prosodically defined chunk, a lexical string that falls under a single intonational contour. Prototypically, these are set off from surrounding phrasal units by pausing and constitute semantically interpretable syntactic entities. As is true of prototype phenomena in general, not all of these characteristics need be present at the same time (Kay & Coleman, 1981). In less prototypical cases, determination of phrase boundaries depends on what divisions make sense in terms of the rhythmic and thematic organization of the surrounding discourse. Even where a phrase seems syntactically incomplete, it is interpretable if we take into account the preceding and following context. Consider turn 1L in the following sequence from a relatively heated argument analyzed in previous work (Gumperz, 1992).

(1) 1D: this is not a-
    1L: ==of *course/ {[ac] it is not a secret//}
    2D: =that it is a secret//=
    2L: =i haven't *said= it's a secret// {[ac] i didn't say it was a secret//}

The "of course" in turn 1L is transcribed as a separate phrase (shown by the slash) although the tape recording does not show a perceptible pause. It is the shift in rhythm in the second part of the line that marks the phrase boundary. The phrasing in this example has interpretive import inasmuch as it suggests that the utterance is not to be understood as "Of course, it is not a secret" but that a different reading involving ellipsis, "Of course it isn't. It is not a secret," more adequately accounts for what transpires in the encounter as a whole. Thus, an informational phrase is basically a unit of cognitive information that, at the level of speaking, can be marked by a variety of co-occurring perceptual cues.

In the first step of the transcription process, we listen to the stream of talk to isolate such units, marking phrase boundaries throughout an event or portion thereof, and then go through the recording again for in-depth analysis. The phrase division is also the main criterion for determining the makeup of transcript lines. Readability is improved by breaking up participants' turns requiring multiple lines at prosodic or syntactic boundaries, rather than running the line to the margin of the page. Some researchers structure the transcript so that each line is a separate phrasal unit. Yet readability suffers when many short phrases each occupy separate lines, thereby requiring considerable space on the page for what was only of brief duration in the saying. We therefore compromise by allowing one, two, or more phrases per line, depending on the length of the lexical string. Each line, of course, must end in a complete phrase, as in (2). Rendering the turn as in (3) violates our principle, not only lessening readability but also making it more difficult to follow the rhythmic organization of the turn. (For a more detailed discussion of the notions of event and activity employed in our interpretive method, see Gumperz, 1992, in press.)

(2) R: now, are the details the same as when you applied?
         you s- living at the same add(ress)?

(3) R: now, are the details the same as when you applied? you s- living at
         the same add(ress)?

2.3. The Lexical Stream

Along with many other discourse analysts, we render most lexical material in conventional orthography. Whereas the use of conventional orthography contributes significantly to readability, it also presents certain problems in capturing significant features of style and dialect that may need to be represented. On the phonetic level, consistency can be difficult to achieve. In attempting to render deviations from what is assumed to be normal, some researchers use what is in effect a pseudophonetic form for certain words in the lexical stretch while maintaining conventional orthography for others in what appears to be an insufficiently motivated way, so that in one transcript the word *is* might be spelled in the normal way, but the word *because* might be spelled *b'cuz*. This approach has been called *eye dialect* due to its comic-strip-like effect. Eye dialect not only reduces the readability of a transcript and interferes with computer retrieval of individual words and strings of text but also, and more importantly, it limits the audience for which data so represented are readily interpretable. Eye dialect relies on spelling conventions that often are not shared by all speakers of English. Readers may be fluent in English but if they are unfamiliar with comic strip conventions or the writings of modern conversation analysts, the deciphering difficulties they encounter may distract their attention from the main features of the analysis. In addition, eye dialect tends to trivialize participants' utterances by conjuring up pejorative stereotypes, while neither representing the phonetic level more precisely nor capturing detail relevant to the analysis.

We need to differentiate, on the one hand, between normal predictable pronunciation of a word for which the conventional spelling is an inaccurate representation of that pronunciation and, on the other, words that have variable pronunciations commonly associated with certain speech styles for which there exist relatively well-known spelling conventions. For example, the use or nonuse of colloquial pronunciation may be a very salient aspect of the data. Stylistic variation in the pronunciation of -*ing* forms can reveal significant differences along the formality/informality dimension from which inferences can be made regarding participants' categorization of an interaction. Colloquial pronunciations of *going to* ("gonna," "gon," "-a") and *want to* ("wanna," "wan") can also be diagnostic of participant categorization. This kind of categorization can have a serious impact on the interpretation of the interaction, especially in cases of stylistic mismatch among participants. One option is to include both the conventional orthography and the popular spelling of the colloquialism, differentiating between the two in some regular way. For example, regularizations may be indicated as in (4) and (5).

(4) H: i'm gonna ("going to") get a job/

(5) H: ahma git ("i'm going to get") me a gig/ (Gumperz, 1982)

With this format, the transcript can be computer searched for register/style symmetry or verbal aspect, both of which may be significant to a particular analysis of the data. This is quite different from "b'cuz" where the pronunciation indicated is predictable rather than being one of several variants commonly associated with certain speech styles. Where, in a particular transcript, all participants consistently use a variety or varieties of colloquial pronunciation and that usage is relevant to the research interests for which the transcript is being developed, a table that indicates what regularizations have been made should be included in prefatory comments to the transcript. Parentheses may also be used in order to add detailed phonetic or phonemic transcription.

A similar technique of juxtaposing two representations of a particular string can be used in the transcription of code switching.

(6) A: to this day he says that ... uh ... it's a shame they don't speak
    ... uh ... spanish/
    están como burros/ les habla uno y,
    ("they are like donkeys, someone talks to them and,")

In this example, the speaker switches from English to Spanish within the same utterance. English appears in standard script, Spanish in italics, and the translation is given using the convention for regularizations.

Unintelligible segments, frequently found in data recorded in natural settings, are conventionally represented with parentheses enclosing either a good guess or blank spaces. Where the number of syllables of unclear speech is countable, one lowercase *x* per syllable can be enclosed within the parentheses. (Other conventions used in the examples are discussed later.)

(7) A: [enters the room]
     H: (take a seat)/
     R: hello m=ister A #surname#/=
     A: =hello/=
     H: ==(   )
     R: ==take a seat/
     A: good morning/

(8) R: now, are the details the same as when you applied?
         you s- living at the same add(ress)?
     K: ==y=es/=
     R: =back= in road A?
     K: ==yes/
     R: ==yeah/

(9) R: can i just check with you a few of the details? are you still living eh ..
         (xxx)?
     B: (xxx), .. driscoe, bar mill/
     R: {[p] bar mill/} bra- brookside is it?
     B: yeah brookside, yeah/

In (9), the fact that the first part of B's turn, although unintelligible, has the same number of syllables as the unintelligible last part of R's turn suggests that B may be echoing R, an interactively significant phenomenon.

As these examples show, we follow the common practice of using the capitalized first letter of a person's name or some other uppercase letter for identifying participants and other individuals named in the discourse while still maintaining their anonymity. This convention can be extended to other kinds of proper names, as in (8), where anonymity of participants may otherwise be jeopardized. We restrict the use of uppercase letters to serving as pseudonyms, having developed another convention for representing loudness as shown in (10) and discussed in more detail later. If we were to use uppercase letters to indicate both volume (or accent) and as pseudonyms, as is often done, then there would be no way to indicate a reference to a person uttered loudly (or with accent), for example. By restricting uppercase letters to pseudonyms, this is easily done. The use of lowercase letters for pseudonyms would reduce transcript readability since the participant-identifying, turn-initial capital so clearly flags turns at talk. Lowercase letter pseudonyms within the text of the transcript may cause readers to confuse a reference to a person or place with false starts or other displays of nonlexical vocalizations. Like a number of other researchers, we use X to identify a speaker where it is not certain which participant is speaking. Colon follows the participant-identifying capital.

(10) B: {[ff] K,} oh .. i didn't see you there/

For purposes of computer-assisted analysis, it may be desirable to be able to isolate and collect or count instances of direct address and references by proper name—perhaps for purposes of identifying and analyzing rapport-building strategies. Reserving capitals for use as pseudonyms facilitates that task. Conventions for representing some common permutations of names are dealt with later.

Reading transcribed material is made easier if the relationship between the symbol and its assigned meaning is as mnemonic and transparent as possible, and if, all things being equal, those symbols that have been used conventionally with a certain assigned meaning in previous work by researchers in the field can be adapted to the current work. Internal consistency is important as well. Part of the interpretive task of transcription is the categorization of both the lexical (e.g., the representation of the speech stream in standard orthography or otherwise) and the nonlexical (e.g., voice quality, laughter, coughing, applause, etc.) phenomena present in the raw data. Internal consistency requires that similar phenomena be represented in similar ways and, conversely, that dissimilar phenomena be represented in dissimilar ways, as far as it is feasible to do so. In what follows, we describe our conventions. (See the appendix for a summary of these.)

2.4. Intonationally Marked Phrase Boundaries

An informational phrase can be described as a stretch of speech that falls under a single intonational contour or envelope and ends in an intonational boundary marker. These boundary markers indicate how the phrase in question relates to what precedes and what follows; they also provide information on such matters as whether the speaker intends to keep or to relinquish the floor, how definite a statement is, and so forth. The most common boundary markers are falling and rising intonation, both of which can be either slight or strong.

Occasionally, it also becomes necessary to mark level endings, that is, where pitch neither rises nor falls. We use double slash (//) to indicate a final fall, which, depending on context, can be interpreted as indicating the conclusion of a stretch of talk, as a signal that the speaker is ready to yield his or her turn, or as a marker of emphasis or definiteness. In some systems, period or dot (.) is used for this because of the relationship between final falling intonation contour and the typical declarative sentence intonation contour. We prefer the double slash since dot serves as the pause marker. We use single slash (/) to indicate a contour terminating in a slight fall, which in some contexts ends a turn and in others suggests that there is more to come. The question mark (?) indicates terminal rise that signals uncertainty, for example, as in yes/no questions. It can also serve to elicit listener feedback or to hold the floor. Comma (,) indicates a terminal slight rise, which can, among other things, suggest that more is to come, as in the intonation typical for listing a series of objects, events, and so on, or act as a turn-holding signal. We use underscore (_) to indicate level ending. The last type of phrase-final marker, dash (-), is discussed later in the section on truncation.

Another way of marking boundaries that may be mnemonically more useful is to adopt / for slight rise, // for strong rise, \ for slight fall, and \\ for final fall. This would also avoid the interpretive problems that arise when listeners automatically associate ? with the speech act of questioning. For practical reasons, however, we have kept to the earlier usage because so much that has been published follows it. Some keyboards, moreover, may not have the \ character.

The following example, taken from an informal narrative of a speaker reporting on her encounter with a waitress in a coffee shop, illustrates our use of phrase boundary markers. The narrator had found a hair in her sandwich and was informing the waitress of this fact.

(11) ...

1. so she said, {[f] [hi] well, whe:re *is it?}
2. ... and i said, whe:re's, {[ac] where's *what/}
3. well, {[very hi, shrill] where's the {[f] ~hair/}}
4. .. {[hi] i can't re*turn it, unless i show them the {[f] ~hair/}}
5. ... and i said, well {[hi] i- i don't, ~know/}
6. you know, when i *noticed,
7. and {[laughing] {[lo] i just started laughing,}
8. you know, when i noticed what it was, i just {[f] threw it a*way/}
9. ... and i- and i'm: . beaming up, ==*at her,
10. and ... {[very lo] no go/}
11. [laugh] and she's staring down at me/

12. so i said, {[lo] well ~look,} i- it's {[lo] somewhere/}
13. i'd- {[ac] it's in my} *na::pkin,
14. and {[ac] i start-} .. {[ac] [hi] and now you (know what-)}
15. {[f] i'm *picking up ~boo:ks,}
16. {[hi] i'm *looking under the ~pla::te,}
17. {[ac] i'm looking all over/}
18. ==and i finally look on my lap/
19. =={[lo] and i see this little curly hair//} [laughs]

    ...

Line 1, spoken in a high pitch register, terminates in a rise. The first two phrases in line 2 end in a commalike, slight rise, whereas the third phrase ends in a slight fall. Terminal contours in the rest of the narrative are marked either by slight falls or slight rises that, in this context, both suggest that more is to come. In the concluding phrase, pitch falls and volume decreases before the final low fall (//), which indicates that the turn has ended.

2.5. Timing: Pausing, Overlap, Latching and Truncation

Informational phrases are often bounded by pauses. We have adopted the convention of indicating short pauses by a series of dots. Generally, two dots indicate a half second or shorter pause; three dots indicate a pause between a half second and 1 second. It may be useful to enlarge this repertoire to include one dot for a brief but perceptible dysfluency and four dots for pauses longer than 2 seconds that are not timed (Tannen, 1984). It is well-known that pause phenomena may be significant to the assessment of the degree of conversational synchrony and cooperation within an interaction. We can easily do computer searches and counts for pauses because we do not use the period to indicate phrase-final falling intonation.

(12) J: so you did motor mechanicking, what sorts of things were you doing/
     M: ... i- i can't remember {[hi] all} things/

(13) K: i think he was coming here on .. prospects/

We are aware that our treatment of pauses differs from that frequently used in conversation analysis, where all pauses are carefully timed (Du Bois & Schuetze-Coburn, this volume; Ehlich, this volume). In view of our interpretive approach to transcription, what we see as important about pausing is what it signifies or how it enters into participants' inferential processes. Following Erickson and Shultz (1982), we assume that when participants are involved in an interaction, they automatically seek to establish a more or less regular rhythm and that, once established, this rhythm becomes the standard against which pausing is perceived. Rhythmic coordination in talk, when seen in this perspective, has somewhat the same character as rhythmicity in music, where deviations from the established beats, as perceived by musicians and audience, have both perceptual impact and signaling value in the performance as such. Our transcription seeks to capture this phenomenon. (See Gumperz, 1992, for a discussion of the signaling value of pausing.)

For some purposes, it may be desirable to provide an approximate numerical value for long pauses. We use angle brackets to display timed pauses (usually pauses over 1 second long). The angle bracket convention facilitates computer searches and frequency counts since angle brackets can be specified in the search command.

One further point: It is our practice, as well as the practice of many other researchers, to enter on a separate line with no participant identifier a lengthy pause that occurs between speakers' turns, thereby not attributing it to a specific participant (Tannen, 1981). We do not usually do so, however, if the same speaker continues after the pause. In this we differ from some other researchers who note that the long pause may be indicative of a missed or passed turn and that the same speaker self-selecting in the absence of another speaker taking over the floor is more accurately viewed as a separate turn, rather than a continuation of the same turn. However, it is not only long pauses that may indicate a missed or passed turn; many other features may do so as well. Among these are lengthening of a segment, rising intonation, reformulation of the proposition of the preceding informational phrase, a short pause, or some combination of these features. Compare the next two examples of talk between an interviewer (T) and a candidate for paid job training (A).

(14) T: so how old are you now, twenty::? ... twenty-two/
      A: yeah/

(15) T: so how old are you now, twenty::?
      A: ...
      T: twenty-two/
      A: yeah/

The second of the two examples more clearly reflects the interpretation that emerges from a detailed analysis of the event as a whole, that is, that A fails to collaborate with T, who is trying to get him to construct a narrative account of his work experience. Where this insight is relevant to the analysis, a researcher may choose either to represent A's missed or passed turns as in the second example or to address the issue instead through an analysis of T's turn-internal pauses, lengthenings, rising intonation contours, and reformulations. Conversely, a turn-internal extended pause may be due to a nonvocal but otherwise unremarkable activity of the speaker that cannot be determined from the audiotape recording. It is no less true of long pauses than of other features that we cannot assign a constant interpretation to any single feature. It is rather a matter of how we choose to represent analytically relevant aspects of interaction.

Traditionally overlap, that is, simultaneous production by more than one participant, has been indicated by enclosing the overlapped portions of multiple participants' turns within long brackets, manually added to the text. For technical reasons, this convention is not feasible for computer stored and distributed transcripts.

In addition to bracketing, spacing may also be used to cue the reader to overlap since the second participant's contribution (utterance, laugh, nod, etc.) is begun at whatever point in the current speaker's turn the second participant begins. Spacing alone, however, is insufficient to indicate where the overlap ends because what was produced simultaneously during the interaction will likely be reproduced in the transcript with different numbers of typographical characters, thereby failing to accurately represent the phenomenon. Also, spacing alone cannot indicate turn-initial overlap. While maintaining the spacing convention, we have added single equal sign (=) before and after the overlapped portions of each participant's contribution. Thus, the beginning and end of the overlap is unambiguous and nothing need be added manually.

(16) R: you haven't {[f] been} to the skill cen=ter,=
      K: =no,=
      =i haven't/=
      R: =so you have=n't seen the .. the workshop there?
      K: no/
      R: <1.2> no?

This convention can also be used to represent overlap of nonlexical material with both lexical and nonlexical material. (Conventions for representing nonlexical material are discussed in more detail later.)

(17) R: so that's ok =with you then?=
      L: ={[nod] sure/}=

(18) R: so that's ok =with you then?=
      L: =[nod]=

(19) R: =[laughing]=
      L: =[laughing]=

With respect to latching, that is, the immediate initiation of a turn following the termination of the previous turn, it has been noted that in much conversation a brief pause regularly precedes each turn at talk. Chafe (1987) has argued that this pause may result from cognitive constraints on language processing, and therefore it is significant and should be represented in the transcript. He indicates this turn-initial pause in the same way as a turn internal pause would be indicated. In his system, then, latching is shown solely by the absence of turn-initial dots. Since the appropriate time interval between turns is (sub)culturally and situationally specific, in our own transcription system we are guided by the pacing characteristic of the event under analysis as a whole and by other relevant empirical findings in determining the time range within which the initial pause is predictable. Taking this predictable initial pause as the default case, we mark the *deviations* from it. Where participants' communicative histories differ as regards the default time interval between turns, one default interval may be chosen to serve as the standard, and that choice noted in prefatory comments. Although this practice obviously biases the transcript to some degree, when it is done consciously and noted explicitly, it can be revelatory of the implicit yet systematic differences among different communities of speakers.

The relationship between overlap and latching is a further consideration for explicitly marking latching. Latching, like overlap, results from participants' judgments about the content and intent of current speaker's turn. When latching is indicated only by the absence of the dots indicating a turn-initial pause, then the relationship of latching to overlap is obscured. Furthermore, it would be more difficult to isolate and count instances of latching because in same-speaker multiple-line turns, lines subsequent to the first line may or may not begin with a pause indicator. To search for latching, one would have to construct more complex commands rather than simply searching for a turn-initial marker.

Researchers working in the conversation analysis tradition or CA, as it is sometimes called (Atkinson and Heritage, 1984) use single equal sign (=) at the end of an utterance that is immediately followed by a second speaker beginning his or her turn, and single equal sign at the beginning of that second speaker's utterance. Because we use single equal signs for overlap, we indicate latching by double equal sign (==) at the beginning of the turn that is latched to the previous turn. In this way, we avoid confusion, while indicating the relationship between the two in an iconic way. In order to use space efficiently, the double equal sign marker and the contribution it precedes are entered into the transcript at the left margin immediately following the participant identifier rather than beginning under the previous turn at the point where the first participant ends, as is often done. This has the additional benefit of maintaining in the transcript a sense of the rapid turn exchange noted in the recording.

(20) R: have you visited the skill center?
     A: yeah once/
     R: ==you have?
     A: ==before this, yeah/
     R: was that on a tuesday?
     A: yeah/

To indicate truncation, that is, (a) a speaker perceptibly breaking off his or her own utterance and reformulating or (b) a speaker breaking off his or her utterance as a second speaker begins, we use dash (-), maintaining the meaning commonly assigned this marker. In addition to level ending, truncation is marked by glottal closure and often also acceleration of the last few syllables.

(21) T: it was about t- ah: nine thirty ten, when we got there/

(22) B: so don't you think it would stand you in *better stead
        to com**plete the engineering course,
        complete the last ten weeks of *that course,
        rather than start out on something you actually know very little a*bout//
     R: .. from {[hi] your} point of view is ok, what you're saying is ok, bu-
     B: ==and as T has already *told you, the preentry test is quite a *stiff one/

To facilitate computer searches and counts, we use the dash only for the representation of truncation and avoid its use word-internally, even in words such as "pre-entry" where standard orthography might use it. However, modifications of the search command to restrict a search to dash followed by a space or by end of line would allow the use of word-internal dash to be distinguished from truncation where readability of the transcript is judged to suffer.

2.6. Characteristics of the Whole Phrase: Pitch Register, Rhythm, and Tempo

Like turn-initial pauses, and many of the other signs we discuss, the signs in this section indicate inherently relational phenomena. They do not have absolute values. Listening to an entire event segment, the transcriber determines what is "normal" for individual participants, then judges given stretches of talk against this norm. We indicate a stretch of a participant's talk relative to other stretches of his or her own or others' talk as higher or lower in pitch register by preceding the relevant lexical stretch with [hi] or [lo] and enclosing the pitch register shift marker and the lexical stretch in curly brackets, as shown in examples (23)–(26).

We use a similar convention to indicate a stretch of talk that is faster or slower in relation to what precedes, follows, or has otherwise been determined as the "norm," using [ac] and [dc], respectively. The communicative significance of this is that it indicates the extent to which speakers are in tune or in sync with each other, that is, whether or not they are in agreement (Erickson & Shultz, 1982). Phoneticians and discourse analysts have described these phenomena under the headings of "rhythm" and "tempo."

(23) W: {[hi] what do you mean/} i mean why are you saying that/

(24) K: {[ac] if you don't ask now,} it'll be too late/

(25) J: {[dc] i suppose} that could be right after all/

The above features can also be nested one within another, extending over different stretches of the utterance.

(26) J: {[lo] {[dc] i suppose} that could be right after all/}

2.7. Phrase Internal Signs: Accent, Loudness and Syllable Lengthening

The terminal markers discussed earlier are only one aspect of intonation. Intonation, along with other signaling mechanisms such as vowel lengthening, increase or decrease in volume or pitch level, also enters into the signaling of communicatively significant prosodic prominence or accent (Auer, 1988; Bolinger, 1986; Couper-Kuhlen, 1986, 1988; Couper-Kuhlen & Auer, 1988; Ladd, 1980). We indicate accent placement within the phrase in the following ways: (a) normal prominence indicated by single asterisk (*) preceding the syllable, (b) extra prominence indicated by double asterisk (**) preceding the syllable, (c) fluctuating pitch over a single word indicated by tilde (~) preceding the syllable. Asterisk and tilde were chosen for their respective tasks because they convey visually something of the quality of the voice as it is perceived auditorally on the tape. These conventions can also be used along with the uppercase letters for person identification within the turns at talk. Our experience has shown that these markings, along with the terminal markers, reflect the most important discourse level signaling characteristics of intonation.

This set of markers conflates some of the detail captured in the systems worked out by British phoneticians (Trim, 1971). For example, we use ~ to indicate fluctuating intonation, without distinguishing rise-fall from fall-rise while that system uses circumflex (^) to indicate rise-fall and haček (ˇ) to indicate fall-rise. The Trim system also allows for the marking of direction of pitch movement where that movement is simple rather than complex, as with the fluctuating intonation. Thus, acute accent (´) indicates rise, and grave accent (`) indicates fall. When more detail is needed, the British system can be used or intonational curves can be drawn and superimposed on the text. Examples of this can be found in the references cited earlier.

(27) N: that's ridiculous, **P gets to stay out until midnight on weekends/
     J: i don't care if ~P gets to stay out until four in the morning, **you can't/

(28) R: he doesn't have any idea what it's all a*bout/

(29) C: there's no ~way he's got all the **right end of the stick/

Some researchers feel that when accent is predictable, it is unnecessary to represent it, as, for example, when the accent falls on the last content word of the informational phrase, as in (28). We tend to follow this convention whenever predictable accent is not relevant for a particular analysis. However, there are instances when what is predictable given the larger context may not be immediately obvious to the reader, yet accenting is relevant to the analysis. In these cases, it becomes necessary to cue the reader as to which word has received accent. The following examples illustrate this. In (30) "swamper" is highlighted and is treated as new information, and thus marked with accent, whereas "S Construction," which also carries some stress but is perceived as less prominent, is not. In the next line, "bricklaying" is used contrastively, and we use double asterisk to mark it off both from "swamper" and from "too."

(30) H: i see you were a *swamper for S Construction/
     B: yeah, i did some **bricklaying for them *too/

(31) H: i see you *also worked for S Construction/
     B: yeah, i did some bricklaying for *them too/

Because the object of study is an interactional sequence as a whole and not isolated utterances, the disambiguating property of context will always be available to the reader.

There is one further consideration, however: the importance of providing support for the claim that dialectal differences between speakers with regard to the prosodic characteristics of talk have significant impact on the success or failure of the interaction. Large corpora of transcripts where a wide range of prosodic features, including accent, are represented (e.g., London/Lund corpus, see Svartvik & Quirk, 1980) facilitate computer-assisted comparison among speech communities that employ lexically and syntactically similar systems within their linguistic repertoires. Talk among people who share ethnicity is the basis for establishing norms which then enter into the analyses of interethnic communication. Furthermore, the explicit representation of predictable accent and many other prosodic features, as well as turn-initial pausing, would minimize the implicit influence of the transcriber who, in listening to the data, must determine what is predictable and what is deviant. Limits on time allowable for transcribing may mitigate against marking these prosodic features, despite the desirable end of developing such corpora. Also, because no transcription is final, we assume that in comparative analyses investigators will always want to go back to the tape recordings to validate findings.

For louder or softer stretches of a participant's speech, we use [f] and [p], respectively, in the same way as was described above for indicating shifts in pitch register and tempo. These two symbols are taken from musical notation and indicate, by analogy with music, "loud" (forte) and "soft" (piano) relative to normal volume level (Tannen, 1984). If capitals were used to indicate loud speech, as is done by some, there would be no comparable way of easily indicating soft speech or shifts in pitch register and tempo, all of which seem to be similar phenomena. It may be useful to be able to isolate, collect, and count such changes in voice quality in an analysis of rhetorical style or as evidence in support of an evaluation of an interaction as a heated exchange, and so forth. Note that in this system shouting could be indicated by "ff" (fortissimo = very loud) and whispering by "pp" (pianissimo = very soft) so that the transcriber need not make the evaluative judgment implicit in designating a stretch of speech as shouting or whispering. These changes in voice quality (hi, lo, ac, dc, f, ff, p, pp) are easily isolated and counted by searching for two or fewer characters within the square brackets. It is for this reason and for improved readability that it was suggested that similar phenomena be represented by similar conventions, dissimilar phenomena by dissimilar conventions.

Segments of a word are sometimes lengthened to increase the salience of the word and sometimes to allow the speaker additional processing time for formulating the rest of his or her utterance. The use of colon (:) to indicate lengthening is conventional in much conversation research and we adopt that usage here. Although not originally chosen with regard to computer-assisted analysis, colon works well for this purpose because it can be suppressed when searching for instances of specific words. The use of reduplicated segments to represent lengthening results in spelling irregularities, which complicate searching. We reject some symbols because they look too imposing when several of them are necessary to indicate (impressionistically) various degrees of lengthening. In our system, the only other use of colon—following the single uppercase letter indicating who is speaking, coughing, and so on—will not be confounded with lengthening since the first two fields of a line are reserved for participant identification.

(32) B: yeah, i've been to the class, and it looks::-
     R: .. yeah,
     B: ==it looked ok really/

The lengthening convention can be used with the person-identifying uppercase letter to indicate that lengthening occurred in the pronunciation of the name even though the particular lengthened segment is not specified. This maintains the anonymity of the referent while losing little interactively relevant material.

(33) G: did you mean F::? you're talking about D's son?
     R: <1> no?

One other signaling mechanism that needs to be discussed under this heading is *rhythmicity*, that is, the spacing in time of successive prosodic prominences, accents or rhythmic beats. One of the first discussions of this can be found in Erickson and Shultz (1982). The phonetic realizations of rhythmicity have recently been described in a series of detailed studies by Auer (1988), Couper-Kuhlen (1986, 1988), and their associates. Rhythmicity can characterize a single person's speech, and it may also occur across different speakers' turns in an interaction. Rhythmic synchronization of participants' turns may play an important part in marking the relative smoothness or communicative success of an interaction or in signaling conversational repairs. One way to mark rhythmicity is by placing the left square bracket ([) at the beginning of the rhythmic unit, as in the following example adapted from Couper-Kuhlen. Couper-Kuhlen and Auer use slash (/) to mark rhythmic units and employ dot (.) to mark falling intonational boundaries. To be consistent with our system, we have substituted [for /.

(34) T: i [didn't even [know him in [nineteen [twenty three [did i [Ernest/
     L: he [wasn't   [born in   [nineteen [twenty three//

Note that the rhythmic units here are aligned to indicate rhythmic integration across speakers. Lack of synchrony can also be indicated by spacing.

2.8. Overlays of the Lexical Stretch

Overlays, as we call them, are nonlexical phenomena produced simultaneously with the lexical stretch by a single participant, as opposed to overlaps, which are the simultaneous productions of more than one participant. When some nonlexical phenomenon is discernible over the lexical stretch, it should be represented in the transcription in a way similar to other such phenomena. For example, if in a given interaction a participant, during one of his or her turns, pounds on a table with a fist punctuating the lexical stretch at certain intervals, some convention should be employed to signal to the reader what was done and when relative to the spoken discourse.

(35) M: {[fist pounding on table = "+"] we've +asked you .. +over and +over again/}

Likewise, if sometime during an interaction a participant punctuates his or her lexical stretch at certain intervals with fingersnapping, some similar convention, suitably adapted, should be used.

(36) L: {[fingersnap = "+"] i +know you +want to +go, so +blow/}

Nonlexical phenomena that overlay continuously rather than intermittently some lexical stretch are similarly represented. For both intermittent and continuous overlays, the lexical material included within the curly brackets is understood as overlaid by the nonlexical material represented by the label within the nested square brackets.

We employ the same convention to represent the superimposition over the lexical stretch of nonlexical phenomena that are discernible (i.e., visible and/or audible) and nonvocal (e.g., (37)–(39)) with nonlexical phenomena that are discernible and vocal (40).

(37) R: {[fingersnap] right/}

(38) S: {[nod] sure/}

(39) P: {[handing paper to doctor] is this it?} is this the one you mean?

(40) M: {[laughing] are you sure of that?}
       because this wouldn't be the first time someone made that mistake/

2.9. Vocal and Nonvocal Interruptions

In the preceding section, we discussed the representation of simultaneity of lexical and nonlexical elements within a single speaker's turn. We now turn to interruptions of the lexical stretch. *Interruption*, as the term is being used here, labels nonlexical phenomena produced sequentially (rather than simultaneously, as with overlays) with the lexical stretch by a single speaker; interruptions by other speakers, whether they are realized as overlapped utterances or latched utterances, were dealt with earlier. Where lexical and nonlexical elements are sequential rather than simultaneous, this can be indicated by the absence of the curly outer bracketing.

(41) T: i asked her to [cough] come in when she can/

(42) L: come in/ [door closing] take a seat/

For timed interruptions, a number following the descriptor indicates its duration in seconds.

(43) T: i asked her to [cough .6] excuse me, to come in when she can/

(44) L: come in/ [door closing 2.5] take a seat/

2.10. Comments about Computer Searches

For practical purposes, if, for example, one wanted to have a computer tabulate instances of laughter, a search for "[laugh" would retrieve both the simultaneous and the sequential. Similarly, all instances of simultaneous realization could be counted by searching for "{"; more specific types of simultaneous realization could be counted by searching for "{[laugh", "{[lo", and so on. All instances of sequential realization could be counted by searching for " [" (where "space" is understood as a character by the computer as it is in UNIX); more specific types of sequential realization could be counted by searching for " [laugh", " [cough", and so on. In general, we try to limit our use of symbols that have special meanings for editing and search programs to avoid complicating the transcription process.

2.11. Background Information

Although background information can precede or follow the body of transcribed text, there may be times when it is desirable to include it at the point within the text where it is relevant to the unfolding of the interaction, particularly noting situations in which some important information is known to some but not all of the participants (S. Ervin-Tripp, personal communication). Background information can be included in the turn at talk where it becomes relevant by flagging it in some way so the reader can easily recognize that it is not part of the recording itself. The pound sign (#) before and after the background information works well to set it off from the transcribed text. Where the information serves as background for the whole turn at talk and is rather lengthy, it can precede the utterance. As in the next example, a dotted line is used to separate the lengthy background information from preceding and following transcribed talk.

(45) --

Family dinner table conversation on a Sunday evening among a husband (J) and wife (L) who are both lawyers and their teen-age son (T). L has just returned to the table following a telephone call.

J: who was it/
L: {[sigh] a **client/}
#J knows that one of L's clients has been phoning her at home and that L is annoyed by his calls#
J: {[laugh] i think he must be in love with you/}
T: who was it mom, got a new boyfriend?

This convention can be extended, as in (46), to specify what kind of name the uppercase participant-identification letter represents: surname, given name, nickname, diminutive, and what grammatical function the name plays: vocative or referential. Such information can be important in determining how participants categorize the interaction along the formality/informality continuum, for looking at rapport-building strategies, and the like. However, it is insufficient for representing the innovative permutations of names that occur in word play, a frequent and significant phenomenon in child language acquisition data. For this type of data, the use of phonologically similar pseudonyms is preferred for obvious reasons.

(46) M: ok, and thank you mr R #vocative surname#/
i'll let you have a chat now with mr C #referential surname#/
C: morning A #vocative given name#/
R: morning/

2.12. Transcription of Languages Other than English

For transcribing languages other than (standard American) English, we use the following format: text line (t), morpheme-by-morpheme line (m), English translation line (e), each line beginning with the participant-identifier and the line-type identifier.

(47) Rt: [text]
     Rm: [morpheme line]
     Re: [English translation]
     Bt: [text]
     Bm: [morpheme line]
     Be: [English translation]

A space between speakers can be added to improve readability for long turns, although this complicates the use of spacing as one of the indicators of overlap. However, since overlap is also indicated by = before and after the overlapped sections, readability should not suffer too much.

(48) Rt: você ta ("está"") estudando pra ("para") =o exame de amanhã=

| | Rm:you are | studying for | the exam of tomorrow |
| | Re: are you | studying for | =tomorrow's exam?= |

	Bt:		=quê droga, ne?=
	Bm:		what drug not-it-is
	Be:		=what a drag, isn't it?=

With this format, one can select to search just the English, just the language of the interaction, all of one speaker's utterances, etc.

As an alternative to the three-line format, parentheses can be used, as in the case of regularization discussed above, but only for brief sequences since readability suffers if the turns are long. Here the morpheme-by-morpheme translation would most likely be omitted. These parentheses should, in any case, be parentheses with quotes. Recall that parentheses without quotes are for unintelligible sequences. As in (5) adapted here as (49), it may, in fact, be preferable to use this convention instead of the tripartite format for regularizations of dialects to the standard form in the language of the interaction.

(49) W: ahma git me a gig/ ("i'm going to get myself a job")

2.13. Nonverbal Phenomena

We have dealt with a variety of common nonverbal signs in various sections. Most common nonverbal signs can be indicated by means of square bracketed comments. The following extract from a recent analysis of a videotape will illustrate this.

(50) 1. A: i went down to (xxxxx) on that site,
    2. B: {[head tilted down but gaze on A] yeah/}
    3. A: in eh- B #place name#) .. i've got to come here now/
    4. B: [bends forward towards A]
    5. A: ... i've been in estimate, eh- if number seventy-six is on the list/
    6. B: .. yes/
    7. A: it is- .. it isn't/ ... for plastering//
    8. B: [slight nod, no other response although A is clearly expecting
            something more]
    9. A: ... and eh- {[hi] when i came down here before,} just a few
            weeks ago, .. {[lifts her hand and points with a jabbing motion
            to someone standing behind A] that fellow there tell me/}
            {[f] it should have been done in march//}
   10. B: =={[ac] i'll just check on it okay?} [gets up and walks away]

Applause is an additional important signaling device. It enters into conversation in several ways. When used by individual participants, it may either overlap, latch or otherwise function as a conversational turn. Atkinson and Heritage (1984) suggest alternately using lower- and uppercase x to indicate increasing or decreasing volume. We suggest using uppercase X, along with the system of signaling loudness described earlier, since lowercase x is reserved for representing unintelligible lexical material. X is repeated to approximate either the length or the manner of the turn. Thus, "X" indicates a single clap, "XXXXX" is repeated clapping, "X-X-X-" signals spasmodic or hesitant clapping. The use of uppercase X turn-internally will not overlap with its use as a participant identifier since the participant capital letter is always in the first field of a line.

An alternate system for nonverbal signs, particularly useful for representing gaze throughout the transcript, is that based on the work of Charles Goodwin. An exposition of this can be found in Atkinson and Heritage (1984).

3. SAMPLE TRANSCRIPTS AND ANALYSES

By way of further illustration of how we use the transcription system, we conclude with a few, somewhat longer examples from texts we are currently working on. The first example is taken from a consultation session between a medical student and her supervising physician. The medical student has just examined the patient and is reporting on her preliminary diagnosis to the physician, who questions her and in the end (not shown here) suggests an alternate diagnosis.

(51) 1. A: {[ac] [p] so what do you think is going on?}
      2. S: {[dc] {[f] well,} i *think her: .. her *leg pain,}
      3.   i mean, her **knee pain, it doesn't seem to be *any te- any tears/
      4.   and doesn't seem to be any u:m *fractures/ {[p] at all/
      5.   and no patella- and no patella dislocation/ or anything/}
      6.   so, {[f] *i think} this *may be like, kind of *post traumatic/
      7.   ==she hasn't *taken anything, *for it/
      8. A: ={[pp] mhm/=}
      9. S: =any= aspirins, or any um .. NXID's, or anything like that/
      10.   ==that may reduce the inflammation, or the swelling there/
      11.   ==so, u:m, .. i'd be inclined to maybe:, {[dc] see how she-}
      12.   to give her some aspirins, see how she d- if the pain resides on that/
      13. A: ==mhm/
      14. S: ==um so, i think this may be just post traumatic/
      15.   ==because it's- {[f] it's been about three months/}
      16.   but the pain's been redu- {dc] has been reducing/}
      17.   ==it's not- definitely not *increased/
      18. A: ={[pp] [hi] (mhm)/}=
      19. S: ={[p] (since)= she . haven't-}
            hasn't had any um .. major problems with tha::t/}
      20.   =={[f] and she gets it *mostly on physical exertion/}
      21.   ==it's not something that comes on .. at rest/
      22.   =={[p] or, while she's, not doing anything, really, u:m}
      23. A: =={[p] mhm/}
      24. S: ==real tiring/

In line 1, our use of [ac] and [p] indicates increased rhythm and quieter tone in comparison with the preceding talk. Similarly in line 2, [dc] and [f] mark slower rhythm and more fortis (more pronounced) tone. The curly brackets in line 1 show that the voice quality markers are to be understood as affecting the whole line. In line 2, the fortis "well" is nested within the curly brackets delimiting the lexical stretch marked by deceleration, indicating that "well" is both louder and slower, whereas the rest of the utterance is only slower than the preceding talk. In this way it becomes possible to locate the sequential positioning of rhythmic shifts, relate them to other cues such as pausing and make more explicit the rhythmic organization of a turn at speaking. Depending on context, these features of rhythmic organization may be quite important in distinguishing between such conceptual level phenomena as planning, hesitation, uncertainty and the like.

The two-dot initial pause in line 2 indicates that S hesitated slightly longer than the predictable turn-initial pause. The colon following the *r* of "her" shows that this segment was lengthened. This pausing, deceleration, and lengthening are likely to be significant to an analysis of the interaction because they suggest that S is carefully planning her turn. For the same reason, the normal accent on "think" is included to suggest our hypothesis that, in accenting "think," S is framing her diagnosis as tentative.

We chose to include the normal accent on "leg" to mark the contrast with the stronger accent on "knee" in the following line. This is also true for the normal accent on "any." This accent is significant to the analysis because "tears" is not accented. It can therefore be understood as being treated as old information despite the fact that no explicit mention of tears had been made before this point in the interaction.

The "at all" in line 4 and the "or anything" in line 5 are treated as separate tone groups primarily on the basis of intonational contour; they are not preceded by detectable pauses. Communicatively, this contouring may say something about the nature of the hedge.

"She hasn't" in line 7, "that" in line 10 and "so" in line 11 follow immediately on the preceding informational phrase without a pause. At the risk of complicating our search procedures, we have adapted our convention for representing latching as discussed earlier to the representation of this intra-turn latching. While rarely described in the literature, intra-turn latching is a common turn-holding device in such diagnostic sessions, where speakers work hard to create the space to make their point. The fact that A's latched "mhm" in line 13 is countered with a latched "um" by S confirms our hypothesis. Note also that in line 18 A raises her pitch register, a common attention-getting device, but her turn is again overlapped by S. A seems to be trying to take over, perhaps to stop S before she commits herself to a potentially embarrassing, inaccurate diagnosis, but gives up when S fails to yield the floor. In these and other ways, the transcription system displays the evidence for our hypothesis concerning participants' conversational management strategies.

The next example, taken from a recording of a televised 1960s debate between the then-mayor of San Francisco and a local African-American community leader, illustrates how the transcription system can be used to illustrate communicatively significant differences in conversational style.

(52) [Responding to B, who has objected to what he has said.]
    1. A: ==( ) {[hi] you'll} see those things/ {[hi] you'll} see those things/
    2.   but the *point **i:s,

3   .. that the *black community in San Francisco Hunter's Point/
4.   is *not giving me the story that they're being excluded
5.   from any kind of positions of responsibility/
6.   .. and i **have *told them, if they're gonna par*ticipate in these
       things/
7.   that there're gonna be *no, .. bequeaths from Mt Olympus
       down *to them//
[One turn by a third speaker omitted.]
8. C: =={[lo] i would just like to say *this/}
9.   that uh .. the mayor, ... is the mayor of San Fran*cisco/
10.   he's not the mayor of the United *States//
11.   .. and uh, that's his area of responsi*bility//
12.   ==an::d, i would like to take exception to uh,
13.   ... the glowing *picture that he's just painted,
14.   .. as to the relationship between uh,
15.   .. his *office, and his admini*stration, and his *government,
16.   .. and the black community//
17.   now it may well *be that he has,
18.   a good rapport with certain people in Hunter's Point//
19.   .. {[hi] at the same *ti:me,}
20.   .. the black community is very well a*ware/
21.   ... that San Francisco, .. *under Mayor A-
22.   ... {[ac] A, excuse me/}
23. A: {[pp] alright//}
24. C: uh ... the same as a::ll,
25.   .. uh city governments across this *country/
26.   ... {[dc] are sharply escalating/}
27.   ... the war against the black community//

Note that A relies mainly on accent and terminal contours to achieve rhetorical effect, and we indicate that by using the appropriate symbols. On the other hand, C relies on phrasing, pausing, and sometimes pitch register shifts. He regularly uses these devices to break up syntactic units in order to highlight his points. There is some suggestion here that the speakers rely on somewhat different contextualization conventions that, depending on power relations and the nature of the audience, may affect rhetorical effectiveness and the outcome of the debate.

In the last example, the first speaker is a native speaker of English and the second, a native speaker of a North Indian language whose English style shows some signs of language interference. The two speakers are arguing about admission to a community college course. The extract begins shortly after the beginning of the conversation.

(53) 2L: what i *said was/
>.. that it was *not a suitable course/ .. for you to *apply for//
>because it is ( )//
>..{[lo] now if you *want to apply for it/}
>.. {[hi] of *course/} you can do what you *want//
>but/ {[hi] if you are *doing the twilight course at the *moment/}
>.. {[lo] it was *not something which-}
>.. mrs N and mr G *thought/ *originally/
>that it was a course to carry *on/ *with the *twilight course/
>but this is {[ff] not} the case//

>3D: no// what you- you take *one thing at a time//
>this case// that whatever {[f] *they know//}
>i get that even .. hmm// for a D .. *me//
>{[lo] and i am *student in E *College//}
>and mr W *knows me// he// .. i am student in the *same school//
>[f] he knows *my qualifications/} and what- whether i'm suitable *or not//

L's use of prosody is typical for British or American native speakers of English. She makes extensive use of accenting to highlight certain aspects of the message and of pitch register shift over a complete syntactic clause to mark such things as the contrast between main information and asides, as well as of terminal contour to indicate interclausal relations. In D's speech, on the other hand, accent does not fall on a single syllable. Typically, his clauses are divided into two strings, one of which is set off from the other by a combination of tempo, rhythm, and loudness. This contrasts with L's use of typically English cues and is most probably a reflection of significant differences in communicative background. More research is needed to understand the details of the prosodic and paralinguistic signals characteristic of D's and many other South Asian natives' English and to determine how these cues enter into his contextualization strategies. Yet, for the purposes of the analysis at hand, it seems sufficient simply to mark the differences between the two speakers' strategies. For this, we chose to use italics in D's case because it is less cumbersome and less intrusive than the bracketing convention, while at the same time it conveys something of what the difference between styles is like. Where this font change causes difficulty in transferring across systems, other conventions can be used.

4. CONCLUSION

The transcription system we have described and illustrated can be used for conversations as well as for monologic texts. In conversation, the focus is on the interactive aspects of conversational management, and on the perceptual cues that speakers and audiences rely on in signaling what they intend to convey and in assessing what they hear. In monologue, it is well-suited for revealing the use of prosodic and paralinguistic signs to establish and maintain coherence.

We are aware that transcription is by its very nature inherently selective and that what is selected depends in large part on the analysts' background knowledge and theoretical perspective. Much has been left out and many of the questions we have touched on are far from resolved. As we said at the outset, our main goal is to reveal the functioning of communicative signs in the turn-by-turn interpretation of talk, not to record everything that can be heard or to provide exact measures of duration and pitch. Yet, at the same time, we seek to remain as comprehensive and attentive to detail as possible in showing what the phenomenological or perceptual bases of our interpretation are.

ACKNOWLEDGMENTS

This transcription system was first developed for use in the University of California, Institute of Cognitive Studies, Disclab, an on-line text archive, that serves as a database for studies of language use in a variety of natural contexts, ranging from institutional settings such as formal interviews, doctor–patient interactions, seminars, or academic lectures to family interaction, children's talk, and informal conversation. We are grateful to members of the Disclab group, Susan Ervin-Tripp, Wallace Chafe, Dan Slobin, Paula Chertok, Jane Edwards, Sarah Freeman, Martin Lampert, and Meryl Siegal, for their many helpful comments. We also thank Peter Auer for his helpful comments on an earlier version of this chapter. The following basic sources have been useful: The approach to pausing, latching, and overlap owes a great deal to Gail Jefferson's transcription system, described in Atkinson and Heritage (1984). Our notion of prosody rests in part on that developed by John Trim (1971). The perspective on rhythm and conversational synchrony is based on that of Erickson and Shultz (1982). We have also profited greatly from reading Couper-Kuhlen (1986).

REFERENCES

Atkinson, J. M., & Heritage, J. (Eds.). (1984). *Structures of social action*. Cambridge: Cambridge University Press.

Auer, P. (1988). Rhythmic integration in phone closings. *KontRI working papers*. Konstanz, Germany: University of Konstanz, Department of Linguistics.

Bolinger, D. (1986). *Intonation and its parts: Melody in spoken English*. Stanford: Stanford University Press.

Bolinger, D. (1989). *Intonation and its uses: Melody in grammar and discourse*. Stanford: Stanford University Press.

Chafe, W. (1987). Cognitive constraints on information flow. In R. S. Tomlin (Ed.), *Coherence and grounding in discourse* (pp. 21–51). Philadelphia: John Benjamins.

Couper-Kuhlen, E. (1986). *An introduction to English prosody*. London: Edward Arnold.

Couper-Kuhlen, E. (1988). Contextualizing discourse: The prosody of interactive repair. *KontRI Working papers*. Konstanz, Germany: University of Konstanz, Department of Linguistics.

Couper-Kuhlen, E., & Auer, P. (1988). On the contextualizing function of speech rhythm in conversation. *KontRI working papers*. Konstanz, Germany: University of Konstanz, Department of Linguistics.

Erickson, F., & Shultz, J. J. (1982). *The counselor as gatekeeper*. New York: Academic.

Gumperz, J. J. (1982). *Discourse strategies*. Cambridge: Cambridge University Press.

Gumperz, J. J. (1992). Contextualization and understanding. In A. Duranti & C. Goodwin (Eds.), *Rethinking context* (pp. 229-252). Cambridge: Cambridge University Press.

Gumperz, J. J. (in press). Contextualization revisited. In P. Auer & A. Di Luzio (Eds.), *Contextualization*. Amsterdam: John Benjamins.

Gumperz, J. J., & Roberts, C. (1991). *Understanding in intercultural encounters*. In J. Verschueren (Ed.), Proceedings of the 1987 Meetings of the International Pragmatics Association. Amsterdam: John Benjamins.

Kay, P., & Coleman, L. (1981). Prototype semantics: The English word lie. *Language, 57*, 26–44.

Ladd, R.D. (1980). *The structure of intonational meaning*. Bloomington: Indiana University Press.

Svartvik, J. & Quirk, R. (1980). *A corpus of English conversation*. Lund, Sweden: C. W. K. Gleerup.

Tannen, D. (1984). *Conversational style*. Norwood, NJ: Ablex.

Tannen, D. (1981). [Review of W. Labov & D. Fanshel, *Therapeutic discourse: Psychotherapy as conversation*]. *Language, 57*, 481–486.

Trim, J. (1971). *English intonation*. Cambridge: University of Cambridge, Department of Linguistics.

APPENDIX
TRANSCRIPTION NOTATION

Symbol	Significance
//	Final fall
/	Slight final fall indicating temporary closure (e.g., more can be said on the topic)
?	Final rise
,	Slight rise as in listing intonation (e.g., more is expected)
-	Truncation (e.g., what ti- what time is it/)
_	Level ending
..	Pauses of less than .5 second
...	Pauses greater than .5 second (unless precisely timed)
<2>	Precise units of time (= 2 second pause)
=	To indicate overlap and latching of speakers' utterances: spacing and single = before and after the appropriate portions of the text to indicate overlap; turn-initial double = to indicate latching of the utterance to the preceding one.

Ex.   R: so you understand =the requirements?=

B: =yeah, i understand them/=

~~~~~~~~~~~~~~~~~~~~~~~~~~~~~~~~

R: so you understand the requirements?

B: ==yeah, i understand them/

::	Lengthened segments (e.g., wha::t)
~	Fluctuating intonation over one word
*	Accent; normal prominence
**	Extra prominence
{[ ]}	Nonlexical phenomena, both vocal and nonvocal, that overlay the lexical stretch (e.g., {[lo] text//)
[ ]	Nonlexical phenomena, both vocal and nonvocal, that interrupt the lexical stretch (e.g., text [laugh] text//)
( )	Unintelligible speech
di(d)	A good guess at an unclear segment
(did)	A good guess at an unclear word
(xxx)	Unclear word for which a good guess can be made as to how many syllables were uttered, with each x equal to one syllable
(" ")	Regularization (e.g., i'm gonna ("going to") come soon/)
# #	Use cross-hatches when extratextual information needs to be included within the text (e.g., R: did you ask M #surname# to come?)

5
HIAT:
A Transcription System for Discourse Data

Konrad Ehlich
Universität Dortmund

1. THEORETICAL BACKGROUND

Linguistic work on spoken language is a relatively new branch of the language sciences. It has been inspired from different theoretical backgrounds that all have one thing in common, namely the conviction that analysis and theory should be based on a corpus of everyday occurring linguistic data. Objects of interest in these approaches include "discourse," "conversation," and "everyday language." The theoretical systems and presuppositions that are involved in the methods of analysis of these disciplines differ widely. Some have been developed in the context of phenomenological sociology ("conversational analysis," "ethnomethodology"; see Atkinson and Heritage, 1984; Jefferson, 1983a, 1983b; Sacks, Schegloff, & Jefferson, 1974). Some are derived from an ethnographic background (e.g., Gumperz, 1982), some are dependent on speech-act theory and presupposition theory (see Levinson, 1983). Some combine different approaches, as does German "Konversationsanalyse" (see Kallmeyer & Schütze, 1976). Some, such as British discourse analysis, are dependent upon specific paradigms in linguistics—mainly the paradigm established by M. A. K. Halliday and his collaborators (e.g., Coulthard, 1977). Some derive from a general theory of action (pragmatics) that has as its aim the reconstruction of linguistic action as part of the overall societal practice (see Ehlich & Rehbein, 1986; Rehbein, 1977).

All of these approaches are characterized by the fact that they do not restrict their linguistic analysis to an abstract linguistic "system," accessible primarily via introspection. They also do not restrict their data acquisition to experimental situations and designs. Instead, these approaches generally assume that a genuine analysis of language should be based on the participants' linguistic activities themselves.

An authentic representation of the oral data—as close to the original as possible—is of crucial importance for linguistic analysis in the theoretical contexts mentioned. Oral data in themselves are evanescent. Preserving them is a first and primary objective for all further steps of analysis. If data are not restricted to an abstract language system, it is also necessary—as a second objective—to account for phenomena that have to do with the interactive character of communication between speakers and listeners. A third objective involves the integration of linguistic activities into larger societal units, such as institutions, which is of major interest to some of the approaches mentioned.

At the same time, the interpretation of language data is seen as a hermeneutic process shared by members of the speech community and by the analysts, leading to an increasing understanding with successive passes through the data. In the analytic approach, some of the characteristics of the hermeneutic process of understanding are considered to be more important than they might be in everyday life.

A basic assumption of discourse analysis is that interaction is a complex phenomenon integrating not just "verbal" but also paralinguistic, nonverbal, and, partly, actional activities. These have to be accounted for in the process of making the evanescent communication events permanent and accessible to further analysis.

The hermeneutic character of understanding discourse requires that the taped data be listened to repeatedly. By this process, the dynamics of the interaction become progressively better understood with each pass through the data.

From a methodological standpoint, the transcript should be so constructed as to facilitate this process of increasing understanding, providing good visualization of the interaction and the interactional dynamics at each point in time together with ease of modification, as the data become increasingly better understood during the course of the analytic process. The transcript must preserve the most essential information in a clear manner, free from excessive amounts of information that might overload the reader and hinder the analytic process. Semiotic plausibility is thus an important property to bear in mind in establishing a transcription system. It is also useful to have conventions that can be flexibly extended and that offer an optimum of readability and interpretability. A lot of decisions that must be made early in the transcription process may lead to problems in its later stages and during analytic work. The continuous enrichment of experience should find its way into the formation of transcription systems (for a critical overview of different types of transcription systems, see Ehlich & Switalla, 1976).

In the following, I provide an overview of a transcription system that has been used for a variety of purposes (see Section 11) and has gained a certain level of acceptance among researchers, especially in Europe. It is used either in the form described here or with some modifications designed for capturing specific aspects of the acoustic data (see Baeyens, 1979a; Brinker & Sager, 1989; Henne & Rehbock, 1982; Schaeffer, 1979).[1] All of these share the basic characteristics of the system, namely its *score notation* (see Section 5).

2. INTRODUCING HIAT

The HIAT system, described in this paper was developed with three criteria in mind: (a) simplicity and validity, (b) good readability and correctability, and (c) minimum of transcriber and user training. The acronym, HIAT, stands for *Halbinterpretative Arbeitstranskriptionen.* "Interpretative" refers to the overall hermeneutic process of understanding the spoken data. That the process is open to further analytical steps is reflected in the qualification of the name as being "semi-interpretative" (*halbinterpretativ*). A fine English version of the name that still preserves the acronym has been proposed by Dafydd Gibbon: "Heuristic Interpretative Auditory Transcription" (with the addition that it can also be extended to nonverbal interaction in the case of audio-visual tapes).

3. BASIC MODE OF TRANSCRIPTION: IPA VERSUS LITERARY TRANSCRIPTION VERSUS STANDARD ORTHOGRAPHY

Although standard written orthography has been the traditional choice for preserving spoken language, this choice is not without problems since written language is known to differ widely from spoken varieties (see Coulmas, 1989). A standard orthography works as a filter whose relationship to the acoustic structures of the data is indirect, serving to regulate the translation of auditory input into written output. The use of standard orthography therefore can lead to considerable loss of information that may be important for later analysis (Sacks, Schegloff, & Jefferson, 1974). Some researchers have proposed using the International Phonetic Alphabet (IPA) or other forms of phonetic or phonemic transcription to solve this problem. Phonetic transcriptions aim at one-to-one relationships between (a) graphemes and (b) phonetic units and other characteristics of the spoken language. The gain in information, however, is offset by a loss in ease of use. Specific phonetic training is necessary in such

---

[1]A broader description of the system can be found in Ehlich and Rehbein (1976, 1979, 1981a, 1981b, 1986).

cases, for both transcribers and transcript users, yet such training is not widespread in all of the disciplines that contribute to the area of discourse analysis (e.g., anthropology, sociology, psychology). Of course, there are many research objectives that make IPA transcription a useful, valuable, and even necessary tool of investigation. But for the analysis of everyday communication from the point of view of discourse structures, and in the context of pragmatic and semantic analyses, in many cases an IPA transcript would contain too much information.

The HIAT system uses, instead, a derivation from written orthography which we call *literary transcription*, or in German, *literarische Umschrift* (see Möhn, 1964; Ruoff, 1973). Literary transcription involves systematic departures from the standard orthographic rendering of an item but in a manner that is meaningful to someone familiar with the orthographic system as a whole, as in the case of *ye* for *your* in the following example (extracted from a larger discourse in which a Yorkshire miner describes certain aspects of his work):

> Miner (speaking in Yorkshire dialect):
> "Then we've had what they call / uh / . ye duffymen
> / ye two duffymen and they come on and they shovel all this
> duff that this machine had made!" (From Schlickau, 1989)

Here, the first syllable of *duffymen* is [dʊf] and the speaker realizes *shovel* as [ʃʊvl], and *your* as [yə].

Although further specification may be added, it is unnecessary for well-known common dialects. In these cases, it may be sufficient to indicate at the beginning of a transcript that the speakers are "speakers of dialect X" and to rely on the reader's stereotypic knowledge of the dialects involved.

When the speaker does not use an established or known variety but rather uses, for example, an "ideolect" or an "ad hoc" pronunciation, it may be desirable to supplement the transcription with the use of IPA or similar systems, as, for instance, in transcribing the speech of aphasics or of foreign language learners. The example in Fig. 5.1, taken from an English lesson among German students, illustrates this possibility.

Literary transcription relies on the standard orthography of a language and presupposes good knowledge of the standard system in use. However, orthographies differ in the degree of regularity with which they map phonetic/phonological sounds onto graphemes. In "deep orthographies" such as English, for easing the recovery of acoustic information from individual words, the transcript should be supplemented with lists of examples and clarifying comments pertaining to use of particular conventions that might otherwise be non-obvious or ambiguous (e.g., *hafta* for *have to, dz* for *does, n*

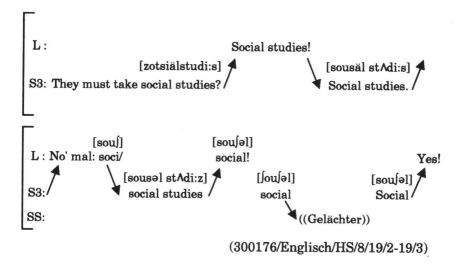

(300176/Englisch/HS/8/19/2-19/3)

FIG. 5.1. Excerpt from an English lesson in a German school.

for *and, cuz* for *'cause*). This is especially important when transcripts are read by nonnative speakers of the language.

4. THE REPRESENTATION OF PAUSES, INTERRUPTION, INTONATION, TONES, AND MODULATION

One of the salient characteristics of everyday spoken language is the distribution of pauses. When reading aloud from written text, the placement of pauses is determined in part by major and minor constituent boundaries (see Chafe, 1986). Pauses in spoken language are known to reflect additional processes, including those related to the planning of utterances and the coordination of turns (Dechert & Raupach, 1980; O'Connell & Kowal, 1983). In HIAT, we preserve the location and duration of pauses by means of periods and explicit timing, as is done also by other researchers (see Chafe, this volume; Du Bois, Schuetze-Coburn, Cumming, & Paolino, this volume; Ehlich & Rehbein, 1976, 1979, 1981a, 1981b, 1986).

Also important for discourse research is the preservation of interruption in the flow of speech, both by the speaker and by others. The identification of interruptions is often based on the linguistic knowledge of interactants, transcribers, and transcript users. This knowledge differs with regard to the various subparts of language. It is generally easier to identify interruptions in words than in larger units, but both are important in discourse understanding.

In HIAT, we use the slash (/), written immediately after the interrupted elements, separated by a space in the case of units larger than words. The slash was chosen because of its iconical plausibility. High frequency of occurrence of slashes suggests a "jerky" production by the speaker, which, again, is of interest for a variety of analytic purposes. As far as syntactic interruptions are concerned, slash distribution hints at the presence of "anacolutha," that is, syntactic reformulations or restarts.

Languages differ greatly with regard to their *intonation* systems. A number of transcription systems have been developed for different languages, but no single system has been generally accepted. In some languages (e.g., German), standard orthographic punctuation offers a sufficiently precise system for representing basic intonation, especially if supplemented by simple conventions for representing "sentence" or "phrase accent." In HIAT we underline words that carry stress that deviates from the standard stress patterns in the language involved (see Section 8.1).

Some systems for a representation of intonation contours make use of "iconic" signs such as the slash (/) for rising tone and the backslash (\) for falling tone or (as in HIAT) the acute accent (´) for rising tone and the grave accent (`) for falling tone (see Cruttenden, 1986; Crystal, 1975; Richter, 1973; Svartvik & Quirk, 1980 for more detailed discussion). The use of symbols of this type is to be restricted in HIAT to a highly specific phenomenon of intonation in the broad sense of the term, namely the so-called *tones* in the phonological sense of the term (see Fromkin, 1978). Tones are present in tone languages such as Chinese or Vietnamese for nearly all lexical entries of these languages. Tonal structures exist also in other languages for small subparts of the lexicon. In German, for example, *hm* and other interjections are combined with several tone structures to generate different "meanings." These tone structures are of high communicative significance (Ehlich, 1986). We have found the following five symbols useful for the representation of tone in German:

Tone Representation Symbols
- ´   rising tone
- `   falling tone
- ∨   falling-rising tone
- ∧   rising-falling tone
- –   even tone

Other important aspects of spoken language are *modulation in volume*, *tempo*, and *quality of articulation*. These are marked in HIAT by means of the following sub- and supralinear notations:

Supralinear notations:

$>$	decreasing loudness
$<$	increasing loudness
>>>>	increasing tempo
<<<<	decreasing tempo
. . . .	staccato (one period per syllable)

Sublinear notations:

_____	emphasized or stressed
_ _ _ _	drawled; poorly articulated

Another type of modulation is the *lengthening* of single phonemes, or gemination. For this purpose, as is done in IPA for gemination of phonetic units, we add a colon (:) after the lengthened phoneme. This is only used in those cases in which the length deviates from "ordinary" spoken language.

5. THE REPRESENTATION OF TRANS-TURN DATA

Only few instances of spoken language are "monologues"; everyday communication generally involves multiple speakers. Even when the discourse involves lengthy turns by a single speaker, the other participants typically engage in activities that contribute to the ongoing interaction. Furthermore, some interactions involve rapid shifts of turn and a great deal of overlapping speech. This simultaneity of speech and action presents a major challenge for all visualization systems of spoken language—namely, how to represent the contributions of multiple participants while preserving an accurate representation of time.

Standard Greek/Latin-based writing systems are inadequate for this purpose because the flow of time is represented from left to right, only one line at a time. In transcribing discourse data, because many things happen at the same time, it is desirable to expand the dimension of a transcript to allow for several simultaneous, ongoing events, in a graphically neat, straightforward manner. A highly effective solution is suggested by the system used in musical representation—the *musical score*.

A musical score makes use of the two-dimensionality of an area for representation purposes. Semiotic events arrayed horizontally on a line follow each other in time, whereas events on the same vertical axis represent simultaneous acoustic events, produced by different musical instruments, such as the violin, the trumpet, and the piano.

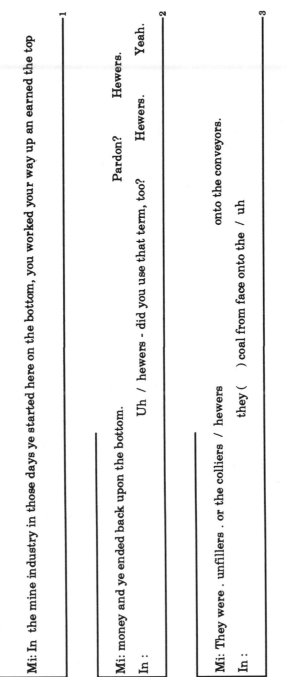

FIG. 5.2. Example of turn-taking using score notation (from Schlickau, 1989).

One can consider simultaneous speech of several speakers at a time as a complex acoustic event similar to the simultaneous realization of a multitude of musical notes in a concerto. Whereas the left-to-right direction preserves the unfolding of events in time, the vertical dimension captures how they overlap at each particular point in time. The score form of representation, or "score transcription," thus offers a good visual representation of one of the most important features of a multiparty communication, namely, simultaneity.

Figure 5.2 illustrates how turn-taking is represented in the score notation. In this example, the interviewer starts his question, "Uh / hewers - did you use that term, too," immediately after the miner's utterance "ye ended back upon the bottom." As the interviewer finishes his question, the miner answers, with "pardon." (For uses of similar format, see Ervin-Tripp, 1979; Tannen, 1984.)

Figure 5.3 shows how the notation is used to capture instances of overlap (see Jefferson, 1983b). Here the interviewee begins his utterance before the interviewer has finished. The beginning of the overlap is marked by the vertical alignment of the two lines.

The length of a word in the written language may prove to be only a partial reflection of its length in the spoken language. Here some ambiguity may arise concerning where an overlap ends relative to the utterance of another speaker. The same may be the case when one speaker speaks considerably slower or faster than another speaker. In order to reestablish synchronicity visually, we use the sign ⌐ or ⌐ drawn vertically across two or more lines of the score. This sign usually is applied to the end of the turn of one of the speakers, as illustrated in Fig. 5.4. It is also possible to adjust the width or number of blanks to achieve visual synchronicity.

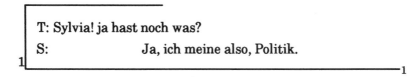

T: Sylvia! ja hast noch was?

S: Ja, ich meine also, Politik.

FIG. 5.3. Example of overlap using score notation.

In: What happened to Bill after his disappearance?

Su: Bill had a pretty hard time.

FIG. 5.4. Example of overlap with lines to indicate synchronicity.

Basic principles underlying score transcription are as follows:

1. Set up an area on the page that has a vertical extent large enough to contain a line for each speaker and enough space to identify intonation, nonverbal communication, etc.

2. Move vertically downward from one line to the next whenever a new speaker utters something.

3. Move vertically upward to the appropriate line when a previous speaker utters something.

4. Continue until you have reached the right margin of the page.

5. Repeat 1–4.

Principle 3 is deviant with regard to usual writing and reading habits, requiring some adjustment of habits by transcribers and transcript users. Experience shows that this system is quick and easy to learn, however.

Concerning the dimensions of the score area, its vertical width is determined by the number of individuals involved in the interaction. Typically, this is less than the full vertical extension on the page, meaning that in most cases it is possible to put more than one score on a sheet. It is necessary to indicate where one score ends and the next begins. In musical notation, a specific brace is used for this purpose. In HIAT, after some experimenting, we have devised a graphical equivalent, namely, a small horizontal line of 1 to 1.5 inches on the left-hand top of the score, a parallel horizontal line on its bottom, and a vertical line on the left-hand side of the score connecting the two horizontal lines. The ease of reading can be improved by drawing the lower horizontal line across nearly the whole width of the page, leaving a small 1-inch open space at the right-hand side. We call this sign the simultaneity brace, and we call the score area that is generated by a simultaneity brace a simultaneity area.

In order to enable the transcript user to adapt more readily to the reading demands of a score, it may be useful to put arrows in the transcript at places of possible ambiguity, as illustrated in Fig. 5.5.

To this basic transcript, only one additional piece of information needs to be added, namely, the attribution of lines to the different parties involved in an interaction. For an entire transcript, individual speakers are distinguished by one- or two-letter codes (e.g., *Mi* for "Miner" and *In* for "Interviewer" in Figs. 5.2 and 5.5). These speaker identifiers are placed on the left edge of each score.

For instances of communication in which speakers are unknown, reserved symbols, such as X, Y, or Z, may be used.

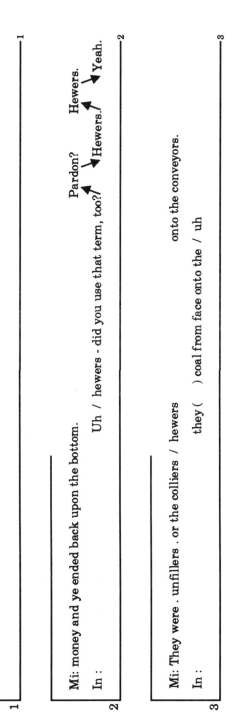

1

Mi: In the mine industry in those days ye started here on the bottom, you worked your way up an earned the top

2

Mi: money and ye ended back upon the bottom.

In :   Pardon?   Hewers.
           Uh / hewers - did you use that term, too?/ ➤Hewers./ ➤Yeah.

3

Mi: They were . unfillers . or the colliers / hewers   onto the conveyors.

In :   they (   ) coal from face onto the / uh

FIG. 5.5. Notation of turn organization.

It may also prove useful to fix the attribution of the first line of each score area to one specific speaker, in particular the speaker who is the focus of an analysis (e.g., the teacher in a classroom or the interviewee in an interview). In these cases, the first line can also be taken as a sort of reference line in the course of transcribed events (see Ochs, 1979).

In some discourse instances, relatively long periods of time are attributed to only one speaker who keeps the turn. In these cases, the transcript will have many score areas with only one line. This, obviously, is a specific case comparable to the solo part of a violin in a concerto.

6. ACOUSTIC DISTURBANCES IN THE DATA

Everyday communication is highly complex in nature. As a consequence, taping is often very difficult, and the data one gets on tape are often less than excellent quality. But if one wants to have authentic data there is no choice except to go into the field with all of its acoustic disturbances and noise.

Often, words and phrases that are initially difficult to hear may be later clarified as the transcriber continues to listen to a tape and gains a greater understanding of ongoing interaction. Upon a first hearing, the transcriber may have a rough idea of what words were said. In HIAT, this tentative conjecture

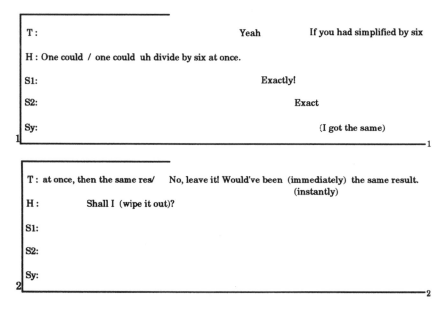

FIG. 5.6. Notation for uncertain hearing: simple and double conjecture (translated from Redder, 1982, p. 182).

is placed within parentheses. When two alternatives seem equally plausible, they are split across the line, one above the other, and both are enclosed in parentheses. Figure 5.6 contains two simple and one double conjecture.

7. NON-PHONOLOGICAL PHENOMENA

Data from the field may contain other types of acoustic information, such as laughter and sneezing. These and other acoustic events that may be relevant to the discourse context, such as a dog barking or the banging of a door, should be preserved in the transcript. To enable good visual separation between these events and spoken events, we use double parentheses. Figure 5.7 illustrates this convention.

For longer description, greater visual separation is needed to avoid ambiguity between spoken events and descriptive commentary. For this purpose we mark the relevant point within the score area and add a full description in the left margin, enclosed in other brackets.[2] (For preserving more detailed descriptions, a different convention is used, as discussed below.)

8. HIAT 2: THE ELABORATION OF BASIC HIAT FOR THE INCLUSION OF INTONATION, NONVERBAL COMMUNICATION, AND ACTIONS

In addition to the basic transcript, which is provided by HIAT, there is sometimes a need for greater elaboration of certain aspects, especially intonation, nonverbal communication, and actions. When further elaboration of

| T: Yeah, that happens quite quickly. |
| P: Uh / What do you understand |

| T: |
| P: by "quite quickly" |
| R: ((laughs)) |

FIG. 5.7. Notation for non-phonological phenomena (translated from Redder, 1982, p. 24).

---

[2]Square brackets ([ ]) or specially designed brackets (/_ _/) may be used for this purpose.

these things is desired, we transform the elementary version of the HIAT transcript into an extended version, which we call HIAT 2.

8.1. Intonation

A basic approach to intonation is provided in HIAT (see Section 4). However, there are cases in which special notation to represent intonation proves necessary, for example, cases in which different intonation contours are possible for different types of questions. For the representation of German intonation, we have decided to use a five-line supra-linear system that is added to the line of the speaker. Figure 5.8 gives examples for the application of the system (see Ehlich, 1981; Ehlich & Rehbein, 1979, for a detailed discussion of some of the most important systems in use).

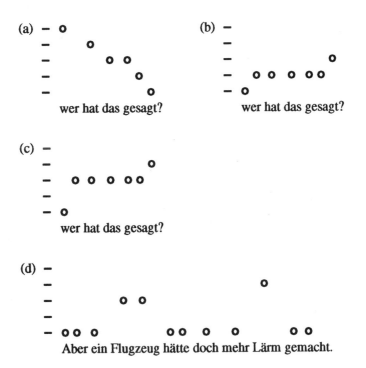

FIG. 5.8. The Representation of intonation using HIAT 2: Four German examples.

8.2. Nonverbal Communication and Actions

In basic HIAT, nonverbal communication and physical actions are handled by means of commentary brackets. Through an extension of the score system, however, it is possible to provide a more detailed account of these aspects including a more precise indication of timing of events relative to each other or relative to the speech stream. As in basic HIAT, there is a single line for verbal communication, but in HIAT 2 this is labeled as VC (VK in German) and is supplemented with additional lines for nonverbal communication and actions, labeled NVC and AC (NVK and AK in German), respectively, for each speaker. The VC line is transcribed as in basic HIAT and serves as the reference for positioning descriptions of nonverbal communication and indicating their relative duration. This series of lines constitutes what we call a *band*.

Though no single system for representation of nonverbal communication has yet gained universal acceptance, some fundamental features of nonverbal communication are of acknowledged importance (see Birdwhistell, 1970, 1986; Ehlich & Rehbein, 1982; Ekman & Friesen, 1969; Erickson & Shultz, 1982; Heath, 1986). These include which part of the body is involved, the nature of the movement, and its duration. The nonverbal event is given a minimal description, aligned with the appropriate portion of the verbal line. Because the score represents the course of time, it provides the graphic space for indicating the duration of an action. We use the letter *o* in combination with a number of hyphens to represent duration:

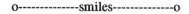

o--------------smiles-------------o

The *o* signs represent the starting and finishing points of the activity in the area of the score, the combination of hyphens represents its duration.

Actions that have very short durations require a modification of the basic convention. For example, the shutting of the eyelid takes less time than the description takes space. In such cases, a percent sign (%) is used to mark the location at which the action occurred, and the associated description is placed immediately after it. The percent sign resembles a pair of *o*s with a slash in-between, and it is therefore a good choice for reasons of semiotic plausibility. Thus, in the following example, the notation indicates that the speaker closed his eyelid when saying *oh*.

VC   oh
NVC   % eyelid closed.

This, and information included in double parentheses (see Section 7) are the only deviation in the system from the rule of direct correspondence between the temporal location of an activity (relative to speech events) and its spatial location in the score.

Finally, we use the following set of two-letter abbreviations to identify the body parts involved in a gesture, in conjunction with *l* and *r*, for "left" and "right," respectively. This contributes to compactness and consistency across transcripts. Of course, the list can be further extended as needed.

Kopf		*Head*	
KO	Kopf	HE	head
GE	Gesicht	FA	face
ST	Stirn	FO	forehead
AU	Auge(n)	EY	eye(s)
LD	Lid	EL	eye-lid
BR	Braue	EB	eyebrow
NA	Nase	NO	nose
MU	Mund	MO	mouth
LP	Lippe(n)	LP	lip(s)
ZU	Zunge	TO	tongue
KI	Kinn	CH	chin
ZÄ	Zähne	TE	teeth

Extremitäten		*Arms/Legs*	
AR	Arm(e)	AR	arm(s)
HA	Hand	HA	hand(s)
HÄ	Hände		
FI	Finger	FI	finger(s)
KF	Kleiner Finger	LF	little finger
RF	Ringfinger	RF	ring finger
MF	Mittelfinger	MF	middle finger
ZF	Zeigefinger	FF	forefinger
DF	Daumen	TF	thumb
FU	Fuß	FO	foot
FÜ	Füße	FE	feet
BE	Bein(e)	LE	leg(s)

Körper		*Body*	
KÖ	Körper	BO	body
SC	Schulter(n)	SH	shoulder(s)

This use of brief descriptions bounded by *o*s and dashes can be extended to capture the temporal location and duration of common actions, or other events or activities (see Ehlich & Rehbein, 1981b, pp. 322–327; Ehlich & Rehbein, 1982, pp. 83–132). Figure 5.9 shows the integration of actions (in this case, "writing") in score areas 3 and 4.

	L VK	Ich werd es auch nacher anzeichnen. Ich bin nicht so optimistisch, anzunehmen,
	NVK	o----*Blickfixierung auf S2*----o o--------*KO nach links zu allen*------------------
		-*HÄ*-oo-*abwert. Geste mit HÄ*-oo--------------------- *HÄ gefaltet*-------------------------
		o--*lächelt*-------------o
	S2 NVK	o--*verschränkt AR trotzig,* o--*nimmt Stift*--o o-----*meldet sich mit ARr*------o
		KÖ vorgebeugt----o *aus MU und*
		setzt zum
1		*Schreiben an*

	L VK	daß wir das hier. voll klären können. Bitte !
	NVK	-------o o-------*KO zurück zu S2*--------------------------------------
		----------------------------*HÄ gefaltet*---
		o----*Hebung des KO*--%--o
L_1 Prä-turn-		L_1 %BR *hochziehen Nicken*
Abgabe		% %LD *schließen (2x)*
		%LP *aufein.* o---LP *aufeinandergepreßt*--------
	S2 VK	( ) mich interessierte nur der Name von dem/ Mich interessierte nur der Name
2	NVK	o-------*bewegt AR winkend*------------o

	L VK	Das war also in einer etwas <u>anderen</u>
	NVK	-------------------------------------- *Blick zu S2*----------------------------------
		--------------------------*HÄ gefaltet*--------------------------------------
		--------LP *aufein.*----------o
	S2 VK	eh, dessen, der dieses .. Experiment . gemacht hat.
3	AK	o-*schreibt*--

	L VK	Form der Herr Foucault . . . mit o u und hinten mit a u el te . . und dieses . . / .
	NVK	--------------------*Blick zu S2*----------------------------------- %-----------o
		AU links zu allen
		--------------------------*HÄ gefaltet*--o
		% *setzt mit* % *spreizt KF ab*
		KO zum Gang o-*lächelt*
		an die Tafel an *andeutungsweise*-o
	S2 NVK	o-*KO hoch, AU zu L-*
		o--*lacht*--------------
		% *Stirnrunzeln*
	AK	--------------------------- *schreibt*-----------------------------------o
	S1 NVK	o-*KO zu S2,*
		AU auf Heft--
	S VK	Meikelsen
4	SS NVK	o--*Lachen*--o

FIG. 5.9. Notation of verbal and nonverbal communication and actions in HIAT 2.

Whereas transcribing 1-minute multiparty verbal interaction in a basic HIAT transcript usually requires 40 to 60 minutes of transcription work, the transcription time needed for the additional nonverbal communication in HIAT 2 takes much longer—up to 240 minutes. This means that the transcription of nonverbal communication usually has to be restricted to small parts of the overall amount of data that are on tape.

9. INFORMATION ON TAPING AND TRANSCRIBING

For archival purposes in both basic and extended HIAT, each transcript should contain information on:

1. the date, circumstances, and equipment of taping,
2. the persons who did the taping,
3. the discourse situation,
4. the participants,
5. the names of the transcribers,
6. the dates of transcription, and
7. the time used for the transcribing.[3]

In HIAT, we use a kind of initial format or *template* to help the transcriber provide all the necessary information in a systematic manner (see Fig. 5.10).

301074 / 7 / D / M / GS : GERMAN – "INTONATION IN GERMAN"

---

2 LES. /CLASS 7 /TEACHER "WIPPERMANN" / COMPULSORY SCHOOL IN NRW

TRANSCRIPTION	:	IRIS FÜSSENICH (1 : 70)
CORRECTION	:	IRIS FÜSSENICH (1 : 100)
INTONATION	:	ANGELIKA REDDER (1 : 30)

FIG. 5.10. Template of transcript information for archival purposes.

---

[3]This also may be of use in applying for grant funds for future projects.

10. THE TECHNICAL LAYOUT OF THE TRANSCRIPT PAGES

A HIAT transcript usually starts with the production of a handwritten transcript, written with pencil on oblong, oversized graph paper. The checkered grid of the graph paper is of great help for the representation of the simultaneous acoustic events on the score area. The transcript is then checked for accuracy, either by the original or a second transcriber. The corrected handwritten transcript is then either typed onto an oblong sheet of paper or entered onto a microcomputer.

If typed, it is necessary to reserve sufficient open space between score areas and between the lines within a score area for good readability. Immediately after the page has been completed the simultaneity braces are marked in the transcript.

For computer entry, we have developed two programs that enable users to transcribe directly from audio tape to HIAT format on their microcomputer, and allow users to do computer-assisted analysis of transcripts. These programs work on IBM-compatibles running MS-DOS (HIAT-DOS), and on Macintosh (syncWRITER, with MacHIAT as a previous version), respectively.[4]

In contrast to other transcription methods discussed in this volume, in which each new turn is positioned at the left margin, turns in HIAT unfold horizontally across the page, meaning that special provisions are needed to maintain vertical alignment across lines within a band. HIAT-DOS version 1 was developed with this problem in mind. HIAT-DOS version 2 provides faster processing, combined with some additional tools designed to facilitate the transcriber's work. The manual is available in German (Becker-Mrotzek, Ehlich, Glas, & Tebel, 1991) and in English (Ehlich, Tebel, Fickermann, & Becker-Mrotzek, 1991).

HIAT-DOS offers a format with the score as its basic graphic unit. It generates on the screen a template for archival information (see Section 9). It then generates a second template for the scores. One work score provides space for 130 signs, split up into two screens. The template also generates the score bracket. Each speaker's line is combined with a supra- and a sublinear line, the first providing the signs described in Section 4, and the latter offering the possibility to include nonverbal data.

HIAT-DOS offers the option to move all data within a score, when insertions or deletions are necessary in any speaker's lines, in the course of correction of previous conjectures and so on. In doing so, HIAT-DOS achieves

---

[4]Further information on HIAT-DOS can be found in Becker-Mrotzek, Ehlich, Glas and Tebel (1989) and on MacHIAT in Grießhaber (1987c, 1988) and Grießhaber and Rehbein (1988). For the PC diskette-versions, please contact one of the following addresses: Prof. Dr. K. Ehlich, FB 15, Dortmund University, P.O. Box 500500, D-W-4600 Dortmund 50, Germany (for HIAT-DOS), and med-i-bit, Hohenfelder Str. 20, D-W-2000 Hamburg 76, Germany (for syncWRITER).

automatic realignment for the transcript as a whole. Before a transcript is printed, a final page set-up is done. Figs. 5.2 and 5.5 are HIAT-DOS examples.

Further development of HIAT-DOS aims at the creation of tools for the computer assisted analysis of transcript data, such as segmentation, and counts of turns.

The Macintosh HIAT program syncWRITER provides an on-screen transcription editor equivalent to that of HIAT-DOS, combining it with the very useful tools of Li-A-M (*Linguistische-Analyse-Makros*, Linguistic-Analysis-Macros) that offers facilities for segmentation, numbering, counting, and various types of data extraction. German and English versions of syncWRITER are available.

By using MacRecorder, the acoustic data can be integrated to the effect that the acoustic equivalents to the transcript data can be made audible in combination with the display of the transcript on the screen. A transcript management system has been developed by Grießhaber (1990). The main menu for this system is illustrated in Fig. 5.11.

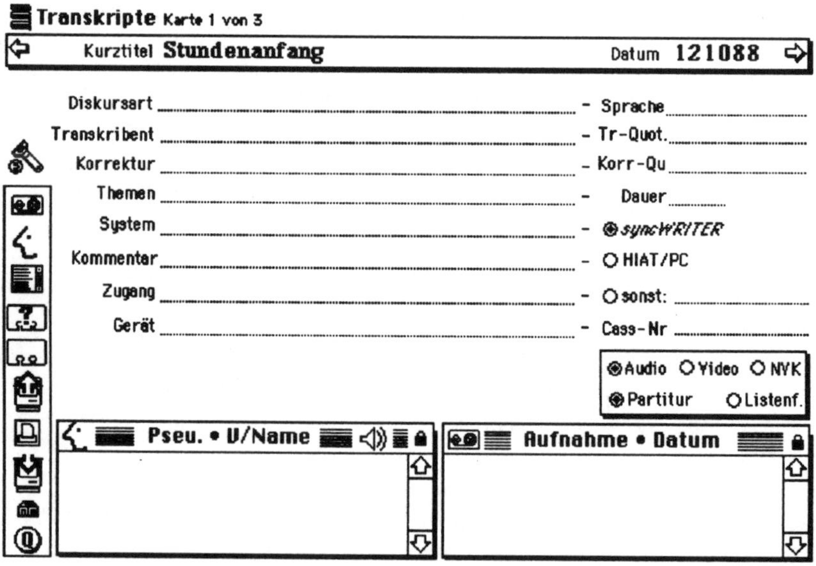

FIG. 5.11. The first page of the menu for MacRecorder.

11. APPLICATIONS

Researchers have applied HIAT to a variety of communicative data from areas such as communication in the classroom (e.g., Ehlich & Rehbein, 1986; Redder, 1984), communication at the workplace (Brünner; 1987; Schlickau, 1989), everyday communication (Ludwig, 1988a, 1988b), discussions (Pander Maat, 1988), communication in the courtroom (Hoffmann, 1983), job interviews and job interview role-plays (Grießhaber, 1987a, 1987b), and child discourse (Reski, 1980). Data cover a range of languages, including German, English (Schlickau, 1989), Dutch (Baeyens, 1979b, Mönnink, 1988; Pander Maat, 1988), French (Ludwig 1988a, 1988b), and Greek (Liedke, 1992; Tsolakidou, 1985). A volume containing HIAT transcripts of data from various institutional and non-institutional settings is in preparation (see Ehlich & Redder, in press).

Brünner (1987) audio- and videotaped the communications between trainers and trainees in a coal mine. For her analysis of discourse processes during training she needed detailed transcripts that included the interrelations between verbal and nonverbal communication and the coal mining actions. These transcripts were done in a HIAT format and provided the basis for a detailed analysis of schemas of verbal interaction in a specific institutional setting.

Redder (1982) provided transcriptions of three classroom lessons. One of these includes the transcription of the nonverbal activities of one pupil, which was the basis of analysis in Füssenich (1981). Füssenich analyzed the complex interrelation of teacher–pupil interaction in the case of a "difficult" pupil, and the effects of different verbal strategies of both interactants.

Reski (1980) reconstructed the process of children's acquisition of the interactional schema for making requests, basing her analysis on HIAT transcripts of kindergarten and mother-child discourse.

12. CONCLUDING REMARKS

HIAT is a system for transcription of communicative data. It offers a tool for representation of verbal, paralinguistic, nonverbal, and actional audio- and videotaped data. Its main characteristic is the use of a musiclike score as a basic graphic unit. Scores offer an appealing format for the visual representation of synchronicity, which is important for the transcription of turn and overlap phenomena. Verbal data are transcribed in "literary transcription," that is, an adaptation of orthographic conventions with the goal of capturing acoustic/auditive variants in a manner useful for analysis yet accessible without requiring specialized phonetic training. Special conventions are provided for pauses, interruptions, intonation, tones, and modulation. Software versions of HIAT are available for use on IBM-compatible and Macintosh computers.

The application of HIAT already covers a large range of data from various types of discourse, institutions, and languages. For the future, additional data can be expected. Compilation of available data is prepared in a "Center for Linguistic and Literary Data Files."

Intercultural aspects of communication and comparison of discourse in institutional settings across cultures and languages are only some of the research areas for which HIAT transcripts may be of use for further research.

HIAT transcripts may also be used in the training of doctors, teachers, lawyers, and other professionals for whom verbal interaction is of major importance. First steps in this direction have been taken (see Ehlich, Becker-Mrotzek, Fickermann, 1989; Fiehler & Sucharowski, 1992).

ACKNOWLEDGEMENTS

I very much thank Bill Elmer (Basle), Dafydd Gibbon, Ingrid Hudabiunigg, (both Bielefeld), Martina Liedke and Stephan Schlickau, and the editors for their considerable help with the English text.

REFERENCES

Atkinson, J. M., & Heritage J. (Eds.). (1984). *Structures of social action: Studies in conversation analysis.* Cambridge: Cambridge University Press.

Baeyens, M. (1979a). Naar een uniform transcriptiesysteem? [Towards a uniform transcription system?]. In A. Foolen, J. Hardeveld, & D. Springorum (Eds.), *Conversatieanalyse* (pp. 17–40). (Lezingen van het congres Conversatieanalyse, December 17–19, 1979, Nijmegen). Groningen, The Netherlands: Xeno.

Baeyens, M. (1979b). Transcriptie 1 [Transcription 1]. In A. Foolen, J. Hardeveld, & D. Springorum (Eds.), *Conversatieanalyse* (pp. 41-44). (Lezingen van het congres Conversatieanalyse, December 17–19, 1979, Nijmegen). Groningen, The Netherlands: Xeno.

Becker-Mrotzek, M., Ehlich, K., Glas, R., & Tebel, C. (1991). *Handbuch zur Erstellung von Transkripten nach dem Verfahren HIAT-DOS 2.0* [Manual for the production of transcripts according to the system HIAT-DOS 2.0]. Dortmund, Germany: Universität Dortmund, Institut für deutsche Sprache und Literatur.

Becker-Mrotzek, M., Ehlich, K., Glas, R., & Tebel, C. (1989). Transkription von Sprachdaten mit Computer-Hilfe: HIAT-DOS [Computer-aided transcription of linguistic data: HIAT-DOS]. *UNI-Report, 9*, 22–24.

Birdwhistell, R. L. (1970). *Kinesics and context: Essays on body motion communication.* Philadelphia: University of Pennsylvania Press.

Birdwhistell, R. L. (1986). A kinesic-linguistic exercise: The cigarette scene. In J. J. Gumperz & D. Hymes (Eds.), *Directions in sociolinguistics: The ethnography of communication* (pp. 381–404). New York: Blackwell.

Brinker, K., & Sager, S. F. (1989). *Linguistische Gesprächsanalyse* [Linguistic conversation analysis]. Berlin: Erich Schmidt Verlag.

Brünner, G. (1987). *Kommunikation in institutionellen Lehr-Lern-Prozessen. Diskursanalytische Untersuchungen zu Instruktionen in der betrieblichen Ausbildung* [Communication in institutional teaching-learning-processes. Discourse analytic investigations into instructions in on-job training] (Series Kommunikation und Institution 16). Tübingen: Narr.

Chafe, W. L. (1986). Writing in the perspective of speaking. In C. R. Cooper & S. Greenbaum (Eds.), *Studying writing: Linguistic approaches* (pp. 12–39). Beverly Hills: Sage.

Coulmas, F. (1989). *Writing systems of the world.* Oxford: Blackwell.

Coulthard, M. (1977). *An introduction to discourse analysis.* London: Longman.

Cruttenden, A. (1986). *Intonation.* Cambridge: Cambridge University Press.

Crystal, D. (1975). *The English tone of voice.* London: Edward Arnold.

Dechert, H. W., & Raupach, M. (1980). *Temporal variables in speech.* New York: Mouton.

Ehlich, K. (1981). Intonation des gesprochenen Deutsch: Aufzeichnung, Analyse, Lehre [Intonation of spoken German]. *Kopenhagener Beiträge zur Germanistischen Linguistik,* **18,** 46–93.

Ehlich, K. (1986). *Interjektionen* [Interjections] (Series Linguistische Arbeiten 111). Tübingen: Niemeyer.

Ehlich, K., Becker-Mrotzek, M., & Fickermann, I. (1989). *Gesprächsfibel. Ein Leitfaden* [A primer of institutional talk]. Dortmund, Germany: Universität Dortmund, Institut für deutsche Sprache und Literatur.

Ehlich, K., & Redder, A. (Eds.). (in press). *Gesprochene Sprache. Transkripte* [Spoken language. Transcripts] (Series PHONAI). Tübingen: Niemeyer.

Ehlich, K., & Rehbein, J. (1976). Halbinterpretative Arbeitstranskriptionen [Heuristic Interpretative Auditory Transcriptions]. *Linguistische Berichte,* **45,** 21–41.

Ehlich, K., & Rehbein, J. (1979). Erweiterte halbinterpretative Arbeitstranskriptionen (HIAT 2): Intonation [Expanded Heuristic Interpretative Auditory Transcriptions (HIAT 2): Intonation]. *Linguistische Berichte,* **59,** 51–75.

Ehlich, K., & Rehbein, J. (1981a). Zur Notierung nonverbaler Kommunikation für diskursanalytische Zwecke (Erweiterte halbinterpretative Arbeitstranskriptionen HIAT 2) [On the notation of nonverbal communication for discourse analytic purposes (Expanded Heuristic Interpretative Auditory Transcriptions HIAT 2)]. In P. Winkler (Ed.), *Methoden der Analyse von Face-to-Face-Situationen* (pp. 302–329). Stuttgart: Metzler.

Ehlich, K., & Rehbein, J. (1981b). Die Wiedergabe intonatorischer, nonverbaler und aktionaler Phänomene im Verfahren HIAT [The representation of intonative, nonverbal and actional phenomena in the transcription system HIAT]. In A. Lange-Seidl (Ed.), *Zeichenkonstitution* (Vol. 2, pp. 174–186). New York: de Gruyter. [This article gives a condensed overview of the authors' articles of 1979 and 1981a.]

Ehlich, K., & Rehbein, J. (1982). *Augenkommunikation. Methodenreflexion und Beispielanalyse* [Eye communication. Methodological reflexion and exemplary analysis]. Amsterdam: John Benjamins.

Ehlich, K., & Rehbein, J. (1986). *Muster und Institution. Untersuchungen zur schulischen Kommunikation* [Pattern and Institution: Investigations in school communication] (Series Kommunikation und Institution 15). Tübingen: Narr.

Ehlich, K., & Switalla, B. (1976). Transkriptionssysteme—Eine exemplarische Übersicht [Transcription systems. An exemplary overview]. *Studium Linguistik,* **2,** 78–105.

Ehlich, K., Tebel, C., Fickermann, I., Becker-Mrotzek, M. (1991). *User's guide for annotating transcriptions by means of HIAT-DOS 2.0.* Dortmund, Germany: Universität Dortmund, Institut für deutsche Sprache und Literatur.

Ekman, P., & Friesen, W. V. (1969). The repertoire of nonverbal behavior: Categories, origins, usage, and coding. *Semiotica,* 1, 47–98.

Erickson, F., & Shultz, J. (1982). *The counselor as gatekeeper: Social interaction in interviews.* New York: Academic.

Ervin-Tripp, S. M. (1979). Children's verbal turn-taking. In E. Ochs & B. B. Schieffelin (Eds.), *Developmental Pragmatics* (pp. 391–414). New York: Academic.

Fiehler, R. & Sucharowski, W. (1992). *Kommunikationsberatung und Kommunikationstraining. Anwendungsfelder der Diskursforschung* [Communication consulting and communication training. Fields of application for discourse research]. Opladen: Westdeutscher Verlag.

Fromkin, V.A. (1978). *Tone. A linguistic survey.* New York: Academic.

Füssenich, I. (1981). *Disziplinierende Äußerungen im Unterricht—Eine sprachwissenschaftliche Untersuchung* [Disciplinary utterances in the classroom—A linguistic analysis]. Unpublished doctoral dissertation, University of Düsseldorf.

Grießhaber, W. (1987a). *Authentisches und zitierendes Handeln, Band 1. Einstellungsgespräche* [Authentic and quoting action: Vol 1. Job interviews] (Series Kommunikation und Institution 13). Tübingen: Narr.

Grießhaber, W. (1987b). *Authentisches und zitierendes Handeln, Band 2. Rollenspiele im Sprachunterricht* [Authentic and quoting action: Vol 2. Role play in language lessons] (Series Kommunikation und Institution 14). Tübingen: Narr.

Grießhaber, W. (1987c). *Li-A-M. Linguistische-Analyse-Makro* [Li-A-M. Linguistic-analysis-macros]. Hamburg, Germany: Hamburg University, Deutsch als Fremdsprache.

Grießhaber, W. (1988). MacHIAT: On-screen transcription editor for use in integrated linguistic data analysis. *Wheels for the Mind Europe,* 1, 51–54.

Grießhaber, W. (1990). *Transkriptverwaltung* [Transcript management]. Hamburg, Germany: Hamburg University, Deutsch als Fremdsprache.

Grießhaber, W., & Rehbein, J. (1988). *MacHIAT. Anforderungen an einen On-screen-Transkriptionseditor für den Macintosh* (Arbeitspapier Nr. 2) [MacHIAT. Demands regarding an on-screen transcription editor for the Macintosh (Working Paper No. 2)]. Hamburg, Germany: Hamburg University, Deutsch als Fremdsprache.

Gumperz, J. J. (1982). *Discourse strategies.* Cambridge: Cambridge University Press.

Heath, C. (1986). *Body movement and speech in medical interaction.* Cambridge: Cambridge University Press.

Henne, H., & Rehbock, H. (1982). *Einführung in die Gesprächsanalyse* [Introduction to conversation analysis]. Berlin: de Gruyter.

Hoffmann, L. (1983). *Kommunikation vor Gericht* [Communication in court] (Series Kommunikation und Institution 9). Tübingen: Narr.

Jefferson, G. (1983a). *An exercise in the transcription and analysis of laughter* (Tilburg University Papers in Language and Literature 35). Tilburg, The Netherlands: Tilberg University.

Jefferson, G. (1983b). *Two explorations of the organization of overlapping talk in conversation* (Tilburg University Papers in Language and Literature 28). Tilburg, The Netherlands: Tilburg University.

Kallmeyer, W., & Schütze, F. (1976). Konversationsanalyse [Communication Analysis]. *Studium Linguistik,* 1, 1–28.

Levinson, S. C. (1983). *Pragmatics*. Cambridge: Cambridge University Press.

Liedke, M. (1992). *Gesprächssteuernde Partikeln im Deutschen und Neugriechischen* [Discourse organizing particles in German and Greek]. Unpublished doctoral dissertation, Dortmund University.

Ludwig, R. (1988a). *Korpus: Texte des gesprochenen Französisch. Materialien I.* [Corpus: Texts of spoken French. Materials 1] (Series ScriptOralia 8). Tübingen: Narr.

Ludwig, R. (1988b). *Modalität und Modus im gesprochenen Französisch* [Modality and mood in spoken French] (Series ScriptOralia 7). Tübingen: Narr.

Möhn, D. (1964). Die Lautschrift der Zeitschrift "Teuthonista." Ihre Bewährung und Erweiterung in der deutschen Mundartforschung 1924–1964 [The phonetic spelling of the journal "Teuthonista." Its proof and expansion in German dialect research 1924–1964]. *Zeitschrift für Mundartforschung, 31*, 21–42.

Mönnink, J. B. M. (1988). *De organisatie van gesprekken. Een pragmatische studie van minimale interaktieve taalformen* [The organization of conversations. A pragmatic study of minimal interactive language forms]. Unpublished doctoral dissertation, University of Amsterdam.

Ochs, E. (1979). Transcription as theory. In E. Ochs & B. B. Schieffelin (Eds.), *Developmental Pragmatics* (pp. 43–72). New York: Academic.

O'Connell, D. C., & Kowal, S. (1983). Pausology. In W. A. Sedelow, Jr., & S. Y. Sedelow (Eds.), *Computers in language research 2: Notating the language of music, and the (pause) rhythms of speech* (pp. 221–301). New York: Mouton.

Pander Maat, H. L. W. (1988). *Harmonie en onenigheid in informele discussies. Gespreksanalytische studies* [Harmony and disharmony in informal discussions. Conversation analytical studies]. Unpublished doctoral dissertation, University of Groningen, The Netherlands.

Redder, A. (1982). *Schulstunden 1: Transkripte* [Classroom discourse: Transcript 1] (Series Kommunikation und Institution 4). Tübingen: Narr.

Redder, A. (1984). *Modalverben im Unterrichtsdiskurs: Pragmatik der Modalverben am Beispiel eines institutionellen Diskurses* [Modal verbs in classroom discourse: Pragmatics of modal verbs, a case study of institutional discourse] (Series Germanistische Linguistik 54). Tübingen: Niemeyer.

Rehbein, J. (1977). *Komplexes Handeln* [Complex action]. Stuttgart: Metzler.

Reski, A. (1982) *Aufforderungen. Zur Interaktionsfähigkeit im Vorschulalter* [Requests. On the interaction competence of preschool children] (Series Arbeiten zur Sprachanalyse 1). Bern: Peter Lang.

Richter, H. (1973). *Grundsätze und System der Transkription—IPA(G)* [Principles and system of transcription—IPA(G)] (Series Phonai 3). Tübingen: Niemeyer.

Ruoff, A. (1973). *Grundlagen und Methoden der Untersuchung gesprochener Sprache, Einführung in die Reihe "Idiomatica" mit einem Katalog der ausgewerteten Tonbandaufnahmen* [Bases and methods of the analysis of spoken language. Introduction to the series "Idiomatica" with a catalogue of analysed tape recordings] (Series Idiomatica 1). Tübingen: Niemeyer.

Sacks, H., Schegloff, E. A., & Jefferson, G. (1974). A simplest systematics for the organization of turn-taking for conversation. *Language, 50*, 696–735.

Schaeffer, N. (1979). *Transkription im Zeilenblocksystem* [Transcription in the line-block system]. Unpublished doctoral dissertation, Saarbrücken University, Germany.

Schlickau, S. (1989). *Methodische und theoretische Aspekte linguistischer Feldforschung im Bereich des Bergbau-Lexikons* [Aspects of method and theory in linguistic field research in the area of the mining lexicon]. Dortmund, Germany: Universität Dortmund, Institut für deutsche Sprache und Literatur.

Svartvik, J., & Quirk, R. (Eds.). (1980). *A corpus of English conversation.* Lund, Sweden: CWK Gleerup.

Tannen, D. (1981). [Review of W. Labov & D. Fanshel, *Therapeutic discourse: Psychotherapy as conversation*]. *Language,* **57**, 481–486.

Tannen, D. (1984). *Conversational style.* Norwood, NJ: Ablex.

Tsolakidoy, K. (1985). Εμπειρικη διερενηση των προσλεκτικων εℬδεικτικων και της συνεπιδρασης τους. [The empirical analysis of illocutionary indicators and their cooperation]. In Τμημα Γλωσσολογιας της Φιλοσοφηκης Σχολης ΑΠΘ (Eds.), Μελετες για την Ελληνικη γλωσσα (pp. 279-295). Thessaloniki: Kiriakidis.

6

Transcription and Coding for Child Language Research: The Parts are More than the Whole

Lois Bloom
Teachers College, Columbia University

1. INTRODUCTION

People have been writing down what infants and young children say at least since Darwin (1877). Two parallel lines of development in this time have influenced how we transcribe the data of children's language for understanding how language is acquired. One of these developments has been conceptual: The different questions that researchers asked have influenced the sorts of data that were collected. At the same time, electronic innovations have provided increasingly more sophisticated equipment to supplement (but not replace) paper and pencils. The purpose of this chapter is to (a) discuss these conceptual and procedural developments that influence contemporary observational research in child language, and (b) describe the rationale and procedures for the computer-assisted transcription and coding we do in my own laboratory for the study of early language acquisition.

2. OBSERVING AND PRESERVING THE DATA OF CHILD LANGUAGE

Conceptual and procedural influences on methods of research are not independent of one another. There is an old adage: "when the only tool you have is a hammer, everything looks like a nail." The tools that we have determine the way in which we approach a task and also determine the sorts of tasks that we consider feasible (Beckwith, Bloom, Albury, Raqib, & Booth,

1985). At the same time, the questions that we ask and the tasks that we address have driven us to pursue alternative methods and means.

This section briefly presents four main themes that provided background and rationale for the transcription system described below. The first of these is the pervasive attention to only the spoken word for the study of language during much of the last century of research. The second is the subsequent recognition of the importance of phenomena hidden within and between individuals for understanding both the nature of language and its development in young children. The third theme has to do with the issue of selectivity that emerges whenever complex events are studied. And the fourth is a perspective on data transcription that evolved from these other themes to take advantage of the sophisticated tools available from parallel developments in electronics, notably the video recorder and the microprocessor. This is the separation of covariables approach to computer assisted transcription that we use in our studies of early language development.[1]

2.1. The Spoken Word

For a very long time, the study of child language was restricted to only the spoken word. The earliest research was the diary study in which parent biographers made the heroic effort to catch and write down all of the sounds and words they heard their infants and young children say. With the rise of behaviorism in the 1930s, the reaction to these diary studies that set in had to do with issues of sample size and observer bias but not with the kinds of data they reported. These studies introduced controls over data collection in their effort to add experimental "rigor" to the enterprise. Their goal was to determine "norms" of development rather than to chronicle the development of individual children. The result was an enormous number of studies that investigated language development by counting particular aspects of the speech of large numbers of children. The typical procedure was to collect a corpus of 50 or 100 utterances from children who differed in age, sex, sibling status, social and economic background, and the like. The features of these utterances were then described by counting such things as the number of different sounds and words, or the number of nouns, verbs, and adjectives, or

---

[1]The research project that is referred to here is a longitudinal study of the development of 14 infants from 8 months to about 30 months of age. The infants were first born, 7 girls and 7 boys, from varied ethnic and economic backgrounds in the New York area. Each infant and mother visited our laboratory playroom every month and were visited in their homes each month until they were 15 months old. This research has been conducted with funds provided by The Spencer Foundation and The National Science Foundation, for which we are grateful. This chapter was drawn from material in the forthcoming book, *Acquiring the Power of Expression: Consciousness, Cognition, and Emotion in Transition from Infancy to Language* (Bloom, in press).

the length of sentences and whether they were complete or incomplete, simple, compound, or complex, and so forth. (See McCarthy, 1954, for a thorough review of this literature and Templin, 1957, for what is no doubt the best and probably the last effort in this era of research.)

These studies were successful in that they provided the "developmental milestones" that are still widely used in pediatricians' offices, day-care settings, well-baby clinics, and the like. Moreover, we learned certain facts about infants' speech in the first 5 years of life that have endured and are still referred to in contemporary research. However, in the 1950s, Roger Brown began a program of research in which he pointed out that the really important questions had to do with the developments in children's *knowledge* that produce the changes in what they say (e.g., Brown, 1957). That knowledge includes the grammar of language.

Linguists, at least in this century, had always operated with the assumption that language was rule-governed. But the galvanizing influence from linguistics on the search for the child's rule system was the theory of generative transformational grammar (Chomsky, 1957). The presumption was that children are learning a grammar when they acquire language, and the grammar they are learning is a transformational one. The search for child grammar in the studies that followed sought evidence of grammatical rules from the regularities in early two-word speech (e.g., Braine, 1963; Brown & Fraser, 1964; Miller & Ervin, 1964). The lasting insight in these studies was that the early word combinations of children are, indeed, systematic. A small number of words are used frequently and in relatively fixed position, with a larger number of other words, each of which occurs relatively infrequently and without predictable word order. However, the resulting 'grammars' were descriptions of the regularities in frequency and word order in children's speech. Even though the goal of research had been to uncover the child's underlying rules of grammar, the data that were used in the endeavor still consisted of only the spoken word.

2.2. Hidden Phenomena

A linguistic fact assumes significance in relation to its "element of experience . . . content or 'meaning'" (Sapir, 1921, p. 10). In 1968, I proposed that the meanings children express in their language learning efforts determine what they acquire of the grammar of a language. These meanings have to do with what the young child has learned and is learning about objects, events, and relations in the world:

> A young child's success in learning to talk depends on [the] ability to perceive
> and organize the environment, the language that is a part of the environment,
> and the relation between the two. . . . Children learn to identify certain

grammatical relations and syntactic structures with the environmental and behavioral contexts in which they are perceived and then progress to reproducing approximations of heard structures in similar, recurring contexts. (Bloom, 1968/1970, pp. 1, 233)

If children acquire meaning from events in the context, then the context ought to be a preeminent source of information about the meanings that children express. I suggested, therefore, that we attend to and use information from the context of children's utterances in our efforts to learn how and what children are learning about language. This meant going beyond the spoken word and inquiring into the underlying meaning of the words as inferred from what children talk about. The suggestion was taken up by Roger Brown, who coined the term *rich interpretation* for what became the dominant method for pursuing the meanings hidden in early speech (Brown, 1973).

Rich interpretation is not without its detractors. In the mid-1960s, when I was doing the original research on which my 1968 dissertation was based, no one wanted to admit evidence about meaning into the study of language. In linguistics, from Bloomfield through Chomsky, the domain of meaning had been avoided like the plague. And still today we have those who feel that what is hidden in the child is not admissable evidence for the language acquisition enterprise. Nevertheless, we do know that individuals provide us with a variety of signals that let us know what they are thinking and feeling, and what individuals think and feel is what they express in language (Bloom, in press; Bloom & Beckwith, 1986). We make use of these kinds of signals quite readily and easily in all of our everyday interactions with one another. Indeed, once context was introduced into the study of language acquisition, not only the meaning of an individual utterance, but developments in pragmatics and the unfolding of discourse between individuals could be studied by attention to "language in context" (Bates, 1976). Moreover, the contexts of language acquisition include not only the immediate circumstances that surround acts of expression and interpretation, but, indeed, the larger cultural world view of the individuals in a society (Schieffelin, 1979).

In sum, contemporary research that takes a developmental perspective is conducted with the fundamental assumption that language is acquired in connection with other developments and events in the life of the young language-learning child. Children acquire the sounds, words, structures, and discourse processes of a language against a background of other cognitive, social, and affective developments. In short, we now recognize the importance of paying attention to a great deal else beside the spoken word in our efforts to understand language development. This recognition has paid off in that we know much more than ever before about the language learning process. However, we have also had to deal with important conceptual issues concerning our methods for deciding what we use as data and how.

2.3. Selectivity[2]

Individuals observe and interpret what children do every day, by necessity, in order to interact with them, and they rarely think about it. But as researchers we have to establish a certain distance from what children do so that we can think about it, describe it, and, hopefully, contribute to explaining it. One reasonable goal might be to approach the task without regard to any expectations that we might have. "On the observational level, the main—one could say the only—rule is that all facts would be carefully observed and described, without allowing any theoretical preconception to decide whether some are more important than others" (Levi-Strauss, 1963, p. 272).

However, our preconceptions cannot help but create and influence our expectations, as many people have pointed out.

> For both logical and practical reasons, there can be no such thing as pure observation . . . one's ideas evolve with one's research, reading and thinking. . . . [T]rying to put oneself at sufficient distance for clear vision is like trying to leap over one's shadow. . . . [Accordingly, we have to] start out with selection of one out of an infinite number of possible descriptive strategies, in accordance with whatever one's wits and experience offer as the best bet (Beer, 1973, pp. 49, 54).

We are then, as researchers, the products of our own intellectual histories, and these cannot help but influence our view of the evidence. Such selectivity, on the whole, is not only to be expected, but even encouraged, as Ochs (1979) pointed out. How else is our current and future work to benefit from what we already know about children, language, and the acquisition process? However, the researcher needs to be aware of the filtering process and take such inherent selectivity into explicit account. Moreover, "the problems of selective observation are not eliminated with the use of recording equipment. They are simply delayed until the moment at which the researcher sits down to transcribe the material from the audio- or videotape" (Ochs, 1979, p. 44).

As soon as we make a recording we have begun a process of data reduction, which is another sort of selectivity. Whether recorded by hand or by audio or video electronics, something is necessarily left out of the record. The microphone and the camera, much less the eye, the ear, and the hand, can never preserve the detail, nuance, and complex circumstances of events. Transcription reduces electronically recorded data even more drastically and provides a serious constraint on the available information. Quite simply,

---

[2]In this section, I borrow heavily from a commentary that I wrote some years ago concerning the accountability of evidence in studies of child language, in the Monographs of the Society for Research in Child Development (Bloom, 1974).

copying the richness of tone and detail that can be preserved on tape, as reduced as it is from the original event, is an impossible task. The process of transcription, then, provides the real moment of truth for the observer.

In sum, transcription presents two problems. The first is the set of biases and distortions that creep in because of the necessarily selective view of the observer. The second is the massive data reduction that results from the sheer physical limitations, through no fault of their own, of electronic devices that make the record to preserve the data and of persons who do the transcribing. The system of transcription I describe below was created in the effort to minimize these problems.

2.4. Separation of Covariables

In effect, a rich interpretation depends on "lean transcription." Not only is it hopeless to attempt to capture everything on a recording, but too much detail in a transcript produces clutter and distraction (Ochs, 1979). Further, the transcription must, necessarily, aim to represent a description of events, rather than an interpretation (Bloom & Lahey, 1978). Admittedly, the bounds for knowing where description ends and interpretation begins are probably not definable. Indeed, one might well say that any description is by nature a form of interpretation. The point is, however, to aim at preserving the data in such a way as to allow for different analyses and different resulting interpretations. The following example is trivial, but only on its surface:

A 1-year-old picks up a small block, says *more*, puts it on top of a bigger block, smiles, and looks at her mother, who smiles back.

This event might be interpreted in many ways. At the minimum, we might want to say something like "initiates activity," "builds a tower," "expresses recurrence," or "expresses pleasure" to capture what happened. However, these or any other evaluations of the event must come from what we have preserved in our transcript after the fact. If all we recorded in the transcript was something like "initiates activity" or "expresses recurrence," we would not be able to use the transcript to make other interpretations. For example, the timing of the baby's smile, in relation to saying the word *more* and the actions with the blocks, is highly relevant to several theoretical concerns. The baby's smile could be interpreted as, again at the minimum, an act of social referencing or, alternatively, a smile of recognition or accomplishment. The fact that the baby did not smile before or at the same time as saying *more* is relevant to understanding the way these two systems of expression, affect and speech, come together in the single-word period (Bloom & Beckwith, 1989). In other words, if one transcribes a piece of behavior only according to its meaning, its function, or its effect, then the information about the event that might contribute to an additional or an alternative interpretation is lost.

When we began to use audiotape recorders, and our research was confined to only the spoken word, we worried about the accuracy with which we represented what was said. For example, we had to decide whether to transcribe orthographically or phonetically, and if phonetically, how broad or narrow a phonetic transcription. When we began to include information from the context in the transcription so that we could interpret something about meaning, we took notes at the time of recording, and then tried to fill in the contextual details surrounding what was said at the time of transcription. The introduction of the video recorder seemed, at first, to solve all our problems. We could use the video data instead of taking notes or trying to remember events and circumstances in the context. Our first video transcriptions were, in effect, modeled after our audio transcriptions and differed only in the added detail (e.g., Bloom, 1973; Bloom & Lahey, 1978).

However, a video record presents other sorts of problems. The amount of detail that is preserved on video tape is, quite literally, enormous, even though the information present in the original event is necessarily reduced in the sense described above. This detail can be overwhelming to the researcher in trying to decide what to include and what to leave out of the transcription. In the effort to preserve a description in the transcript rather than an interpretation, we could easily be engulfed by the details.[3]

In our current research, we have not attempted a full transcription of all relevant behaviors and accompanying contexts, which has been the standard operating procedure with audio and video data. Instead, we have pulled the video record apart, exploded it, so to speak, and separated out the variables of interest according to one or another research question. The advantage of having the video record is that it is impervious to these operations that we perform on it. This was pointed out as long ago as 1935 by Gesell, who pioneered in using film to study infant development:

> The behavior record becomes as pliant to dissection as a piece of tissue. Any phase or strand of behavior may be exposed to view. If the view is an intricate one it may be repeated numerous times without in anyway damaging the original record. Here the dissection of behavior forms has a striking advantage over anatomical dissection. Bodily tissue suffers from the scalpel, but the integrity and conformation of behavior cannot be destroyed by repeated observation. A behavior form can be dissected over and over again in

---

[3]The level of detail preserved on video can also be seductive in leading the transcriber down one or another garden path. The effect of watching a small scrap of an interaction over and over again is to reveal some incredibly fine details. The result is often a severe narrowing of focus and excessive attention to what may turn out to be, in the final analysis, irrelevant.

increasing detail without loss of form. (Gesell, 1935, p. 6; quoted in Beckwith et al., 1985)

Thus, more than 50 years ago, Gesell anticipated the way in which we have exploited the technology available to us today. We can separate the variables for examination to study the relationships between them in many different ways without sacrificing the integrity of the original record.

If we return to the mother–infant episode above, we can see what this means. Our research project concerns developments in cognition and affect expression in relation to the transition from infancy to language. The relevant variables in our research so far have included child speech, mother speech, the situation accompanying mother speech, child affect expression, mother response to child affect expression, child object play, child object search, and so forth. Certain of the questions we ask have centered on object play as a window on developments in cognition (e.g., Lifter & Bloom, 1989), and on affect expression in relation to the emergence of expression through speech (e.g., Bloom, Beckwith, Capatides, & Hafitz, 1987). With data such as in the example above, we separate the covariables in independent passes through the video record and transcribe or code (a) child speech *(more)*, (b) child affect expression (a smile with +1 intensity), (c) mother response to child affect expression (a smile with +2 intensity), (d) child object constructions (putting one block on another), and so forth. Independent coders are assigned to transcribe or code only one variable at a time. For instance, one person would only transcribe child speech; another would only code child affect expression. The beauty of the system is that we can go on to code or transcribe however many variables we would need, bounded only by the conceptual issues that we pursue (and the vagaries of available funding).

3. A PLAN FOR COMPUTER-ASSISTED TRANSCRIPTION[4]

3.1. The computer system

Because the variables in the stream of activity do, in fact, covary, we had to have a way of putting them back together again. This is the distinctive feature of the system. The system we devised uses state of the art (circa 1981) equipment and is schematized in Fig. 6.1. The hardware is either still commercially available or reproducible in some other way. At the time of the original observation, the audio signal from the interaction is recorded on one sound track of the stereo video tape while a computer-readable audio time code is recorded on the other. Videotape runs at 30 frames per second and the

---

[4]This section contains material presented originally in Beckwith, et al. (1985).

timecode generator (SMPTE FOR-A) lays down a unique discrete audio signal for each frame, that is, 30 times every second. At the time of playback, the videodeck (Sony stereo Betamax) is interfaced with a microprocessor (Apple II Plus) via a timecode reader. This entails a simple multiplexing circuit made to connect the 32-bit timecode readers with the 8-bit Apples.

The Apple controls the videodeck, turning it on, moving it forward or backward, slowing or speeding the playback, freezing the frame, and so on. More important, the Apple can also read the timecode, giving it the ability to find any particular frame in the recorded observation.

A coder sits at the Apple keyboard watching the video monitor and decides when a behavior occurs that is relevant to the variable being coded. The coder uses the keyboard to stop the playback and then must decide on which frame the behavior begins and/or ends. This is done by telling the computer to move the videotape forward or backward a specific number of frames until the desired frame is targeted. Accuracy in determining onset and offset times, after training, is remarkably high. For example, the mean discrepancy between pairs of independent coders was 2 video frames (.07 second) for speech onset time and 5 video frames (.17 second) for speech offset. The accuracy in finding onset time of an affect expression was somewhat less due to the fact that several kinds of cues were used to code affect (i.e., facial expression, body tension, affective vocalization). The mean discrepancy in

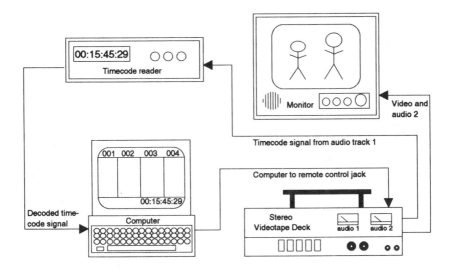

Coding Station

Fig. 6.1. Schematic representation of coding equipment.

locating affect onset was 16 frames (.50 second). (The offset of an affect expression was the onset of the next expression because affect was coded as a continuous variable.)

When the onset or offset frame is found, the coder enters an edit mode and types in the data. Data can be entered as a string of up to 255 characters and can include anything that can be typed. The four columns on the computer monitor in Fig. 6.1 (here labeled 001, 002, and so forth) represent any four of the 135 separately coded variables that the system is capable of handling. At the time of transcription, the researcher can call up any three variables in order to code a fourth variable. For instance, in coding the situation that mothers' sentences were about (Beckwith, 1988), the coder asked the computer to locate each mother sentence in column 002 and then typed in the situation code in column 050.

Once entered, the data are stored in files that are ordered sequentially according to time code. An extract from a data file is presented in Fig. 6.2. Each line in the file represents one record. Each record has three fields. The first field is a hexadecimal number (two columns) that identifies the particular variable coded (child speech is 01, mother speech is 02, and so forth). The second field in the record is a hexadecimal number (six columns) that represents the frame count for hour, minute, second, frame. The third field consists of text of variable length (up to 255 characters). This text may be transcription of speech or any one of a number of codes that we have devised for representing the information from different data variables.

The coded data can be manipulated to (a) generate a hard copy transcript for traditional sorts of descriptive analyses and (b) perform a variety of quantitative analyses for statistical treatments.

3.2. Generating a Transcript

Because the data are stored electronically, they are flexible for manipulation before output. Thus, transcripts can be set up in any number of ways with different combinations of the separate coding passes. Moreover, because the computer can read the timecode and every coding decision is associated with a time of onset and/or offset, the separate codes can be merged sequentially. The merging produces an integrated account with the relevant behaviors lined up according to the original temporal relations between them. An example of such a computer-generated transcript is presented in Fig. 6.3 using the data from the example in Fig. 6.2. The codes represented in the data displayed in the two figures are explained briefly in Table 6.1.

```
01  CHILD SPEECH
02  MOTHER SPEECH
04  CHILD SEARCH
05  CHILD OBJECT PLAY
14  CHILD AFFECT
19  CHILD SPEECH CONTENT
32  MOTHER SENTENCE/SITUATION
19  005325 v:a<go(bff in (slide-in))>d/n
01  005325 in/
01  005337
02  005340 In?/
02  005342 N
02  00534E
05  0055357 CO-SN-IM-GE-NA-NA
32  00535A [GO](ENTITY = child)(CAUSE = child)(SRCE = NIL)(PATH = NIL)
            (DEST = slide-in)
02  00535A You can put the boy in./
02  00537C
32  00539F [GO](ENTITY = bff)(CAUSE = child)(SRCE = NIL)(PATH = NIL)
            (DEST = slide-in)
02  00539F Boy in./
02  0053B6
19  005407 v:a<go(fff in (slide-in))>a/n
01  005407 in/
01  005419
32  00541D [GO](ENTITY = fff)(CAUSE = child)(SRCE = NIL)(PATH = NIL)
            (DEST =slide-in)
02  00541D Put the man in./
02  00543D
05  00547A CO-SN-IM-GE-NA-IM
19  005483 v:a<go(fff in (slide-in))>d/n
01  005483 in/
01  005498
32  0054A5 [GO](ENTITY = child)(CAUSE = child)(SRCE = NIL)(PATH = NIL)
            (DEST = mff)
02  0054A5 Go get the, yeah, go get the girl./
14  0054AC + 1
04  0054D5 LO-XC-NA-NA-MR-AR-GE
02  0054D9
32  0054DD [GO](ENTITY = mff&fff&cff)(CAUSE = child)(SRCE = NIL)(PATH = NIL)
            (DEST = slide-in)
02  0054DD Put them all in./
02  0054F4
```

FIG. 6.2. Data file example. (Note: The duration of this example is 15 seconds, 13 frames. See Table 6.1 for a description of these codes.)

CHILD SPEECH	CHILD SPEECH CONTENT	MOTHER SPEECH	MOTHER SENTENCE/SITUATION	CHILD PLAY	CHILD AFFECT
00:11:49:15 in/ 00:11:50:03	00:11:49:15 v:a<go(bff in (slide-in))>d/n				00:11:50:14 N
		00:11:50:12 In?/ 00:11:50:26			
		00:11:51:08 You can put the boy in./	00:11:51:08 [GO](ENTITY = child)(CAUSE = child)(SRCE = NIL)(PATH = NIL)(DEST = slide-in)	00:11:51:05 CO-SN-IM-GE-NA-NA	
		00:11:52:12 00:11:53:17 Boy in./	00:11:53:17 [GO](ENTITY = cff)(CAUSE = child)(SRCE = NIL)(PATH = NIL)(DEST = slide-in)		
		00:11:54:10			
00:11:57:01 in/ 00:11:57:19	00:11:57:01 v:a<go(fff in (slide-in))>a/n	00:11:57:23 Put the man in./	00:11:57:23 [GO](ENTITY = fff)(CAUSE = child)(SRCE = NIL)(PATH = NIL)(DEST =slide-in)		
		00:11:58:25			
00:12:01:05 in/ 00:12:01:26	00:12:01:05 v:a<go(fff in (slide-in))>d/n	00:12:02:09 Go get the, yeah, go get the girl./	00:12:02:09 [GO](ENTITY = child)(CAUSE = child)(SRCE = NIL)(PATH = NIL)(DEST = mff)	00:12:00:26 CO-SN-IM-GE-NA-IM	00:12:02:16 +1
		00:12:04:01 00:12:04:05 Put them all in./	00:12:02:09 [GO](ENTITY = mff&fff&cff)(CAUSE = child)(SRCE = NIL)(PATH = NIL)(DEST = slide-in)		
		00:12:04:28			

FIG. 6.3. Transcription generated from data file. (Note: The duration of this example is 15 seconds, 13 frames. See Table 6.1 for a description of the codes.)

Table 6.1
Explanations of Example Codes in Data File and Transcription

---

19 CHILD SPEECH CONTENT
19 005325 v:a<go(bff in (slide-in))>d/n
=a child volition (v:) that is achieved (a) to put the boy family figure (bff)
into (in) the interior space of the slide (slide-in); said during the action (d)
and not directed (n) to the mother.

05 CHILD OBJECT PLAY
05 005357 CO-SN-IM-GE-NA-NA
=a construction (CO), without support (SN), that was an imposed (IM),
general (GE) relation; (NA) = not applicable

04 CHILD SEARCH
04 0054D5 LO-XC-NA-NA-MR-AR-GE
=locating one object (LO), in order to construct a relation (XC), which
mother had suggested (MR), when the child was attending to another
object (AR), and the resulting relation was a general one (GE); (NA) =
not applicable

14 CHILD AFFECT
14 005342 N
=neutral affect expression; only onset times coded because affect
expression was coded as a continuous variable (onset of an expression
= onset of the previous expression)

14 CHILD AFFECT
14 0054AC +1
=affect expression with positive valence and low level intensity

32 MOTHER SENTENCE/SITUATION
32 0054DD [GO](ENTITIY = mff&fff&cff)(CAUSE = child)(SRCE = NIL)
(PATH = NIL) (DEST = slide-in)
=the child (CAUSE) moving ([GO]) the mother, father, and child family
figures (ENTITIY = mff&fff&cff) to the interior of the slide (DEST = slide-
in); (SRCE) = source; (PATH) = path; (NIL) = not applicable

This example of a transcript reproduces the five separate columns containing (a) transcription of child speech, (b) the code for the underlying cognitive representation attributed to child speech, (c) mother speech, (d) the situation code for mothers' sentences, and (e) child object play. Each entry in each column is associated with the times of onset and offset (for child and mother speech) or the times of onset (for the two codes associated with child and mother speech and for object play). The five columns are integrated with one another sequentially according to the timestamp. This restores the temporal relations that existed among child and mother speech and child object play at the time of the observation in the original video recording.

A transcript such as this one can be used in much the same way as a traditional transcription. We can examine the unfolding of events in regard to one or another research question, perform descriptive analyses, generate new hypotheses, and so forth. In addition, however, because the data are electronically stored, the computer can also perform many of the data analyses we need.

3.3. Quantitative Analyses to Assess Qualitative Domains

The coded data are transferred from the Apples onto an IBM-PC and stored in a standard form—delimited ASCII—that allows access from any number of different programs. Most recently, we have developed software for converting the data into database format using DBASE+ (Ashton-Tate) run by the Clipper Compiler (Nantucket). This allows us to run a variety of data manipulation programs.

Most simply, the different codes within a variable can be counted to look at relative frequencies and contingent probabilities. We know, for example, as a result of several such analyses, how frequently our subjects expressed positive and negative affect; the relative time spent in nonneutral, positive, and negative affect expression; and their average duration (reported in Bloom, Beckwith, & Capatides, 1988). We also know how the children's ages at certain language milestones (a) correlate with these measures of affect expression (reported in Bloom & Capatides, 1987), and (b) correspond to developments in object play (reported in Lifter & Bloom, 1989). We have looked at the relative frequency of expression of different kinds of meaning content through affect and words in the single-word period (reported in Bloom, Beckwith, Capatides, & Hafitz, 1987). In studies of later developments in the children's multiword speech, we have reported how they acquired the distinction between transitive and intransitive verbs (Rispoli & Bloom, 1988), and the correspondence between the sentence types in mother and child speech (Beckwith, 1988). In still other studies of how the mothers in our sample have influenced their children's development, we have studied the mothers' behaviors that surround their children's affect expression (Capatides, 1990) and play with objects (Harner, Bloom, & Gronell, 1991).

But, in addition, we can look very carefully at the timing of one behavior relative to another. Thus far, we have done this for expression through affect and speech and been able to show how the two systems—one of which (affect) has been in place since early infancy and the other (speech) is just emerging— come together in the single-word period (reported in Bloom & Beckwith, 1989). The system would also allow us to look at this contingency in the multiword period, as well as other contingencies, such as between mother speech and child speech and gaze. Most recently, we have looked at the profiles of speech and affect expression in the moments before and after episodes of object play (Bloom, Tinker, & Beckwith, forthcoming).

To be sure, very many qualitative phenomena will always resist such quantitative treatment. This is to be expected whenever we delve into the domain of human expression. Nevertheless, in our efforts to understand how young children acquire the power of expression we must, of necessity, make the relevant phenomena accessible for study. This means recording the phenomena so as to preserve them in the first place, and transforming the recording for the analyses that we do. The plan for computer-assisted transcription described here has made use of the technology that is currently available in order to respond to the problems of selectivity in transcription cited earlier.

4. CLOSING THE GAP

This chapter has continued the dialog, begun in Bloom (1974) and taken up by Ochs (1979) and Beckwith et al. (1985), concerning the *accountability of evidence in child language research*. The problems of selectivity in transcription will always be with us. However, we believe that we have succeeded in making at least modest progress toward closing the gap between an act of expression and the record we make of it in our efforts to understand it.

On the face of it, separating the covariables that are contained in an act of expression in order to attend to only one variable at a time would seem to be a radical reduction of the data indeed. However, separation of covariables is not the same as isolating the variables, because we necessarily attend to whatever surrounds the target variable in making coding decisions regarding it. Furthermore, separating a variable for the purpose of coding or transcription assures us that we have preserved the integrity of that particular variable beyond what would be possible if we tried attending to many or even several aspects of behavior at the same time. The effect of narrowing the focus in this way is to enlarge the view we have of the target variable, enabling us to see it more clearly and consider it more carefully. In addition, transcription problems having to do with training and reliability are far more manageable than they would otherwise be. But most important, *we can always add variables.* Our transcript is never limited by whatever questions or concerns motivated our research at one particular time. Thus, separation of covariables reduces the data only to enlarge our view of the evidence.

Two other factors contribute to our confidence that we avoid at least some of the susceptibility to investigator bias inherent in observational research. The use of coders and transcribers who are uninformed as to the research questions and hypotheses in one or another study reduces the threat that we will tend toward interpretation rather than description in the decisions that are made during transcription. Another factor is the delicate balance in confidence we have between persons and machines for making decisions regarding timing in events. Persons make the original decisions regarding onset and/or offset of a particular piece of the action. But machines are far more adept than persons at putting the pieces of the action back together again.

In sum, the system for coding and transcription described here is an example of how conceptual developments in the field and developments in technology came together in the last two decades of child language research. Studying language in context, and studying the development of language in the context of other developments in the child, require that we preserve far more than just the spoken word in the record we make of the data we collect. Nonindustrial video recording became available at just about the time that context was introduced into the study of child language in the late 1960s. A video record confronts us with an overwhelming amount of information, even recognizing how much is lost in the inevitable reduction of the data that occurs through recording. The resulting problems of selectivity for transcription have begun to seem more manageable with the development of the microprocessor and personal computers in the last 10 years. We wonder how the ways in which we study children's language might change in the 21st century as a result of what we learn from our present research and the developments in technology to come.

REFERENCES

Bates, E. (1976). *Language in context.* New York: Academic.

Beckwith, R. (1988). *Learnability and psychologically constrained grammars.* Unpublished doctoral dissertation, Teachers College, Columbia University.

Beckwith, R., Bloom, L., Albury, D., Raqib, A., & Booth, R. (1985). Technology and methodology. *Transcript Analysis, 2,* 72–75.

Beer, C. (1973). A view of birds. In A. Pick, (Ed.), *Minnesota symposia on child psychology* (Vol. 7, pp. 47–86). Minneapolis: University of Minnesota Press.

Bloom, L. (1970). *Language development: Form and function in emerging grammars.* Cambridge MA: The MIT Press. (Original doctoral dissertation, Teachers College, Columbia University, 1968)

Bloom, L. (1973). *One word at a time: The use of single-word utterances before syntax.* The Hague: Mouton.

Bloom, L. (1974). The accountability of evidence in studies of child language. Comment on Everyday preschool interpersonal speech usage: Methodological, developmental, and sociolinguistic studies. In F. Schacter, K. Kirshner, B. Klips, M. Friedricks & K. Sanders (Eds), *Monographs of the Society for Research in Child Development,* **39** (Serial No. 156).

Bloom, L. (in press). *Acquiring the power of expression: Consciousness, cognition, and emotion in the transition from infancy to language.* Cambridge: Cambridge University Press.

Bloom, L., & Beckwith, R. (1986). *Intentionality and language development.* Unpublished manuscript.

Bloom, L., & Beckwith, R. (1989). Talking with feeling: Integrating affective and linguistic expression in early language development. *Cognition and Emotion,* **3**, 313-342.

Bloom, L., Beckwith, R., & Capatides, J. (1988). Developments in the expression affect. *Infant Behavior and Development,* **11**, 169-186.

Bloom, L., Beckwith, R., Capatides, J., & Hafitz, J. (1987). Expression through affect and words in the transition from infancy to language. In P. Baltes, D. Featherman, & R. Lerner (Eds.), *Life span development and behavior* (Vol. 8, pp. 99-127). Hillsdale, NJ: Lawrence Erlbaum Associates.

Bloom, L., & Capatides, J. (1987). Expression of affect and the emergence of language. *Child Development,* **58**, 1513-1522.

Bloom, L., & Lahey, M. (1978). *Language development and language disorders.* New York: John Wiley & Sons.

Braine, M. (1963). The ontogeny of English phrase structure: The first phase. *Language,* **39**, 1-13.

Brown, R. (1957). Linguistic determinism and the part of speech. *Journal of Abnormal and Social Psychology,* **55**, 1-5.

Brown, R. (1973). *A first language, the early stages.* Cambridge MA: Harvard University Press.

Brown, R., & Fraser, C. (1964). The acquisition of syntax. In U. Bellugi, & R. Brown, (Eds.), *The acquisition of language, Monographs of the Society for Research in Child Development,* **29** (Serial No. 92).

Capatides, J. (1990). *Mothers' socialization of their children's experience and expression of emotion.* Unpublished doctoral. dissertation, Teachers College, Columbia University.

Chomsky, N. (1957). *Syntactic structures.* The Hague: Mouton.

Darwin, C. (1877). Biographical sketch of an infant. *Mind,* **2**, 285-294.

Gesell, A. (1935). Cinemanalysis: A method of behavior study. *Journal of Genetic Psychology,* **47**, 3-16.

Harner, L., Bloom, L., & Gronell, T. (1991). *Social construction of object knowledge from preverbal through multi-word stages.* Paper presented to the Jean Piaget Society, Philadelphia, PA.

Levi-Strauss, C. (1963). *Structural anthropology.* (C. Jacobson & B. Schoept, Trans.). New York: Basic Books.

Lifter, K., & Bloom, L. (1989). Object play and the emergence of language. *Infant Behavior and Development*, **12**, 395-423.

McCarthy, D. (1954). Language development in children. In L. Carmichael, (Ed.), *Manual of child psychology* (2nd ed., pp. 492–630). New York: John Wiley & Sons.

Miller, W., & Ervin, S. (1964). The development of grammar in child language. In U. Bellugi, & R. Brown (Eds.), *The acquisition of language, Monograph of the Society for Research in Child Development*, **29** (Serial No. 92).

Ochs, E. (1979). Transcription as theory. In E. Ochs & B. Schieffelin, (Eds.), *Developmental pragmatics* (pp. 43–72). New York: Academic Press.

Rispoli, M., & Bloom, L. (1988). The conceptual origins of the transitive/intransitive distinction. In *Papers and Reports of the Child Language Research Forum.* Stanford, CA: Stanford University, Department of Linguistics.

Sapir, E. (1921). *Language.* New York: Harcourt, Brace & Company.

Schieffelin, B. (1979). Getting it together: An ethnographic approach to the study of the development of communicative competence. In E. Ochs, & B. Schieffelin (Eds.), *Developmental pragmatics* (pp 73–108). New York: Academic Press.

Templin, M. (1957). *Certain language skills in children.* Minneapolis: University of Minnesota Press.

II CODING

7

Structured Coding for the Study of Language and Social Interaction

Martin D. Lampert
Holy Names College

Susan M. Ervin-Tripp
University of California at Berkeley

1. INTRODUCTION

The classification and labeling of natural events into discrete categories is a central part of most research in the social sciences (see Babbie, 1989). It allows investigators to identify and group similar instances of a phenomenon together for systematic study and is essential to any quantitative analysis.

The process of classification and labeling is commonly referred to as "coding," and on the surface, coding appears to be a relatively simple task: (a) identify the information that you wish to recover, (b) select mnemonic abbreviations or numbers as codes to represent that information, and (c) do it— match codes to actual cases in your data base. In language research, this can involve the characterization of a number of linguistic and contextual features from phonology to event structure. For example, consider the following exchange:

Wife: Katie left her coat.
Husband: Uh oh.

If we were interested in syntax and morphology here, we could set up coding categories for *noun, verb, tense, determiner, preposition, possessive,* and so forth, and then assign codes for each category in such a way as to symbolically represent the original structure of each sentence. Du Bois and

-Coburn provide a description of how to do this later in this volume, ~~~ simple illustration here, we might represent *Katie left her coat* as

Noun Verb+Past Possessive Noun

In addition to sentence structure, if we were further interested in the structure of discourse, we could also code for the roles that utterances play in an exchange. Following McTear (1985), for example, we could break down blocks of speech into initiations and responses, using *I*s and *R*s, respectively, to represent each. We might code the above exchange then as

Wife: Katie left her coat.   *I*
Husband: Uh oh.   *R*

All of this seems quite straightforward. However, coding is not just a matter of deciding what to classify and how to represent it. In fact, when more than a single variable is involved, coding frequently requires the development of a highly structured and hierarchically arranged system that can be used not only to relate variables to one another, but also to generate and test hypotheses.

In this chapter, we address many of the issues surrounding the development and use of a structured coding system by focusing on four fundamental and interrelated steps in the coding process: *construction, implementation, evaluation,* and *application.* The first of these deals with the initial step of designing the system; the second involves the business of doing coding, including the development of techniques and making objective coding decisions and training coders; the third focuses on the adequacy the system and the reliability of coded data, and the fourth deals with how best to organize coded data in order to do meaningful comparisons and statistical analyses.

To illustrate what is involved throughout the coding process from construction to application, we have also selected as a case study the Control Exchange Code (CEC), a coding system developed under the direction of the second author at the University of California at Berkeley (Ervin-Tripp, 1988a).[1] This particular system was designed to characterize the

---

[1] The Control Exchange Code was originally developed in 1976 but has been revised in subsequent years. The original version of the code was developed by Susan Ervin-Tripp for family interaction videotapes collected in collaboration with David Gordon and Jenny Cook-Gumperz. There was a radical expansion of the code later by Julie Gerhardt and Iskender Savasir, who introduced a considerable deepening of the contextual information. Subsequent revisions and changes to make coding easier and more "user-friendly" and to adapt it to computer on-line coding were made by Martin Lampert working with classes of student coders. An additional section on overall request strategies was later borrowed from Shoshana Blum-Kulka, with some additional examples and definitions. Copies of the complete manual can be obtained from Susan Ervin-Tripp, Institute of Cognitive Studies, University of California, Berkeley, CA 94720, USA.

organization of verbal and gestural moves intended to control the behavior of others, and includes at present categories for some 66 facets of 17 dimensions considered to play a role in the organization of the control moves of children and adults in interaction. Because of its size and manageability, the CEC is a prime example for the issues and concerns encountered at each step of the coding process from construction to application.

2. THE CONSTRUCTION OF A CODING SYSTEM FOR LANGUAGE RESEARCH

Every coding project typically begins with some goal in mind. This can simply be to provide data with which to test a hypothesis or to explore possible dimensions of some phenomenon—as in the present situation, language. Once research objectives are in place, investigators can then begin to work on the construction of a coding system, a job that can proceed either in a top-down fashion, based on some theory, or from the bottom up, based on the raw data at hand.

In the former instance, investigators can and often do turn to a well-established theoretical framework as a guide to how to construct coding categories. In the case of language research, this means that a researcher may choose as a first step to select or develop a theory that explains how speech is organized and how certain variables are likely to influence language use. Once this is accomplished, the next step is then to figure out how to use the theory as a guide for what linguistic and paralinguistic phenomena to code (e.g., syntax, exchange structure, speech acts, prosody, etc.) and, more specifically, how to define these phenomena and break them up into coding categories.

The selection or development of a guiding theory is not easy. This requires not only a consideration of what theory, if any, suggests the best taxonomy for what the researcher wishes to study, but also a realization that whatever theory the researcher chooses is likely to have an influence on the kinds of analyses and results that are possible. In fact, two investigators can propose to study the same thing (e.g., speech acts) and code the same natural language set, yet if they begin with different theoretical orientations, they are likely to end up with different coding categories. They are likely to have different characterizations of the coded data and, in turn, different interpretations of the linguistic material studied. This point must always be kept in mind when dealing with theoretically derived coding categories.

On the other hand, of course, a coding system can be derived atheoretically; that is, established primarily to characterize what data are like, or altered when a theory turns out not to fit the data well. When researchers are not absolutely sure what categorical distinctions should be made, they can start with a few rudimentary and loosely defined coding categories, and as they study texts add to these when they discover instances that do not quite fit the original categories. In fact, the behavior of studied individuals can suggest what are the "natural" categories for actors and provide an index for what categories the researcher should include in the final coding system. For example, Gee and Savasir (1985) studied children's differential use of *will* and *gonna* in this fashion. They first identified instances of *will* and *gonna* and then identified and categorized the contextual features that co-occurred with each. They subsequently labeled the types of exchanges that they found *undertaking* and *planning*.

Although based on the researcher's data, empirically derived categories are not necessarily theory-neutral, however. Once coding dimensions and categories have been sketched out, researchers must still define these explicitly and describe how they differ from one another, and in doing this, they create an outline for how exemplars in a particular domain are to be viewed and classified. As a result, this outline forms its own implicit theory of how language is organized and how future data are to be coded.

Regardless of whether a coding system begins with a theory or evolves one as part of the coding process then, every investigator who studies language must recognize that underlying assumptions have an influence on the decisions that are made at every step of the construction process with each decision affecting subsequent ones and the end product as a whole. All organizational decisions, therefore, must be carefully weighed, and as we see it, these occur at two levels: (1) deciding how to segment texts for analysis and (2) determining how to describe, or rather code, these segments. We will address each of these in turn.

2.1. Segmentation of the Data

Units of Analysis

The first and perhaps most obvious decision that a language researcher must make is what exactly gets coded in a transcript. In some research, the answer to this is easy. In survey work, for example, what gets coded is typically the response to a question. When dealing with natural language, however, the answer is not so simple. Here the researcher must make a deliberate effort to decide (a) what size unit of text should be studied and (b) whether all stretches of text of this size should be coded.

The coding of language therefore begins with the decision of how to divide up texts into bounded segments. The scope of each segment, which we refer to as the *basic unit of analysis*, can be of any size. It can cover an entire exchange, a single utterance, or even a single word. The only requirements are that this unit remain a constant throughout all coded texts and that, as with everything else, it be consistent with the investigator's research objectives.

For example, if an investigator is interested in the structure of discourse, the conversational turn may be a more appropriate unit of analysis than the sentence. On the other hand, if the interest is in syntax, the intonation unit or the clause probably would be more useful.

In the Control Exchange Code, our basic unit of analysis is the speech act with each act differentiated from the next by a shift in theme, purpose, or goal. In the following exchange, for example, we would divide the text into three separate segments:

Mother: Wash your hands then come down for dinner.
Child: Okay.

The mother's directives *wash your hands* and *then come down for dinner* would constitute the first two segments, because they specify two different actions, and the child's response would constitute the third.

Cases

Every segment of text defined by the basic unit of analysis, however, does not necessarily constitute a codable case. By "case," we mean specifically a segment that meets a set of coding prerequisites set down by the researcher. In many instances, a researcher may be interested in characterizing every segment in a transcript. For instance, someone interested in the structure of mother–child interaction might choose to code every turn, whereas someone curious about syntax may wish to code every clause.

However, if interest is on only a subset of exchanges, utterances, or acts, coding every segment in a text may not only be unnecessary but in some instances counterproductive. In the CEC, because our main objective is to study only control-oriented speech, we select for coding *only* those speech acts intended to change the behavior of someone else, such as a request for goods or services. We do identify how assertions, greetings, explanations, and other noncontrolling speech serve as support for or a reply to a control act; however, these acts do not receive separate coding records of their own. For instance, we would establish a separate record for each of the mother's directives in the example above, but not for the child's response. The child's *okay* would not be considered a case for coding purposes; however, in the coding records for the mother's directives, we would indicate that the intended addressee did agree to comply. In this respect, the CEC is radically different from coding systems that identify the function of every utterance.

Restricting what qualifies as a case has two advantages. First, it allows the researcher to design the coding system specifically around that aspect of language that is of interest, and second, it provides for a more productive use of time. If a coding system in fact makes many distinctions, the amount of time necessary to code every utterance in a text could be enormous, with the payoff for the additional work minimal, especially if only a subset of cases will ever be analyzed.

On the other hand, coding only select segments also has its disadvantages. First, it is single-purposed in that it allows only for a characterization of the cases sampled and not the full data set. And second, when only some segments are analyzed, the potential exists to overlook important dynamics in the overall interaction. Clearly, there is a need to weigh the short-term efficiency of coding only parts of a transcript against the long-term benefits of having fully coded texts.

2.2. Description of the Data

Once the decision has been made as to what cases to code, the next step is how to describe them. This typically involves setting up a record for each case that contains coded information placed in some systematic order. The coding system that one adopts generally lays out the form of this record by outlining three levels of description that we discuss in this section: (a) *topics*, the actual dimensions that are used to describe cases, (b) *categories*, the values that are assigned to the individual topics, and (c) *codes*, the abbreviations associated with categories that make up the coding record itself.

Topics

A coding system generally begins with the development of a series of coding topics. Some topics may be set up strictly for bookkeeping purposes, for example, to provide the line number of the coded utterance in the original transcript, the location of the utterance on the tape, or other identification information. Having coding records and their corresponding transcript lines begin with the same identification number is often useful for easily separating the two or sorting them together for various analytic purposes. For bookkeeping purposes, one could also include as a topic a numerical index to link related cases, such as repetitions, elaborations, and question–answer pairs.

Most topics in a coding system, however, are generally suggested by theoretical orientation and research goals. The Control Exchange Code, in particular, was designed to study the relationships between certain contextual variables and the types of control acts used by parents and their children.[2]

---

[2]In a coding system designed to classify the functions of every line of dialogue, topics would most likely include a richer list of exchange features, speech acts, and activity types than those identified under the CEC. For example, in a more comprehensive coding system designed to study classroom

Our initial model for the structure and coding of control acts was based on two sources. The first was Catherine Garvey's (1975) work on the domain of a request, in which she described children's requests sequentially in terms of the request itself, its adjuncts or support moves, responses and remedial tries.

We wished to include around each request this full array of structure. We believed that there was a "head act" or focal request that most explicitly represented a speaker's move, modified socially in various ways. Accordingly, we chose to describe the form of a request as well as capture any build-ups, modifiers, justifications, or remedies associated with the head act that could be seen as tactical. We also chose to capture as fully as possible the contextual circumstances that might affect the form of the request. Our hope was that by identifying a request's form, modifiers, and context as topics in the CEC, we would be able later to study how the form of a request changes as a function of context and addressee.

The second source for our coding model was experience. Actual coding experiences, in fact, led us to introduce two major changes in our original model. One was a conceptual shift from our earlier view of a control act as simply a request to a broader definition that encompassed a wider range of "instrumental moves" (e.g., offers, permissives, claims, etc.). This shift came about because we found that the boundaries between requests and other types of moves were not clear, and they had many similar properties. Accordingly, we introduced a topic to the CEC to identify different types of control moves (see the definition of *Purpose* below).

Our other change also involved a shift in view, a shift that led us to think that not all that happened was strategic. That is, our original notion that speakers always knew what they wanted from the beginning of an exchange and designed their tactics for certain results gave way to a view that many moves are emergent from the interaction and do not start out as instrumental in nature. The CEC does not fully capture this latter view; however, the system does represent in part the relationship between a control act and earlier discourse by linking the act to preparatory moves and providing indices to earlier attempts at control.

In all, the CEC currently spans a wide range of topics. For coding purposes, we have grouped these into three larger areas that we believe reflect

---

interaction (Ervin-Tripp, 1988b), we identified exchange features for every utterance, including whether a turn initiated an exchange, maintained it with new information, questions, and back-channeling, or terminated it altogether. Ninio and Wheeler (1984) provided a similar system for the line-by-line function coding of mother–child interaction.

In the CEC, we did not examine noninstrumental acts or the overall structure of an interaction as these were not of primary concern. We did, however, capture certain exchange features with respect to the onset of an instrumental move—for example, the activity context, and whether the move initiated or continued an exchange.

the construction of a control act. The first set of topics identifies the *context* in which a control move occurs. These include not only topics for identifying participants and events but also intent and the nature of the situational context and discourse leading up to the control move. The topics in this group are as follows:

Speaker: The individual who initiates the control move.

Addressee: The individual or group intended to act (or not to act) as a result of the control move.

Event: The activity context in which the control move occurs.

Timing: The level of engagement between the speaker and the hearer at the time of the control move.

Repeated Tries: The relationship between the current move and earlier related ones that may or may not have been successful.

Cost: The likelihood of the speaker being rebuffed or ignored as a result of making the control move.

Purpose: The reason for or underlying intent of the control move.

The second set focuses on the *characteristics* of the control move itself and of the supporting or tactical moves that Garvey (1975) identified as being within the domain of a request. These include topics to describe the linguistic form of the move as well as supporting linguistic and paralinguistic devices used to increase the move's chances of being effective. This group includes:

Basic Form: The sentence structure of the head control move.

Explicitness: The extent to which the action, goal, and actor of the desired move are expressed or have to be inferred.

Verbal Attention Forms: The linguistic devices used to get an addressee to pay attention to the control move.

Adjuncts: The reasons, justifications, threats, and mitigators used to increase the likelihood of compliance with the control move.

Gestures: The facial expressions, postural shifts, and hand motions used either to direct an addressee's attention to the control move or to emphasize its imperativeness.

Vocal Mode: Shifts in register or pitch intended to get an addressee's attention or qualify or emphasize the move.

The third and final set includes topics that describe the *effect* of the control act on the intended addressee. The topics here include:

Verbal Reply: The verbal response of the addressee to the control move, expressing either a willingness or unwillingness to comply and why.

Behavioral Compliance: The level of success of the control move in getting an addressee to act.

All of these topics were incorporated into the CEC system so that specific empirical questions could be addressed. These included whether there were age changes in children's tactics in getting attention, persuading addressees to act, and remedying failure; and whether relative age or other characteristics of the addressee affected forms used and the probability of success. A series of articles has examined these and other findings from the coding of family interaction (Ervin-Tripp, 1982; Ervin-Tripp & Gordon, 1986; Ervin-Tripp, Guo, & Lampert, 1990; Ervin-Tripp, O'Connor, & Rosenberg, 1984; Gordon & Ervin-Tripp, 1984).

Topic Fields

In the coding record, it is usual to reserve a space at a specific location and of a fixed length to enter information on each topic. We refer to these reserved spaces as *topic fields.*

In many instances, a topic will have just one field set aside for it. To flesh out a topic, however, it is often useful to make finer distinctions in the form of subtopics. A topic, therefore, can have just one field associated with it or serve as an umbrella for several interrelated fields, depending on the researcher's needs. A researcher may choose to use more than one field to provide more comprehensive information on a topic. In some systems, for instance, the only space needed under *Speaker* might be a field for the speaker's name. In the CEC, however, we also include fields for the speaker's age, gender, and role-playing in the interaction because we see these variables as likely to influence the form of a control act as well as the compliance of addressees.

A researcher may also employ multiple topic fields to provide not only a more comprehensive description but also a richer characterization. For instance, while developing the Event topic for the CEC, we found that it was common for children to be distracted temporarily from one activity to engage in another or to embed one activity in another as a kind of aside. At these points we could tell that one was more foregrounded with respect to the control act but that the other was still in a way there, for the children picked up where they left off. Accordingly, we included fields to indicate a foregrounded as well as a backgrounded activity if both existed.

A final use of multiple fields is for simplifying the business of coding by breaking up a single topic, which may require a rather complicated coding decision, into less complicated subtopics that individually require fewer decisions to code effectively. This last consideration is discussed more fully in the section on implementation.

Coding Categories

Once topics have been outlined, the next step in the construction process is to lay out the categories that will be assigned to each topic field. One way to achieve this goal is to adopt the top-down approach of applying an already existent or theoretically derived classification system to ones data. For example, if we wished to code the speech act performed by every utterance in a text, we could adopt Searle's (1976) speech act taxonomy and classify utterances with some success into the following five categories:

Representatives: Speech that commits a speaker to the truth of the expressed proposition (e.g., assertions, suggestions, conclusions).

Directives: Speech where a speaker attempts to get an addressee to act (e.g., requests, prohibitions, questions).

Commissives: Speech that commits a speaker to some future action (e.g., promises, offers, threats).

Expressives: Speech that reveals a speaker's current psychological state (e.g., apologies, greetings, thanks).

Declarations: Speech that immediately changes a current state of affairs (e.g., christenings, firings).

In adopting this taxonomy, however, we must recognize that we are assuming that it will allow for the kinds of distinctions that we wish to make. This may not always be the case.

Frequently, especially if we are interested in only a subclass of language or have a novel perspective on language use, we cannot always use another investigator's coding system. In the CEC, for example, we study a subclass of speech acts, which would suggest that we could have used Searle's or a similar taxonomy to classify control moves. Searle's system, however, would have been inappropriate here for it suggests categories that we would never use to classify control acts, such as *apologies* and *christenings*. Furthermore, based on Searle's definitions, what we have termed a control act would always be coded as a directive (i.e., language where the speaker attempts to get the addressee to act). Yet, it is possible to see acts labeled as representatives and commissives as intended to change the behavior of an addressee in some fashion. For example, an offer of goods, which would be classified as a commissive in Searle's system, could be viewed as a request for an addressee to act, that is, to accept the goods provided.

When an appropriate classification system is not available, the alternative is to adopt the bottom-up approach, that is, to begin with selected transcripts and identify categories that appear to occur naturally in the data. This was the method that we adopted for the CEC. Under the topic of *Purpose,* for example, we developed a field labeled *Type of Act,* with empirically derived categories to capture speaker intent. We began with obvious categories, such as *request* and *prohibition,* but added categories for other types of speech that appeared to require an addressee to acquiesce or comply. In all, we developed the following six coding categories:

Directives or Positive Requests: Utterances that require that an addressee act to provide either goods or services.

Prohibitions or Negative Requests: Utterances that require that an addressee stop or avoid a line of action.

Permissions or Allowances: Utterances that either request from or grant to an addressee permission to obtain goods or services.

Intentions: Utterances that commit the speaker to a line of action that an addressee is expected either to facilitate or at least not block.

Claims: Utterances that require an addressee to recognize a speaker's right to certain goods, activities, or services.

Offers: Utterances that invite an addressee to accept goods or services.

Notice here that the CEC's categories encompass a much narrower band of language use than Searle's speech act system as a result of our focus on just control acts. Also, notice that the CEC divides up control acts in a manner different than that suggested by Searle's directive category. Like Searle, we identify requests and prohibitions as language intended to get others to modify their behavior; however, we also pull in intentions, claims, and offers, which, if we had used Searle's categories and definitions, would not be considered control acts at all, let alone coded for type. In short, by looking at our data first, we were able to see the kinds of things that speakers attempt to get addressees to do (e.g., accept offers, respect ownership, allow a stated intention), and accordingly, we were able to construct categories that were appropriate for our research needs.

Coding categories, then, can be suggested by theory, borrowed from another investigator, or empirically derived. Irrespective of the method used, however, we would like to suggest three rules of thumb. First, coding categories should follow directly from research goals and should not include distinctions that have little or no utility for future research objectives. That is, investigators should not employ another's coding scheme simply because it is accessible and there may already exist available texts coded with this system. An earlier coding system, although appearing to capture the dimensions an investigator wishes to study, may in fact be inappropriate for a research objective other than the one for which it was initially created.

In the case of *Type of Act* in the CEC, the six basic categories were selected after a consideration of how a range of different types of speech acts were likely to affect the behavior of an addressee.   Accordingly, we included categories for types of speech that could be seen as intended to get an addressee either to act (or not to act) or to facilitate (or at least not block) the speaker's current plans.

A second rule of thumb is that categories within a field should be clearly defined so that it is clear not only what each represents but also how each one differs from the rest. In short, the categories should be defined, if possible, so that they are mutually exclusive.[3] This is not to say, however, that a case cannot be, and should not be, coded into more than one category. In fact, given the plurifunctionality pervading language, double coding may not only be useful, but desirable.

For example, consider *Do your own work* said by a teacher to a student caught looking at a neighbor's exam during a test. At one level, in the CEC system, this utterance could be coded as a directive, because the teacher is directing the student to do something (i.e., work on his own exam).   On another level, however, the statement can also be heard as a prohibition because the teacher is also trying to prevent the student from doing something (i.e., from copying from a neighbor).

For cases like this, there are two mechanical conventions available for the double coding of data. The first is to create not one but two coding fields to allow for a primary and a secondary coding. As mentioned earlier, this solution was adopted in the CEC system to deal with event codes. This solution could have also been adopted to handle the coding of acts with multiple functions. By opening up a second field for type of act, it would have been possible to code *Do your own work* as both a directive and a prohibition. Notice, however, that this particular coding solution requires a reorganization at the topic level.

An alternative solution is to set up a series of "joint" coding categories, ones that represent the co-occurrence of two possible outcomes, such as an

---

[3]Some may argue that this is an impossible task, requiring the identification of core features that may or may not, in fact, be representative of all exemplars of a category. This criticism, however, overlooks the fact that, for descriptive and analytic purposes, it is in the researcher's best interest to use care and objectivity when defining the criteria for distinguishing categories, so that cases can be assigned to categories effortlessly and unambiguously.

utterance that may serve as both a directive and a prohibition, as in the case of *Do your own work*. When constructing a joint category, however, care needs to be taken not to violate the rule of mutual exclusivity. This is accomplished by making clear in the definition of a joint category that it applies only to those cases that fit the definition of a first category *and* that of a second. If only one definition applies, then the appropriate stand-alone category (e.g., *directive*), and not the joint category (e.g., *directive-prohibition*) is used. In the CEC, we employed this second solution to capture control acts that could serve as both a directive and a prohibition (e.g., *Do your own work*) as well as those that could serve as a directive and an intention (e.g., *Let's go to the movies*).[4]

The final rule of thumb is that all categories within a field should be not only mutually exclusive, but also exhaustive. That is, within each field, the coding categories should be extensive enough to be able to provide a classification for every foreseeable case, even if this requires including a *miscellaneous* or *other* category.

Some researchers may have theoretical reasons to force cases into a limited set of categories. However, one cannot always predict what all possible cases might be like. The hope is that through careful consideration of how cases may differ for a particular topic area, it would be possible to isolate all possible coding categories. Work by other investigators and various theories on how language is organized can provide clues here. However, for a newly constructed topic field there is likely to be a case that just does not quite fit into any category.

The solution to this problem in the short run is to create an *other* category. The value of such a category is that it provides not only a place for uncodable cases but also an avenue for exploring how to revise and expand the coding system.

When an *other* category begins to catch a substantial number of cases, the coding field as originally conceptualized needs to be modified in some fashion. The ways in which *other* cases cluster may suggest that either a new coding category should be added or that the definitions and distinctions between the

---

[4]The reader may appreciate at this point that based on the six original coding categories under type of act, 30 different joint coding categories would have been possible. However, we did not choose to provide codes explicitly for the remaining 28 possibilities for empirical reasons. After having coded some 20 transcripts with the CEC, we encountered few utterances codable as serving dual functions, and those that have been encountered are of the two types already identified. It is primarily because of the infrequency of dual function control moves that we did not opt for the two-field coding solution (i.e., the second field would have been left uncoded most of the time) and why only the two mentioned here are formally defined in the CEC coding manual.

Because of the recognizable problem in cases like this, some code designers do provide preference hierarchies, instructing coders how to make a forced choice between the two categories in joint cases. We did not do this.

original categories should be revised in order to incorporate the unclassifiable cases.

The inclusion of an *other* category should not be seen as a weakness in an ongoing coding project, but in fact a strength. Such a category helps to guide revision of the coding system as a whole and to make clear that the development of a coding system is not a static one-time operation that occurs before the coding of the first case. Rather, the construction of a coding system should be seen as a dynamic and ongoing process that benefits at the start from original theories and research goals, yet has enough flexibility so that later revisions can be made to capture unexpected and interesting distinctions.

Coding Labels

The final consideration in the construction process is the selection of codes or coding labels. A coding label is the abbreviation or tag added to the data to represent a coding category. In principle, they can consist of any alphabetic or numeric characters, but errors in data entry are less frequent when they have some mnemonic resemblance to the name of the coding categories they represent (e.g., *D* for *Directive*, *I* for *Intention*, etc.) than when they are arbitrary numbers (e.g., *1* for *Directive*, *2* for *Intention*, etc.).

For minimizing error and easing data analysis, it is preferable for all the labels within a particular field to be of the same length, that is, the same number of characters. Computer analysis programs such as the *Statistical Package for the Social Sciences* (SPSS) require the researcher to indicate the number of characters for each field and expect it to conform to the specification. If a code label is said to be two characters long, it must fit within two characters or else the data will be read incorrectly. Although spaces can be used to pad shorter values to make them equal, this increases the possibility of error, as coders may not place spaces uniformly and some software packages may not interpret " D" and "D " as being equivalent.

If labels differ in length within a field, they can be modified by global substitution prior to the actual analysis to conform to the requirements of the software package. The main thing, however, is that codes should be systematically differentiable and easy to check for errors, and both of these goals are facilitated when field lengths are kept constant.

2.3. Some Limitations

Every coding system has limitations that become more apparent as one attempts to reduce the complexities of recordings and transcripts to coding categories. Even after initially designing and periodically adjusting the CEC, we continued to be troubled by the fact that we had forced ourselves to deal with only one level of a highly complex layering of functions. A narrative, for example, can be embedded within and support a control act, and a control act can be embedded within and support a larger scheme or strategy. Labov and Fanshel (1977) discuss this layering most fully; we did not deal with it at all except at the Speech Event level. Not surprisingly, we found that coders often differed in choosing the level at which to interpret an activity or event.

Another limitation we uncovered arose from our choice for unit of analysis. Because we focused on and evaluated only one speech act at a time, we developed a kind of myopia to certain features in the dynamics of a conversation. For example, in one of the tapes we had used many times for training coders in the CEC, we noticed that one child always dominated another, in every context. Her preference always won, her topics won, her choices of play won. She was, in fact, a few months older than the other child; her strategies were subtler. We had looked in the text only at the dynamics of each act, one at a time, not at their relation or organization. We did not get the overall picture of the relationship. Our failure to see these dynamics even though they were pertinent to the issues in our research is evidence of how narrow one's focus can become in coding. This limitation may be impossible to remedy in the framework of a coding study, because it depends on constantly reframing one's perspective on the data. Coding is based on maintaining a consistent and shared perspective. This is why qualitative study of the same texts is always necessary as a complement to the coding process.

3. THE IMPLEMENTATION OF A CODING SYSTEM

3.1. Coding as Language Planning

Once the basic outline for a coding system is in place, the next step is to put the system to work—that is, to train coders on how to use the system to describe a set of texts. But what is this process like? How can it be organized to the researcher's greatest advantage?

The learning of a code in essence can be compared to the learning of a vocabulary in a second language: Both require learners to develop a sense of prototypical cases as well as categorical boundaries for newly acquired terms. As in second language acquisition, the easiest coding categories for a learner to acquire are those that involve a familiar concept such as *adult* or *past tense*. This sort of category is comparable to learning a new word in a second language that has an equivalent in one's first language. However, the *faux amis* of translation reminds us that analytic codes may restrict meaning more than is conventional in ordinary language. For instance, the word *nom* in French in most contexts means "name," but in the context of filling out official forms it means just "family name." Many an erasure testifies to this problem for English speakers learning French in France. An example from transcription is the use of the question mark for rising intonation alone, not for grammatical interrogation, as in *What do you want.* versus *What do you want?* Some code-builders avoid such forms altogether to prevent interference from conventional usage.

Safeguarding against interference from differences in range of reference requires prudence and foresight, or the luck to discover coder confusion early enough to change the code. Ideally, codes should draw on concepts that are natural, already familiar from practical experience, or very easy to learn. Thus, the process of coding can lead coders to identify "natural" behavior units. When codes create theoretical, arbitrary, artificial units and artificial coding concepts, there is a high risk both that the concept will be short-lived in the coders' minds and that it will be short-lived in the history of the research field.

When presented with categories named by a researcher, coders become in essence newcomers to a new group who must learn the group's jargon. In natural language learning, we rely on context to teach; in code instruction, we cannot do this, and instead must be as explicit as possible. Extensive training against modeled coding supplies the equivalent of context. The problem with training by coding of natural texts is that due to natural frequencies some categories are not trained at all; others are very well taught. Experience with children's learning of vocabulary tells us that variety of contexts of exposure is crucial to new learning. So for every category, a range of examples needs to be available.

Extensive training and examples, however, do not guarantee perfect coding. Even after being thoroughly trained, coders may still apply a category in a manner different from that laid out in the coding system because of a "drift" in meaning. What is likely to happen is that the conceptual correlates for coding terms may tend to move toward a coder's natural category system. As codes are defined verbally, variations in the coders' sense of word meanings can therefore lead their personal definitions for a coding category to drift apart from one another as well as away from the original intended definition.

An additional problem is that coders from different backgrounds often bring with them different presuppositions and concepts that can influence their decision making, and subsequently, their coding judgments. For example, we discovered that coders would often disagree about whether a request for goods involved a high or low cost to a speaker because of different familial and cultural views about who has rights to such things as food and toys and therefore can ask for these things directly without the fear of criticism. We further observed examples of such bias in a project in which we coded for conversational humor. Cultural background, gender, political viewpoint can all influence the identification of the basis of humor, and we found that recent immigrants did not recognize idioms or cultural allusions at all.

In short, coders typically have *implicit ideas* about how certain phenomena correlate with one another, and consequently, they may code topics—albeit at times unintentionally—so that these underlying assumptions are corroborated. This is why constant communication and retraining is needed to keep meanings calibrated and mutually acceptable. In addition, the communication helps clarify ambiguities in the researcher's thinking and helps in code revisions to add examples, clarify definitions, and even identify new categories that are needed. A regular "Round Robin" with paired duplicate coding is one way that coding projects do this; it plays the same role as talking about the same visible referent does in language learning.

We can see then that there is a paradox in the coding process: that is, even a carefully outlined system with clearly defined topics and categories does not guarantee that coders will be able to use the system to make valid and reliable coding decisions. In the CEC, for example, we define directives under *Type of Act* as simply speech that requires or requests an addressee to provide goods or services. This definition, however, does not say anything about what a coder should and should not consider when making a decision about whether an utterance should be classified as a directive or not. Based on the definition alone, we have no clue, for example, as to whether a statement such as *Katie left her coat* should be seen as an assertion and left uncoded or seen as a subtle hint to act and coded as a directive.

The second major task in the coding process, therefore, is not simply to write better definitions—as better definitions are not likely to solve the problems cited here—but rather to figure out how to present and teach the coding system so that coders can learn its language and use it to assign cases smoothly and objectively to categories. In this section, we provide suggestions that can be used to meet these goals by looking at the organization of topics, the presentation of coding categories, and the mechanics of data entry.

3.2. The Organization of Topics

The researchers in charge of a coding project may do their own coding; in which case, they may already have a good idea of what distinctions they wish to make within each topic area. Frequently, however, individuals not involved in the planning and development of the original coding system are solicited to do coding work, and they have to be provided with an outline for doing coding and taught how to use it.

Topic Definitions

The initial problem, as already highlighted, is that newcomers often come to the task of coding with their own definitions and ideas about such things as syntax, speech acts, turns, gestures, and other language-related phenomena.

These prior definitions could conceivably facilitate the coding process to the extent that the new coders' definitions match those employed by the coding system. To the extent that they do not, however, old definitions could easily interfere with and cause confusion over what the researcher actually wants coded under a given topic and could lead to invalid coding decisions.

A standard example in the study of requests involves a phenomenon known as *prerequests*. These are strategic, preparatory moves intended to get an addressee to orient toward a desired object, or to gather information on the likelihood of compliance, prior to the actual delivery of a request. In the following sequence of turns, the problem is how to consider the first two turns. They can be seen either as preparatory moves before the head request in the third turn, or they could be considered part of a series of repeated requests, increasing in explicitness when the first moves fail.

(1) I don't have enough stickers.

(2) Are you all done?   (Nods)

(3) Could I have some?

Levinson (1983) has argued that the genesis of conventional indirect requests might be exchanges in which the preferred outcome was a compliance by the addressee who infers what is desired, leaving the requestor successful without having taken the risks of refusal of an explicit, on-record request. Therefore, in any particular exchange we cannot know for sure, especially if the speaker is a young child, whether the moves were essentially a strategic sequence or a sequence of repeated tries. Undoubtedly, coders are affected by their beliefs about age and capacity in this judgment and must be given rules for making these distinctions in some standardized way.

Accordingly, a coding system must not only lay out what each topic involves from the researcher's perspective, but also how its current conceptualization differs from some dictionary, folk, or previous theoretical definition. When we define the topic of *Purpose* in the CEC, for example, we spell out exactly what coders must and must not consider when making judgments here:

> Control acts are attempts to get another person to act, often with strong social purposes as well. In terms of the action component, we can conceive of a variety of goals in terms of changes in location of goods, activities, and states, varying beneficiaries, and different levels of the conscious attention of the speaker. In common sense language, these variations are coded into terms such as order, offer, prohibition, and so on. For instance, an offer has the addressee as beneficiary.
>
> The point of this topic is to determine what the speaker wants to accomplish through each control act. The first judgment is to decide whether

the desired outcome of the act will primarily involve action by the hearer or by the speaker. If the action is by the speaker, then we are talking about offers, intentions, and soliciting permission. If the expected action is by the hearer, we are talking about directives, prohibitions, claims, and permission-giving. The analysis of purpose often can go deeper. We are looking at purpose just behind the surface forms, not in terms of deeper unconscious goals. Try to decide what the goal is for the speaker. This will help you see whether the speaker's focus is on the goal, on the means, or on what is annoying, that is, on what is to be changed.

Our comments here also apply to the definition of coding categories within each topic area, and we readdress this issue in the section on categories below.

Topic Order

Clear-cut definitions can reduce coding problems, but they do not eliminate them. Another difficulty stems from the effect that earlier coding can have on later work. Coders may at times code a particular topic field in line with an earlier one because they (a) rely on the earlier field to help them in making later coding decisions, (b) have implicit notions of how the two fields should be related, (c) hope to confirm a theory, or (d) hope to disconfirm one. For example, if a coder identifies two statements as successive control acts, he or she would be unlikely to code the first statement as a preparatory move for the second, even if the two moves could be seen in this way. Similarly, what coders identify as a Foregrounded Event is likely to influence their view of the power structure, and later on their judgments of Cost.

Given all this, how topics are arranged within a coding system and assigned to coders becomes a critical issue, especially if the same individual is expected to code all topics for each individual case in a text. Left unchecked, the effect of earlier on later coding could invalidate the coding system.

As discussed by Bloom (this volume), this problem can be minimized by having individuals code different topics. Having a different coder for every topic, however, may not be particularly efficient, especially if the coding project has only a few coders and many fields. Another solution is to have the same individual code each topic but to do so on a separate day without reference to any earlier coding. This, however, has the disadvantage of increasing the amount of time it takes to code a single text.

In the CEC, we employ a combination of both solutions. For any given transcript, we have different people code different topics, but this is not a one person–one topic arrangement. Coding assignments are done primarily by splitting the system in thirds according to the three larger topic areas identified earlier. Because the system was designed mainly to study how context and intent are related to the form of a control act and how form in turn is related to compliance, we felt it wise to have different individuals code the context, form, and compliance variables in order to avoid any bias toward or against a particular hypothesis.

For each assigned block of topics, we also instruct coders to make several passes through a text and to code a different topic on each pass. The reason for this is to minimize the effect that an earlier coding decision in one topic area for a case could have on the coding decision in a subsequent topic area. We have developed computer software to facilitate the coding of one topic at a time, which we describe in more detail in the section on data entry below.

Field Order

The concerns that apply to the arrangement of topics also apply to the organization of fields within each topic area: namely, the concern that the coding of one field may influence the coding of another. Depending on what the topic fields reflect, however, the previous solutions could turn out to be unnecessary and, in some cases, even problematic.

First, separate coders and separate passes are not necessary when it is clear that decisions required for two fields are completely independent of one another and can be objectively made. For instance, under *Speaker* in the CEC, a decision concerning the coding of a speaker's age is unlikely to influence a decision concerning the coding of the speaker's gender. These two fields can be safely coded together.

Second, separate coding may in fact be undesirable when the coding of one field is dependent on the coding of another, such as two fields used to specify the type and location of a linguistic feature.

For example, in the CEC, we code attention forms that co-occur with a main control act. These can be of various types (vocatives, epithets, exclamations, turn takers, etc.) and can appear in different locations relative to the act itself. There can even be more than one attention form. If an attention form is identified, its type and location need to be coded at the same time. Otherwise, it is possible that in a first pass the attention form may be caught and its type coded, but in a second pass overlooked with its location left with a null code (a code that indicates that location is not specified because there is no attention form to identify). In sum, these two fields must be coded together because they are mutually dependent on one another (i.e., if one field has a non-null code, the other must have one as well).

Third, separate coding may also be undesirable when one field constitutes a subclass of another. In this instance, not only must each field be coded in the same pass, but in a specific order. Employing fields that are subclasses of one another, in fact, can be quite helpful in making category decisions. As mentioned earlier, when a coding decision may be rather complicated, it is sometimes helpful to break the decision making process into two steps: a first step where a primary coding decision is made, and a second where a subsequent and finer distinction is worked out.

In the CEC, in fact, we employ two separate and hierarchically arranged fields to code adjuncts (i.e., statements that support or justify a control act). The first is used to provide a major type category (i.e., "reason," "threat," "history," "clarification," etc.), and the second is used to make a finer distinction depending on what was coded in the first field. For example, if a control move involves an adjunct (some do not), and the adjunct is coded as a reason in the first field, then the system allows for one of several types of reasons to be specified in the second (i.e., "external state," "internal bias," "situational norm," etc.).

The use of subclasses as fields is a technique that can also be employed at the topic level to facilitate the coding of categories. Other techniques involving the coding categories themselves can also be used, and we now turn to these.

3.3. The Presentation of Coding Categories

When setting up a topic fields, it may appear sufficient to provide a clear definition of each coding category and examples of illustrative cases. However, as with topic definitions, seemingly well-defined categories do not take care of the second language problem.

First, coders may use inappropriate criteria for deciding whether or not a case fits a particular category definition. Second, although definitions may suggest mutually exclusive categories, real world cases may still be difficult to classify, especially if whether or not a case can be classified into a particular category depends on making inferences from overt behavior and speech that are not part of the category's definition. And third, even with clear-cut definitions, there may still be fuzzy cases that can fall into more than one category.

The overriding problem here is the possibility that coders will classify cases into a particular category based on the category's probability of occurring within a given context or with an identifiable linguistic form that has nothing to do with deciding whether or not the category should be used. This problem would not be so serious—although it is a serious one—if not for the fact that analysis often involves relating topics to one another. To the extent that relationships between topics pertaining to context, form, and other language-related dimensions are to be studied, such coding could lead to spurious correlations.

For example, we might end up with a perfect correlation between form and purpose if all declarative sentences were coded as assertions and all imperatives and interrogatives as directives. Statements such as *The window is open*, *It's naptime*, and *Katie left her coat* would all be coded as assertions although under some circumstances they could be interpreted as directives.

The point is that a coding system must make clear what is and is not to be considered—or at least what criteria should be given primacy—when deciding in which category to place a case. In short, the coding categories *must be operationalized*. That is, guidelines must be set for what coders must observe in the natural language data before they select a conceptually defined category. Some guidelines can be anticipated; others, however, can only be found in the course of actual code use.

As a result of coding experiences, for example, under *Type of Act*, the CEC does not simply define a directive as speech that requires or requests an action from an addressee, but rather also instructs coders that they should not be distracted by the surface form and that they should consider factors that indicate (a) that the speaker is in need of certain goods or services, (b) that the hearer can be expected and/or is expected to meet that need, and (c) that the hearer does not have the option to refuse. Under this definition, *Have an orange* looks like a directive but might be considered an offer, and *I'm finished* to a waiter becomes a directive that does not look like one.

Stipulating that coders should look for specific observables in a text before they select a category, however, does not guarantee that they will do so effectively. One solution to this dilemma is to outline for each topic a step-by-step procedure for making a classification. This can be guided by category definitions and take the form of a hierarchical flowchart with each level of the chart representing a different yes–no decision as to whether something is true about a case or not. To be easy to use, a coding chart should follow the normal path that coders use to make decisions, and the final level should contain the individual coding categories. Figure 7.1 provides a possible flowchart for coding *Type of Act* in the CEC.[5]

One obvious flaw in this hierarchical arrangement is that some cases may be viewable in several different ways. As we have seen, for example, the utterance *Do your own work* can be interpreted as a directive and a prohibition. Under these circumstances, what do we do?

One solution, of course, is to code only one interpretation. However, some researchers may wish to represent this duality. Other solutions are ones we have already suggested. First, separate coding fields could be open for each possible interpretation, with each following a different path down the hierarchical flowchart. And second, joint coding categories could be created, and these could be configured into the hierarchical arrangement.

---

[5]A hierarchical arrangement for making coding decisions, of course, can be built into the code itself by creating a separate field for each coding decision as was illustrated for the coding of adjuncts in the preceding section.

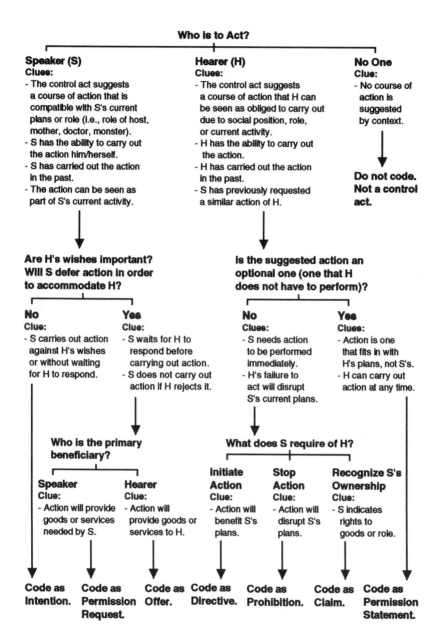

FIG 7.1. Flow chart for coding CEC topic field, *Type of Act*. (This chart was designed to help coders classify the purpose of ambiguous control acts.)

hierarchical flowchart. And second, joint coding categories could be created, and these could be configured into the hierarchical arrangement.

Even with operational definitions and flowcharts, however, a coding manual is not complete. To guide them along, coders not only need definitions but also examples of prototypical and boundary cases to give them a sense of what they are looking for with respect to a particular category. Because instances occurring at boundaries, or points of potential ambiguity between categories, may be rare in natural texts, the code or the training materials need to oversample at boundaries where coders are most likely to disagree. Along with good definitions and flowcharts, a broad range of examples can also provide coders with the tools they need to code successfully. As an illustration, Table 7.1 contains the CEC manual page for *Type of Act*, complete with definitions and examples.

TABLE 7.1
Manual Page from the Control Exchange Code for *Type of Act*

Topic 7: Purpose of the Control Act

Control acts are attempts to get another person to act, often with strong social purposes as well. In terms of the action component, we can conceive of a variety of goals in terms of changes in location of goods, activities, and states, varying beneficiaries, and different levels of the conscious attention of the speaker. In common sense language, these variations are coded into terms such as order, offer, prohibition, and so on. For instance, an offer has the addressee as beneficiary.

The point of this topic is to determine what the speaker wants to accomplish through each control act. The first judgment is to decide whether the desired outcome of the act will primarily involve action by the hearer or by the speaker. If the action is by the speaker, then we are talking about offers, intentions, and soliciting permission. If the expected action is by the hearer, we are talking about directives, prohibitions, claims, and permission-giving. The analysis of purpose often can go deeper. We are looking at purpose just behind the surface forms, not in terms of deeper unconscious goals. Try to decide what the goal is for the speaker. This will help you see whether the speaker's focus is on the goal, on the means, or on what is annoying, that is, on what is to be changed.

Field 26: Type of Act

D - Directives. An action is required or requested of the hearer, involving goods or services. Don't be distracted by the surface form which is coded in Topic 10. The critical issue is WHO IS GOING TO ACT. If it is the addressee, it is a directive.

Can I have some of that?
Is there any of that cake left?
Your brother wants some too.

(cont.)

Table 7.1 Continued

I'll smack the living daylights out of you . . . (if you don't get off the mantel).
If you want to play with these you could. (needed to solicit partner in a game.)

P - Prohibitions. The addressee is expected to avoid doing, or stop doing something undesirable. Prohibitions can be realized either by telling the addressee to stay there, go on doing something, primarily to keep them from the alternative, or to stop doing or avoid doing something (e.g., "don't do that"; "stop that"; "leave that alone").

You stay right there!
Stay out of here!
Pick that up and I'll slug you.
I'll tell Mom (that you've been pestering me).
You can't have that one!

C - Claims. This primarily includes ownership claims. May or may not have legitimacy. Don't worry about the hidden prohibition. "That's mine" is aimed at keeping goods, in the present. Claims can occur at the time when free goods are claimed, or when someone has taken goods which one wants back. If used to prohibit, when there is immediate threat, probably is a prohibition in purpose.

A - Permissions or allowing. Requesting or granting permission, which is usually targeted at a later end state, and the beneficiary differs in the two cases. Where the addressee is a superordinate, permission might be solicited.

Do you want me to bring my stuff over there?
May I please go out in the rain?
Will you let me go out in the rain?

I - Intentions. Statement of intention by the speaker to commit an act which will affect the hearer, hearer's goods, or will require the hearer not to controvert speaker action. These are related to permission requests in that the hearer is involved in accepting a proposed act by the speaker. However, a request permission calls for a reply and implies the speaker will refrain if not approved. Intend does not call for a reply. In fact, by virtue of its assertive character Intend hopes to preclude any objection. A possible point of confusion to avoid: announcements, boasts, which control hearer's awareness but not actions except looking. Tend to include modals and focus on the end state. Do not code intentions as control acts unless you can rephrase them as directives or prohibitions. Be sure the hearer is the target and the speaker isn't just thinking out loud. S wants to let H know what he's gonna do and he doesn't want H to interfere with plans.

I'm gonna sit on your lap.
I'm drinking up all the orange juice. (you can't have any).
I'll knock down your tower.

(cont.)

Table 7.1 Continued

O - Offers, invitations, or promise of goods or action. We are coding these as control acts because they are initiated by the speaker and affect the hearer. Some benefit to the donor will accrue in almost every case, but to be an offer the speaker must believe that the recipient must also benefit. Of course many speakers will use offers to gain their own ends in a respectable way. One way to determine an offer is to judge how likely a refusal is on the part of the hearer. If the hearer is unlikely to refuse, or if a refusal is due to factors unrelated to the desirability of the offer then a felicitous offer has occurred.

Would you like some of this cake? No, I'm on a diet.
Can I help you do that? (where help would benefit addressee)
I want to do that for you.

J/L- Joint action. A combination of directive and prohibition (J) or directive and intention in which both speaker and addressee are going to equally act (L). Do not use unless you find yourself torn between these two categories.

Get your *own fork*! (J)
Let's watch television. (L)

3.4. Coding and Data Entry

Once a researcher has laid out conventions and methods for doing coding in an easy-to-follow manual, the actual business of coding can begin. This process can be a rather time-consuming task, requiring, not one, but several passes through individual texts. However, there are a few things that coders can do to simplify and speed up the process.

The first step, of course, is for them to familiarize themselves completely with the coding manual. We have found it extremely useful for novice coders to work alongside the researcher on a practice transcript. This experience affords the newcomers the opportunity not only to discuss how to make specific coding decisions but also to check their coding judgments before they move on to code their own texts.

After learning the manual, the second step is for coders to go through their assigned transcripts and to identify all codable cases. In some instances, this can be done from the transcript alone. Frequently, however, coders must do this from the original recorded data. In the case of the CEC, for example, we realized that control acts had to be initially identified from a first pass through the video recording; this could not be done from the transcript alone because outside observers often need to see how actors behave in order to infer a request or prohibition, especially if these moves are not explicit.

The third and final step is to work through the topics for each case, assigning a code to each field, and entering it into a typed or computer record for that coded case. The transcript alone may be sufficient for coding some topics, whereas others may require referring to the audio- or videotape. In using the CEC, for instance, *Speaker Identity* could be coded from the transcript alone, as could fields relying solely on the surface structure of an utterance, such as *Basic Form* or *Adjunct*. In contrast, topics requiring extensive knowledge of context, such as *Speech Event, Purpose,* and *Compliance,* had to be coded from audio or video tape. Failure to do this could cause a coder to inaccurately identify the purpose of an act, which requires knowledge of what speakers and addressees do, or to overlook role-play, which requires knowledge of a speaker's manner and voice.

The coding process can be greatly speeded up if coders make a single pass through the tapes to first upgrade their transcripts to include those features that will be coded later on. In the CEC, in fact, we identified 10 topics for which contextual information could be added to a transcript to facilitate coding. Coders were instructed to make a special pass through our videotaped data with an eye toward incorporating features such as tone of voice, addressee, gestures, and behavioral compliance. In the process, of course, the richness of the transcript also increased.

A final consideration here is how to minimize "slips of the pen" or mistyping. When data are entered into a computer, it is useful to have a data-entry program that prompts the user for individual fields and checks their entered responses against a set of allowable values for that field.

Our data entry program is called "codedit" (Lampert, 1985). It provides the user with a visual display of the coding record, in which rows represent the individual cases and columns, the topics and fields. When the cursor is moved across the terminal screen from one field to the next, a header appears at the top of the screen to indicate which topic and field the coder has entered, and a line appears at the bottom to indicate all the possible codes that can be entered into that field. If an incorrect code is entered, the editor sends a beep, and an error message appears at the bottom of the screen, instructing the coder to use only the codes indicated. The coder cannot move into the next field unless an acceptable code is entered or the field is left blank.

This code editor, written for a UNIX environment, also allows the user to have selective access to a subset of topics, so that a coder may enter just the codes for a single topic or field in one pass through the data. This can be more efficient for some topics as well as minimize the influence of coding from other fields.

4. EVALUATION

Once coded texts have been produced, the question naturally arises as to whether the codes adequately capture the distinctions they were designed to make. If the guidelines outlined above have been followed, we would expect that we could address the theoretical and empirical questions for which the system was originally designed. There are, however, a few potential problems.

If coders cannot agree on how to classify specific cases, or if it turns out that the codes reflect factors other than the categories they were intended to capture, then the validity of the coding system as well as any coded information resulting from it would certainly be compromised. In this case, it would be difficult, if not impossible, to do any meaningful analyses with the data.

Assuming that codes are reliable and valid, however, there still remain problems regarding how to organize the coding to investigate relationships between variables. Again, improper compiling of the data for analysis would severely compromise the interpretation of any results.

In this section, we address issues that pertain to the reliability of a coding system—that is, the extent to which coders agree on how to characterize individual cases—and in the next we focus on problems and solutions for organizing data for analysis.

4.1. Reliability

One of the most fundamental coding problems is whether or not individuals can agree on how to code a case. The more they agree, the more confident we can be that the coding of each can be trusted as reliable. However, to the extent that they do not agree, this can point to problems within the coding system itself, suggesting that the criteria for coding certain topics and categories may not be outlined clearly enough. In fact, when disagreements exist among well-trained and like-minded coders, the grounds for suspecting problems with the code system are particularly strong. When this is the case, the coding system may have to be revised and any earlier coding redone accordingly.

One way to check the reliability of categorical data is to calculate the proportion of coder agreement. That is, we can have two individuals code the same cases, and for any selected coding field, tally up the number of times they agree on a coding category for a case and compare this number to the total number of cases overall. For example, if two individuals coded 100 cases and assigned the same codes to 92, their level of agreement would be .92 or 92%. The closer the proportion is to 1.00, the better the level of agreement and the higher the degree of reliability.

The problem with using only a proportion to check reliability, however, is that a proportion does not take into account chance factors. In fact, two individuals could code the same cases with one of them assigning codes at random yet, strictly by chance alone, still end up with a reasonably high proportion of agreement.

To illustrate this problem, consider a topic with only two coding options (*yes* or *no*) and the following matrix representing the decisions of two coders (A and B) for 100 cases. The columns represent the decisions for coder A, the rows represent the decisions for B, and the cells along the downward sloping diagonal indicate the number of times they agree.

		A	
		Yes	No
B	Yes	75	25
	No	0	0

This matrix suggests 75% agreement for all 100 cases. However, such an outcome could result with only A making true distinctions across the 100 cases and B indiscriminately coding everything as *yes* without even considering a single case. When we get patterns of agreement like this one, it becomes difficult to say with any certainty whether agreement is in fact due to carefully weighed judgments or is simply a chance outcome due to a bias for a particular coding category on the part of one or both coders, irrespective of the cases considered.

For any set of cases, we can expect a certain amount of chance agreement. The question, however, is how much is due to chance and how much actually reflects carefully made discriminations?

One descriptive statistic that is used to answer this question is Cohen's Kappa (Cohen, 1960). Kappa or κ represents the proportion of observed agreements that is not attributable to chance. This value can be calculated by (a) determining for each coding category the number of agreements that would be expected strictly by chance if one or both coders were assigning codes indiscriminately, (b) subtracting the expected number of chance agreements overall from the actual number of observed agreements, and (c) dividing this difference by the total number of cases minus the number of expected agreements due to chance.

The formula for κ is as follows with O and E, respectively, representing the number of observed and expected agreements for each category, and T equal to the total number of judged cases.

$$\kappa = \frac{\sum O - \sum E}{T - \sum E}$$

Based on this formula, κ would equal 0 for the data in the previous matrix. This suggests that although there appears to be 75% agreement, all of this agreement is what we would expect from chance alone, based on the distribution of judged cases overall.[6]

In our own reliability work, we have found values of κ to vary quite dramatically from topic to topic as well as from one coding team to the next. As part of our coding process, we typically have two coders go through a text together to decide jointly which utterances constitute control moves. Once they have done this, however, we then have them code the identified moves separately, and afterward, we compare their work.

We have found that topics requiring relatively objective decision making, such as speaker information or sentential form, tend to produce relatively high levels of coder agreement. For example, we have had proportion agreement as high as .97 (κ = .95) for the topic field *General Sentence Type*, where coders must decide whether an utterance should be classified as a declarative, interrogative, imperative, or ellipsis. Agreement for this field generally ranges from .70 to .90 with κ's from .60 to .80. On the other hand, fields that rely to a larger extent on a coder's intuitions about language tend to reveal lower levels of reliability. For example, we have never found percent agreement for *Type of Act* to be higher than .78 (κ = .66) with agreement here ranging roughly from .60 to .70 with κ's from .50 to .60.

These differences across fields of varying degrees of subjectivity are not surprising. They do, however, emphasize the importance of doing periodic reliability checks to determine where problems lie in the coding system. These checks have helped us in the past to discover coding difficulties with such topics as *Purpose*, *Timing*, and *Cost*, and have led us to rewrite definitions, realign categories, and introduce flowcharts.

In addition to differences across topics, reliability checks have also allowed us to spot differences across pairs of coders. Some pairs, for instance,

---

[6]If coders assign categories indiscriminately, then their coding judgments should be statistically independent of one another. Using the probability rules governing independent events, we can calculate the expected number of chance agreements for any category as $(A)(B)/T$, where A and B, respectively, are the number of times a coder A and a coder B use a given category, and T equals the total number of judged cases. For the yes–no matrix, the expected number of chance agreements overall is

$$\Sigma E = \Sigma \frac{(A)(B)}{T} = \frac{(75)(100)}{100} + \frac{(25)(0)}{100} = 75$$

and Kappa equals

$$\kappa = \frac{\Sigma O - \Sigma E}{T - \Sigma E} = \frac{75 - 75}{100 - 75} = 0$$

Alternative methods for calculating κ can be found in books on nonparametric statistics (e.g., Fleiss, 1981) as well as Cohen's original article (Cohen, 1960).

consistently reveal a high level of agreement from topic to topic, whereas others are consistently low.

In general, these differences could be taken to suggest varying degrees of familiarity with the coding system involved and to indicate the importance of providing similar instructions and training experiences to all coders. In the case of the CEC, however, we believe that these differences more likely reflect a tendency among coders from different backgrounds not to view and interpret language in exactly the same way, irrespective of the amount of training they receive.

In our coding project, in fact, individuals who are assigned to the same text are often trained together, receiving the same instructions and the same practice exercises. However, these individuals often do vary in terms of their familiarity with and similarity to one another, and we have observed anecdotally that coders who are friends and who are from similar backgrounds tend to show a higher rate of agreement than coders who begin as strangers and come from different backgrounds.

This observation is not so surprising given the well-established finding that speakers who are in maximum communication as peers tend to talk alike and to share vocabulary and points of view. Because coders form a social group, the sharing of perspective and the frequency of communication between them should influence the reliability or agreement in their use of the coding vocabulary, and close friends, having had a longer association than most, would be expected to show more agreement in their coding.[7]

In addition, similarity of social background and orientation could also be expected to increase coder agreement independent of friendship, because of conceptual similarity. If reliability measures are intended to predict probable agreement for a new set of codes, reliability should be tested with a sample of unrelated strangers whose only training is reading the code itself. This would be a very stringent test. In fact, current views of coding reliability consider high reliability to be solely a reflection of the code, rather than of both the code and the specific group of coders used for the reliability assessment.

Given all this, researchers aiming at high reliability measures might be well advised either (a) to hire coders who are quite similar to one another and have an understanding of language similar to the researchers themselves or (b) to get coders from diverse backgrounds but train them to think about language in the same way that the researchers do. We offer, however, what we believe to be a more productive solution in the long run: namely, to hire coders from diverse

---

[7]The second author had a vivid experience of this type. The content coding for her dissertation had such a high reliability the faculty committee was suspicious. The reliability coder was her roommate—presumably in better rapport regarding goals and perspectives than hired coders.

backgrounds and use their different interpretations of language as an index for redefining topics and realigning categories. Such an outcome would make the code far more valid and usable across a range of cultural contexts.

4.2. Disagreements and Revision

The hope with respect to reliability, of course, is that after fine tuning a coding system, the level of coder agreement should be or be at least close to 1.00. Perfect coder agreement is so rare, however, that very high agreement arouses suspicion. Reliabilities are typically less than 1.00, and this leads us to an important question: When you do not have perfect agreement, whose codes do you include in the data base?

We have employed two solutions to resolve this dilemma. The first is one of discussion and negotiation. After coders have finished their work, all members of the coding project come together to discuss the difficult cases. The group as a whole goes over and settles on the best way to characterize these cases, and the consensus of the group is then used to decide how to identify these cases in the data base. This method is not only useful for resolving coder disagreements but also for providing another forum for identifying problems for future revisions of the coding system. By identifying the types of coding disagreements that keep recurring, we can identify which coding alternatives are the most difficult to differentiate.

When there are many disagreements, however, the group method becomes impractical, and in these instances, we employ a second, more expedient method in which we assign a third coder to the difficult cases. This third coder goes through only the difficult cases and makes a third set of coding decisions. The codes chosen by two of the three coders (the recoder and the original two) are then selected for inclusion in the data base. If it turns out that all three coders disagree on how to code a particular case, then this case is turned over to the project group, and the first method is used to resolve the disagreement.

In all such cases, it is important to keep a record of what has happened and to use the experience to improve the examples in the code and to reorganize categories.

5. APPLICATIONS

Once a data base of coded information has been assembled, the final question is how to put it to use. Assuming that the codes have been laid out in some systematic fashion, there are two possibilities here. The first is to use the codes to search for all cases of a particular type for a more qualitative examination; the second is to use them to perform statistical analyses on the relationships between coding dimensions.

5.1. Codes and Qualitative Research

Regarding searches, researchers often wish to retrieve similarly coded lines of text so that they can be systematically compared with one another. Searches with this purpose in mind can be easily accomplished by providing an index with each line of coding that identifies the line of text that corresponds to it. In the CEC, for example, we lay out our codes in single-line records with an index that identifies the location of the original line of text at the head of each record. When we wish to search for utterances of a particular type, for instance, prohibitions, we simply skim through our data base and locate all the code lines with P in the topic field *Type of Act* and then use the record index to find the corresponding prohibitions in the original transcripts.

In addition to indexing, we have also done two other things with our computerized data base. First, we have developed our own text-scanning software, labeled "textscan" (Lampert, 1986). This software allows us to specify any pattern of text and returns all lines containing these patterns. What makes this search program unique compared to others is that it allows the user to specify what topic fields to search and which code letters to match in those fields, provided that the fields are in the same fixed location from case to case. Because multiple fields can be scanned together, the program can search for and return any pattern of coded information.

To simplify searches, we have also found it useful to interleave our codes and transcripts to create computer files that contain lines of text followed by the corresponding records of coded information. The original code and transcript files are left intact for other purposes. The new files are then used for searches with textscan, which has the capability to match any line and to return up to 12 of the lines before and after the matched one. This feature allows us to recover the context in which a match occurs.

5.2. Codes and Quantitative Research

In addition to aiding searches, codes can also be used to perform statistical analyses. Currently, there are a number of statistical packages available for calculating various descriptive statistics (i.e., means, standard deviations, correlation coefficients, etc.) and performing inferential tests. Along with the Statistical Package for the Social Sciences mentioned earlier, these include the Statistical Analysis System (SAS) and the Biomedical Computer Programs-P series (BMDP).

Many of these packages require that the values for each variable appear in the same location from case to case. If a coding system assigns codes to fields with fixed locations, this does not pose a problem: Most statistical packages can read in an entire data base provided that every field's location and length are included as input for each program. In short, if a data base of codes is highly structured to begin with, it would appear that very little has to be done to prepare it for computer analysis. However, this is not necessarily the case.

Whereas an original data base may not have to be realigned for computer analysis, some reorganization is often necessary to create variables that can be meaningfully studied. Reorganization is especially needed if the researcher wishes to compare the language of different groups of people. In such a case, the researcher must have records that reflect not only which categories were used from case to case but also how many times any given individual employed a particular category.

This is a serious consideration, for once a data base has been compiled, the temptation often is to simply correlate one topic field with another. This procedure would be fine if all the data came from a single individual and all the researcher wished to do were to show relationships between variables (i.e., form and purpose) for just *one* person. However, when we wish to make statements about groups of people, we have to take into account individual differences, as the unusual behavior of just one person can distort the picture of the group as a whole. This problem is best illustrated by example.

Suppose, for instance, that we were interested in whether 4-year-olds used more hints to make requests than 3-year-olds (hints are picked up in the CEC under the topic *Explicitness*) and that we had four children at each age level with each level providing 200 coded cases. To address our research question, we could tally up and compare the total number of hints for the two groups. If we did this, we might then discover that the 3-year-olds and the 4-year-olds produced a total of 28 hints each. Such an outcome might suggest no relationship between age and hinting. However, if we inspected the data a little closer we might have discovered that although each group produced the same number of hints, each 4-year-old produced 7 hints whereas a single 3-year-old produced all 28 for the younger age group. This outcome suggests a totally different picture. In fact, if we went by the number of children who actually provided hints, we might conclude that there was an age trend (inferential tests aside).

In short, data that do not reflect individual performance can lead a researcher to conclude no group differences when differences do exist and, conversely, to claim differences when there are none at all. This problem of treating individual observations as if they each were independent of one another and came from a different person is not new to the social sciences. In fact, textbooks in behavioral statistics often admonish students not to do this and refer to this problem as the case of the inflated N (see Runyon & Haber, 1991).

A language researcher can avoid having an inflated N by simply providing separate scores for speakers across coded transcripts. In fact, it is useful to have individual speaker scores or totals for each topic area that will be analyzed. However, even individual totals are often not adequate for analysis, for these too can be artificially inflated (or deflated) in natural language research as a function of the length of observation or involvement. For example, two children may be equally likely to use indirect requests; however, because one is observed for 1 hour and the other for 2 hours, the latter may appear more likely to hint when the total number of indirect requests are finally tallied. This particular problem can, in fact, be exacerbated when longer observations occur and longer transcripts are produced for all individuals in one comparison group as opposed to those in another.

The solution to this problem is often to weight the individual totals in some fashion; that is, to create a score that reflects the number of instances for a given behavior per unit of time or some other common denominator that, in language research, could be number of utterances or turns. For instance, if we were trying to compare the frequency of hinting for two children in similar situations, observed for 1 and 2 hours, respectively, we could divide the number of hints each produced by the amount of time each was observed to obtain two scores reflecting the number of hints per hour. In this way, the length of observation can be controlled.

If each code line in a data base provides fields to identify the speaker and the amount of time the speaker was observed within a particular transcript, or a particular activity within a transcript,[8] these fields can be used to create weighted totals for individual speakers. Most statistical packages, in fact, can be programmed to create these totals without the user having to manually realign the original data.

Once individual totals have been assigned, these can then be analyzed according to age, sex, or any other subject or contextual variable. Group means and standard deviations can be calculated, and parametric and nonparametric tests (e.g., analysis of variance, Kruskal-Wallis test, Friedman test, etc.) can be performed. For further information on how to calculate statistics and carry out the various inferential tests, we suggest Hatch (1982), Hays (1988), Marascuilo and McSweeney (1977), Marascuilo and Serlin (1988) and Woods, Fletcher, and Hughes (1986).

---

[8]Providing each case with an index for the amount of time that the speaker was engaged in a current activity has the advantage of allowing the researcher the opportunity to study weighted means for any activity type. If only the length of the transcript is recorded, this would not be possible, as total time observed is likely to be longer than the time in any given activity, leading to an inaccurate weighting.

Needless to say, statistical analyses are important for uncovering relationships among variables, leading to lawlike generalizations. However, they also play an important role in the evolution of a coding system. As we have stated throughout, most coding systems are guided by either an explicit or, at least, implicit theory about language. By analyzing coded data, researchers have an opportunity to evaluate whether there is any empirical support for their original hypotheses. Sometimes these will be borne out; sometimes they will not. Lack of support, however, may suggest either that the original theory needs revision or that the coding system needs to be reorganized to be more sensitive.

In the case of the CEC, for example, our original code did not include the topic of cost. When we initially analyzed the data in terms of the relation of politeness of request to compliance, we found that there was a very strong relationship: the more polite the request, the *less* the likelihood of compliance. We realized that what we had overlooked was that both politeness and noncompliance with requests increase when what is requested is difficult, expensive, time-consuming, or valuable to the addressee. As a result, we developed the variable of cost to control for this factor and found that when cost was low to moderate, politeness was indeed unsuccessful in gaining compliance (Ervin-Tripp, Guo, & Lampert, 1990; Ervin-Tripp, O'Connor, & Rosenberg, 1984), and in fact increased refusals by most listeners, especially adults. Only high-cost requests to peers and older children were more effective if polite.

We expected that requests directed toward a superior would reveal greater deference, and for the most part, this is what we found. While doing pilot work with the cost code, however, we were further surprised to discover that, counter to our initial hypotheses, young children's directives to mothers (but not fathers) were quite direct and showed little deference. This led us to rethink the definition of cost, at least as it applied to caregivers. We eventually modified the code so that requests for things that were within the addressee's cultural role to provide were coded as having a neutral cost.

What we have hoped to illustrate by this example is that once again the code-building process does not necessarily have a specific end, but rather can be ongoing, involving revisions even during and after a phase of statistical analysis.

Coding and statistical analysis of coded material are not, of course, the only ways one can analyze verbal discourse. This type of analysis can be done either before or after qualitative studies that provide a more vivid account of specific cases and reveal more clearly the tactical choices that speakers make. Coding and statistical analysis done after qualitative studies can then provide reliable tests or confirmation of patterns found in the qualitative studies, as well as suggest additional hypotheses for further testing.

6. CONCLUSION

In this chapter, we have attempted to outline the evolution of a structured coding system for the study of natural language by taking the reader through four separate phases of the coding process: construction, implementation, evaluation, and application. We have presented some of the basic problems that researchers encounter when developing a new coding system and have offered some solutions to these problems based on our own experiences with the Control Exchange Code. We have also attempted to illustrate how many of the problems and solutions encountered in instituting and learning a code have much in common with the learning of a second language. Our hope in doing this is that we have provided not only insight into the coding process but also have offered some ideas on how to organize future coding projects.

REFERENCES

Babbie, E. (1989). *Practicing social research.* Belmont, CA: Wadsworth.

Cohen, J. (1960). A coefficient of agreement for nominal scales. *Educational and Psychological Measurement,* **20,** 37–46.

Ervin-Tripp, S. M. (1982). "Ask and it shall be given you": Children's requests. In H. Byrnes (Ed.), *Georgetown roundtable on languages and linguistics* (Vol. 35, pp. 235–245). Washington, DC: Georgetown University Press.

Ervin-Tripp, S. M. (1988a). *Control exchange code.* Berkeley: University of California, Institute of Cognitive Studies.

Ervin-Tripp, S. M. (1988b). *Interaction coding manual.* Berkeley: University of California, Institute of Cognitive Studies.

Ervin-Tripp, S. M., & Gordon, D. P. (1986). The development of children's requests. In R. E. Schiefelbusch (Ed.), *Communicative competence: Assessment and intervention* (pp. 61–96). San Diego, CA: College Hill.

Ervin-Tripp, S., Guo, J., & Lampert, M. (1990). Politeness and persuasion in children's control acts. *Journal of Pragmatics,* **14,** 307–331.

Ervin-Tripp, S., O'Connor, M. C., & Rosenberg, J. (1984). Language and power in the family. In C. Kramarae & M. Schultz (Eds.), *Language and power.* (pp. 116–135). Urbana: University of Illinois Press.

Fleiss, J. L. (1981). *Statistical methods for rates and proportions* (2nd ed.). New York: John Wiley.

Garvey, C. (1975). Requests and responses in children's speech. *Journal of Child Language,* **2,** 41–63.

Gee, J., & Savasir, I. (1985). On the use of *will* and *gonna*: Towards a description of activity-types for child language. *Discourse Processes,* **8,** 143–176.

Gordon, D., & Ervin-Tripp, S. M. (1984). The structure of children's requests. In R. E. Schiefelbusch & A. Pickar (Eds.), *The acquisition of communicative competence.* (pp. 295–321). Baltimore: University Park Press.

Hatch, E. M. (1982). *Research design and statistics for applied linguistics*. Rowley, MA: Newbury House.

Hays, W. L. (1988). *Statistics* (4th ed.). New York: Holt, Rinehart, and Winston.

Labov, W., & Fanshel, D. (1977). *Therapeutic discourse*. New York: Academic Press.

Lampert, M. (1985). *Codedit* [Computer program]. Berkeley: University of California, Institute of Cognitive Studies.

Lampert, M. (1986). *Textscan* [Computer program]. Berkeley: University of California, Institute of Cognitive Studies.

Levinson, S. C. (1983). *Pragmatics*. Cambridge: Cambridge University Press.

Marascuilo, L., & McSweeney, M. (1977). *Nonparametric and distribution-free methods for the social sciences*. Monterey, CA: Brooks/Cole.

Marascuilo, L., & Serlin, R. (1988). *Statistical methods for the social and behavioral sciences*. New York: W. H. Freeman.

McTear, M. (1985). *Children's conversations*. Oxford: Basil Blackwell.

Ninio, A., & Wheeler, P. (1984). *A manual for classifying verbal communicative acts in mother-infant interaction*. Jerusalem: Hebrew University, Martin and Vivian Leven Center.

Runyon, R. P., & Haber, A. (1991). *Fundamentals of behavioral statistics* (7th ed.). New York: McGraw-Hill.

Searle, J. (1976). A classification of illocutionary acts. *Language in Society*, **5**, 1–23.

Woods, A., Fletcher, P., & Hughes, A. (1986). *Statistics in language studies*. Cambridge: Cambridge University Press.

8
Coding Child Language Data for Crosslinguistic Analysis

Dan I. Slobin
University of California at Berkeley

1. INTRODUCTION

In carrying out crosslinguistic research, the investigator is faced with all of the issues raised in this volume, multiplied by two or more. Data in each of the languages involved in a crosslinguistic project must be transcribed, coded, and analyzed. But, in addition, the descriptive categories used in these tasks must be applicable in comparable fashion across languages. Comparability applies to both form and function. Put most simply, a researcher needs a uniform coding system that facilitates the comparison of language-specific forms with respect to common functions.

We can schematize the task as involving three broad types of information:

1. utterances and accompanying nonverbal acts, with their context (as discussed in Part I of this volume)

2. coding categories for linguistic *forms* (phonology, morphosyntax, prosody)

3. coding categories for *functions* (semantic, pragmatic)

Transcription practices in crosslinguistic studies are the same as for single-language studies, except for the possible addition of an English gloss of the utterance. In principle, the analytic categories for forms and functions should be drawn from "universal" theories, applicable to any and all studies. In practice, though, special care must be paid to ensure comparability across languages within the study at hand. Ideally, of course, all single-language studies would be comparably coded as well, allowing for future crosslinguistic comparisons.   However, we are far from the sort of theoretical and methodological consensus that would allow for such easy comparative use of data from different studies.   Thus, a central challenge of crosslinguistic research is to arrive at codes for forms and functions that "mean the same thing" for each language of the study. This is as true of formal analysis as it is of functional analysis.

The "grain" of coding is determined by the goals of the investigation. For example, suppose one were interested in studying the acquisition of casemarking in Russian and Turkish, and that one were concerned only with the semantics of case categories. For such an analysis, it would be irrelevant to code for phonological form or for language-specific features (e.g., *gender* and *number*, which figure in Russian, but not in Turkish). Thus, for such a project, the relevant form category would be simply the case category (e.g., *accusative*). Depending on the goals of the study, formal coding of other parts of the utterance might also be necessary (e.g., *person, tense, aspect, modality*). However, note that overcoding is time-consuming and expensive and should be carefully avoided. The level of coding can always be made more fine-grained on a second pass, if additional features turn out to be important.

For function-level analyses in this hypothetical project, one would have to devise a coding scheme based on the semantic categories that are of theoretical interest to the study, being sure that these categories can be determined independently of the language of the utterance and of the form of the utterance within each language. Depending on the goals of the study, such a category might be as general as *count noun* or as specific as *movable object currently under child's control*. It is important that such categories be assignable to nouns that are both properly and improperly casemarked in the utterance, for without an independent way of assessing form and function it is impossible to study their interaction in development. Thus, it would be uninformative, for example, to code every noun with an accusative inflection as having *accusative* case form and as *patient* function, with no independent means of identifying "patient," other than by the form of the utterance.

There are no established guidelines that a new researcher can refer to in establishing form and function codes for crosslinguistic research. Essentially, codes are tailor-made for particular studies, within the frameworks of particular theories. Unpublished coding manuals are available for various projects and can generally be obtained from the investigators.[1]   Rather than summarize entire coding systems here, I briefly present several case studies, drawn from investigations based at the Child Language Research Laboratory in

---

[1]Projects at Berkeley have developed such manuals over the past 30 years. Details are available from project directors: Susan Ervin-Tripp (Department of Psychology), Lily Wong Fillmore (School of Education), Alison Gopnik (Department of Psychology), and Dan I. Slobin (Department of Psychology)—all at the University of California, Berkeley, CA 94720, USA.

Berkeley. The first set of examples focuses on *functions* (the semantics of locative relations and temporal contours), seeking to relate them to the acquisition and use of *forms* (prepositions, postpositions, tense/aspect inflections). The second set of examples focuses on a single class of forms (relative clause), seeking functional explanations of crosslinguistic differences in its development and use. All of the issues raised below will be familiar to linguists who carry out comparative and typological studies; people from other disciplines can find theoretical orientation in such works as Comrie (1981), Croft (1990), Dahl (1985), Hawkins (1983), and Mallinson and Blake (1981).

2. FROM FUNCTION TO FORM

2.1. Locative Elicitation in English, Italian, Serbo-Croatian, and Turkish

Johnston and Slobin (1979) examined the development of a collection of locative notions in a sample of languages, with the following theoretical aim: "[W]e expect to be able to account for sequences of the development of linguistic forms on the basis of two interacting classes of variables: (1) *conceptual* development and (2) degree of difficulty of *linguistic* processing" (p. 529). Children aged 2;0–4;8 were presented with the task of describing arrays of objects that were constructed to tap particular locative relations. Accordingly, the codes for form consisted of the relevant locative expressions in each of the languages; and for function, codes were simply an indication of the locative features on each of the object arrays. The arrays were designed to embody spatial arrangements of increasing conceptual complexity, from containment and support (e.g., 'in', 'on') to projective relations (e.g., 'front', 'back'). Four languages were used, contrasting in the grammar of locative expressions: prepositions (English, Italian, Serbo-Croatian) versus postpositions (Turkish), non-inflectional (English, Italian) versus inflectional (Serbo-Croatian, Turkish), and several other features.

One dependent variable was the number of locative arrays that were described appropriately by a child. In all four languages, it was found that children in each successively older age group produced more appropriate locative expressions than those in the previous group, thus showing a general crosslinguistic developmental trend. However, it was also found that children learning Turkish or Italian produced more different locative expressions at each age than those learning English or Serbo-Croatian. We will return to this crosslinguistic difference.

Another dependent variable was order of acquisition of encoding of locative notions, as measured by the percentage of children at each age who appropriately encoded each notion. A common developmental order of groups of concepts was found across languages, indicating cognitive "pacesetting" of development (from topological notions to projective notions), with some crosslinguistic variation within conceptual groups (e.g., terms for 'back' were acquired earlier than terms for 'front' in all of the languages except English).

In order to account for fine-grained differences between languages in developmental patterns, it was necessary to enrich the formal analysis, doing additional coding for dimensions on which the languages differ. It appeared that several factors function to increase the "processing load" of locative terms, and that such dimensions interact in complex fashion to determine the acquisition of linguistic means to express each of the locative notions in the study. Relevant factors include:

Synonymity: For example, English has two terms, *behind* and *in back of*, where Italian has one, *dietro a*.

Morphological Complexity: English *in back of* is morphologically complex in comparison with *behind*.

Clear Etymology: English *in back of* contains the body-part term *back*, whereas *behind* is probably morphologically opaque to preschoolers.

Position: Postpositions are more perceptible than prepositions.

Coding for these factors of processing load made it possible to account for the overall developmental advantage of Italian and Turkish in this sample, as well as for detailed developmental differences among the four languages in order of acquisition of terms for particular concepts.

Finally, an additional aspect of development was revealed by an examination of *inappropriate* uses of locatives. Correct use of a locative term was frequently preceded by substitutions and circumlocutions using known linguistic forms. Such "old forms expressing new functions" (Slobin, 1973) were especially evident in attempts to describe an array in which the target item was located between two reference items. For example, children frequently described an object between two blocks as *beside the blocks* or *in the blocks*. Coding such responses for locative features indicates that the child has correctly encoded the plurality of the referent objects (*blocks*) and a general relation of adjacency (*beside*) or containment (*in*), before having acquired *between*, which expresses the relationship in a single term.

The analyses of processing load and substitutions demonstrate ways in which analysis can lead to new details of coding—Function-level coding in the first instance, Form-level coding in the second. The overall study indicates the role of form and function coding in the application of a simple experimental paradigm across languages. The linguistic data in this case were limited to prepositional or postpositional phrases. Similar issues arise in the coding of more extended speech data.

2.2. Narrative Elicitation in English, German, Hebrew, Spanish, & Turkish

Berman, Slobin, and co-investigators elicited narratives from children and adults in a number of languages, using Mercer Mayer's *Frog, Where Are You?*, a wordless picture book about a boy searching for his lost frog (Berman & Slobin, 1987, 1993; Slobin, 1987, 1990a, 1991a, 1991b). In these studies, the linguistic data consisted of extended narrative texts, sharing a common set of participants, situations, and plotline. Detailed coding was carried out, following a coding manual designed for English, German, Hebrew, Spanish, and Turkish—and potentially applicable to all languages (Berman & Slobin, 1986).

The first decision on data organization dealt with the unit of analysis. Because our interest was in narrative organization, with particular focus on expressions of temporality, we chose the *clause* as the basic unit of analysis, defined as "any grammatical unit which contains a predicate." This unit was defined in a manner that could be applied to the diverse range of language types in our sample (Indo-European, Semitic, Turkic), with an eye to issues of narrative structure. The manual offers the following basic definition:

> We define a clause as any unit that contains a *unified* predicate. By *unified*, we mean a predicate that expresses a *single* situation (activity, event, state). Predicates include finite and nonfinite verbs, as well as predicate adjectives. In general, clauses will be comprised of a single verbal element; however, infinitives and participles which function as complements of modal or aspectual verbs are included with the matrix verb as single clauses—e.g., *want to go, started walking*. These matrix verbs plus modifiers should not be confused with utterances that clearly express two "situations," as in subordinate complement clauses—e.g., *I thought that I would go.* As illustration, each of the following phrases would be analyzed as a single clause with a unified predicate: *running through the woods, taken by surprise, (in order) to help his friends, was angry*.
>
> In general, then, treat as a single clause those utterances that have two verbs but one subject, and treat as two separate clauses cases when each verb has a different subject—e.g., *I want to go* vs. *I want you to go*. (Berman & Slobin, 1986, p. 37)

These conventions can be used in segmenting any kind of continuous text. An additional convention was added for purposes of *narrative* analysis, since our focus was on clauses that function to advance a narrative:

> Predicates that are clearly narrator-comments are kept with the matrix verb in a single predicate—e.g., *I assume that the boy is happy.* / *It appears that the dog is going to fall.* These phrases constitute one clause with the main verb coded under *V: Verb Form* and the comment noted under *M: Modality* (usually Inferential).

The manual provides the following examples of clause types, following these definitions (each line represents a separate clause):

Single Clause Examples:

Single clause with two verbs and one subject:

He stopped running.
They had begun to search all over.

Single clause with different subjects (narrator comments):

I think the boy misses the frog.
It appears that the frog is happy.

Two Clause Examples:

Subordinate complements, same subject NP:

He thought
he could get the bees.
He said
he would find the frog.

Subordinate complements, different subject NP:

He decided
that it was an owl.
He told the dog
to be quiet.

In addition, rules had to be provided for special cases, based on the grammars of particular languages. For example, copular sentences in Hebrew and Turkish have zero-expression of the copula in the present tense. Such sentences are coded as separate clauses. Gapping and ellipsis in a language like English require special treatment:

Treat as separate clauses strings in which the verb is lacking due to grammatical reductions such as gapping and where the verb semantics is fully recoverable from the text, or structures which can be analyzed as clauses where the copula has been deleted.

The boy looked in his boots
and the dog in the jar.
With the frog not there
the boy felt very upset.
He began searching for the frog
and the dog too.   (p. 38)

With regard to functional coding, the manual provides for a variety of plot-level categories dealing with such issues as sequentiality/simultaneity of events, foregrounding/backgrounding, and expressions of contingency, causality, and motivation. These will not concern us here. The most basic content-oriented coding indicated the picture in the story to which each clause applied. This made it possible to search for various formal features with respect to the narrative scene to which they referred.

As an example, consider tense/aspect marking of clauses that refer to the same scene across languages and ages (detailed in Slobin 1987, 1991a). One of the pictures depicts two simultaneous events, one *completed* and the other *in progress*: a boy who has fallen from a tree while a dog runs past, chased by bees. Beginning with this functional (semantic) characterization, we can examine the tense/aspect forms of the verbs in the clauses that encode these two events. English and Spanish allow for distinctive aspectual marking of an event as "progressive," and Spanish, in addition, contrasts "perfective" and "imperfective" events. German and Hebrew do not provide such grammatical marking of aspect on the verb. We were interested in learning if narrators are guided by the aspectual contrasts in their grammars while narrating this scene. Specifically, would the two clauses have the same or different tense/aspect marking of their verbs? German and Hebrew speakers have the option of encoding the completed event in the past and the ongoing event in the present (e.g., 'the boy fell down and the dog runs away') or marking the ongoing event with some sort of adverbial repetition (e.g., 'the boy fell down and the dog ran faster and faster'). English and Spanish speakers also have the option of using a simple verb form in both clauses, as in German and Hebrew (e.g., 'the boy fell down and the dog ran away'). We searched for descriptions of the bee picture and counted the narrators who used the same verb form in both clauses. The figures are presented in Table 8.1.

Looking at the overall figures, it is evident that Hebrew and German speakers tend to use the same form about three-quarters of the time, whereas English and Spanish speakers tend to use different forms about three-quarters

TABLE 8.1

Percentage of Narrators Using Same Tense/Aspect Form for *Fall* and *Run* Clauses in Tree/Bee Scene

	Preschool (Ages 3-5)	School (Age 9)	Adult	Overall
Hebrew	71	100	63	78
German	54	80	78	71
English	26	22	33	27
Spanish	23	18	0	21

of the time, thus indicating that they are guided by their languages in the attention that they pay to temporal contrasts between events. The fact that these figures are not 100% or 0% indicates that some speakers do take nonstandard options in each language, showing that they are not completely bound by language-specific grammatical options. The developmental data show these tendencies to hold at all ages, with some crosslinguistic developmental differences that need not concern us here.

The purpose of this small example from an extended study is to show how one can go from a uniform Function-level task definition to language-specific Form-level analysis. The uniform coding of functions is determined by the picture in the story and a language-neutral characterization of the temporal contours of the two events. The crosslinguistic comparison of linguistic forms is made possible by a uniform segmentation across languages into clauses, and language-specific coding of verb forms for tense and aspect and adverbial expressions—within a uniform linguistic approach to the marking of temporality.

3. FROM FORM TO FUNCTION

In the second half of this chapter we focus on a single grammatical form, the relative clause, searching for functional correlates of differing acquisition patterns across languages.

3.1. Relative Clauses in English and Turkish Conversation

English and Turkish relative clauses differ radically in their surface syntax and morphology and can only be compared within an overarching grammatical framework that provides for functional relations between clauses of varying surface forms. This, of course, is a prerequisite to all crosslinguistic and typological research. For example, Comrie (1981) compares English and Turkish relative clauses, using the following example:

Hasan-ın Sinan-a ver-diğ-i patates-i yedim.
Hasan-of Sinan-to give-NOMINALIZATION-his potato-ACCUSATIVE I-ate.
'I ate the potato that Hasan gave to Sinan'.

He points out how different these two structures are:

The verb form *ver-diğ-* is a non-finite form of the verb *ver* 'give', with the nominalizing suffix *-diğ*; like other nominalized verb forms in Turkish, it requires its subject (*Hasan*) in the genitive and the appropriate possessive suffix (here *-i* 'his') on the verb noun. Thus a literal translation of the head noun and relative clause *Hasanın Sinana verdigi patates* would be 'the potato of Hasan's giving to Sinan'. (p. 135)

However, in order to study the development of comparable forms across languages, one must compare them in broader terms. Comrie goes on to note:

> In English traditional grammar, the term clause is often restricted to constructions with a finite verb, so in terms of this definition the Turkish construction is not a clause, therefore not a relative clause. However, this terminology simply reflects a general property of English syntax: subordination is carried out primarily by means of finite clauses; whereas in Turkish subordination is in general by means of non-finite constructions. The claim found in some discussions of Turkish that Turkish does not have relative clauses is thus in one sense correct, but from a wider perspective, it is clear that the Turkish construction illustrated [above] fulfills precisely the same function as the English relative clause: thus, in its restrictive interpretation, there is a head noun *patates* 'potato', and the relative clause restricts the potential reference of that head noun by telling us which particular potato (the one that Hasan gave to Sinan) is at issue. *The lesson of this comparison is thus that we need a functional (semantic, cognitive) definition of relative clause, on the basis of which we can then proceed to compare relative clauses across languages, neglecting language-specific differences in our over-all definition of relative clause. . . .* [emphasis added]. (p. 136)

Using such a definition of relative clause (the details are not relevant here), one can identify such clauses in both English and Turkish transcripts. When one does so (Slobin, 1986), one finds that relative clauses are far less frequent in Turkish speech than in English—in child speech, in adult speech to children, and in speech between adults. At this point, language-specific details enter the analysis. It appears that morphosyntactic facts account for a heavy processing cost in producing relative clauses in Turkish, apparently decreasing their utility. In addition, because Turkish is a verb-final language, relative clauses precede their head noun, which limits their usefulness in providing additional information about a new participant in narrative. For example, in the narratives discussed above, English-speaking children often begin the story by introducing a protagonist and adding information in a relative clause, such as: *There was a boy that caught a frog.* It would be awkward to begin a Turkish narrative with: 'A having-caught a frog boy there was', because the boy has not yet been introduced.

Once we have accounted for the relative infrequency of a construction in a language, we can go on to ask what happens to the functions that can be fulfilled by that form in such a language. With regard to the tense/aspect contrast discussed above, we found that Hebrew and German speakers simply make fewer references to the completed/ongoing distinction between events in their narratives. It is unlikely, however, that Turkish speakers have less of a need to restrict the potential range of referents of a noun (the basic function of relative clauses). Armed with a functional definition of relative clauses, we can then search Turkish transcripts for alternative constructions that perform the same function.

Note the cycling between function and form. We began with a functional definition that allowed us to compare English finite subordinate clauses with Turkish nonfinite subordinate clauses. Comparing these forms in English and Turkish, we found the Turkish forms to be less frequent, for various functional reasons (processing load, order of information flow). We now return to the functional definition, asking whether other construction types perform a similar function in Turkish. And here we find a frequent construction, in both child and adult speech, that serves to identify referents. It is a sort of periphrastic or elaborated version of a relative clause, in which the qualifying information is bracketed by two discourse particles, *hani* and *ya*. For example, in a conversation between a 3-year-old and an adult visitor, the child wants to describe his parents' bed as similar to the one he has seen in the visitor's house. In English he might say, *It's like the big bed that's in your house.* Avoiding a complex relative clause construction, the Turkish child says the equivalent of, '*Hani* there's a big bed in your house *ya*—it's like that one' (something like: *Y'know, there's a big bed in your house? Well, it's like that one.*). Now we can cycle through our transcripts again, looking for the variety of means used by both Turkish- and English-speaking children to introduce qualifying information into discourse, using a crosslinguistically applicable functional definition. In so doing, we arrive at a "family of construction types" (Slobin, 1991b) that perform a common function, thereby enriching our understanding of the interactive development of form and function.

3.2. Relative Clauses in Spanish, English, and German Narratives

In the elicited narrative study described above, it is possible to do a fine-grained analysis of developmental differences in the use of relative clauses in languages that are typologically similar. Lisa Dasinger and Cecile Toupin (Dasinger, 1990; Slobin, 1990b; Toupin & Dasinger, 1993) found striking differences in the frequency of use of relative clauses in Spanish, English, and German, as shown in Table 8.2.

TABLE 8.2
Percentage of Narrators Using at Least One Relative Clause

| Language | Age | | | | |
	3	4	5	9	Adult
Spanish	50	50	55	92	100
English	17	42	25	50	100
German	8	no data	17	50	92

Throughout childhood, Spanish is in advance of English, and English is in advance of German, and even in the adult sample, fewer Germans use relative clauses in their stories. Here the issue is not one of acquisition: The form is acquired by age 3 or younger in all three languages. Rather, Toupin and Dasinger found intersecting factors of linguistic complexity and narrative function which may account for the crosslinguistic differences in narrative use. Again, this is not the place to present the details of their findings. Of relevance here is rather the manner in which their use of coding helped bring out this pattern in the data.

Form-level coding in these studies isolated a number of formal features that point to processing factors. Spanish has an all-purpose relativizer, *que* 'that', making no distinctions of number, gender, case, or animacy. English provides *who*, *that*, and *which*, allowing *that* to be used for both animates and inanimates. German is most complex, with a set of forms that mark number, gender, case, and animacy. In addition, English and German have syntactically conditioned word-order changes in the subordinate clause. Coding for formal features thus suggests that the frequency of use shown in Table 8.2 may be partly determined by processing load.

Toupin and Dasinger went on to Function-level issues, asking whether the differences in frequency of use were also reflected in differences between the languages in the development of discourse functions of relative clauses. This required construction of codes for such functions. It was found, across languages, that the earliest functions were to name and describe participants in the story, followed by their reidentification. Other narrative functions of relative clauses developed later, reflecting more sophisticated narrative organization (e.g., motivating or enabling the main clause event, providing anticipatory information from the narrator's perspective of a later event, summing up previous events).

Overall, then, there was a parallel development in the functions of relative clauses—across all five languages of the study. However, the processing ease and frequency of use of relative clauses in Spanish may lead Spanish speakers to use these constructions for two particular functions at an earlier age: to *motivate* or *enable* actions (e.g., 'there was something that wanted to eat the boy' [age 3;11]) and to *continue* the narrative (e.g., 'an owl came out that threw the boy (down)' [age 5;4]). Detailed functional coding of a given form thus reveals crosslinguistic developmental patterns in each function of that form. Toupin and Dasinger conclude that such patterns are an integral part of language development:

> Factors such as morphosyntactic complexity, the relationship between form and function, system influences, and alternatives for expressing various functions within a language, all interact in determining the course of acquisition of a particular form. Such an approach demonstrates that language

development includes more than just the grammar of one's language (in this case the relative clause construction), where grammar includes syntax, semantics, morphology, and phonology. In addition to the above, language development involves an increasing capacity to express what language is and can be used for, and this aspect of language development (as the analysis of the development of the functions of relative clauses shows), continues throughout childhood and perhaps throughout adulthood. *Interestingly, what linguists classify as a particular construction type does not always function in the same ways or to the same extent in all languages. Such findings strongly point to the need for functional analyses of constructions as well* [emphasis added]. (Dasinger, 1990, p. 42)

This conclusion is an appropriate final word to this chapter, emphasizing the need for crosslinguistic researchers to attend to both form and function in coding, analyzing, and theorizing about language in general and child language development in particular.

REFERENCES

Berman, R. A., & Slobin, D. I. (1986). *Coding manual: Temporality in discourse.* Berkeley: University of California, Institute of Cognitive Studies.

Berman, R. A., & Slobin, D. I. (1987). *Five ways of learning how to talk about events: A crosslinguistic study of children's narratives.* (Tech. Rep. No. 46). Berkeley: University of California, Institute of Cognitive Studies.

Berman, R. A., & Slobin, D. I. (Eds.). (1993). *Different ways of relating events in narrative: A crosslinguistic developmental study.* Hillsdale, NJ: Lawrence Erlbaum Associates.

Comrie, B. (1981). *Language universals and linguistic typology: Syntax and morphology.* Chicago: University of Chicago Press.

Croft, W. (1990). *Typology and universals.* Cambridge: Cambridge University Press.

Dahl, Ö. (1985). *Tense and aspect systems.* Oxford: Basil Blackwell.

Dasinger, L. K. (1990). *Towards a functional approach to the acquisition of language: A crosslinguistic study of the development of the functions of relative clauses in narrative.* Unpublished manuscript, University of California at Berkeley, Department of Psychology.

Hawkins, J. A. (1983). *Word order universals.* New York: Academic.

Johnston, J. R., & Slobin, D. I. (1979). The development of locative expressions in English, Italian, Serbo-Croatian and Turkish. *Journal of Child Language, 6,* 529–545.

Mallinson, G., & Blake, B. J. (1981). *Language typology: Cross-linguistic studies in syntax.* Amsterdam: North-Holland.

Slobin, D. I. (1973). Cognitive prerequisites for the development of grammar. In C. A. Ferguson & D. I. Slobin (Eds.), *Studies of child language development* (pp. 175–208). New York: Holt, Rinehart and Winston.

Slobin, D. I. (1986). The acquisition and use of relative clauses in Turkic and Indo-European languages. In D. I. Slobin & K. Zimmer (Eds.), *Studies in Turkish linguistics* (pp. 273–294). Amsterdam: John Benjamins.

Slobin, D. I. (1987). Thinking for speaking. In J. Aske, N. Beery, L. Michaelis, & H. Filip (Eds.), *Berkeley Linguistics Society: Proceedings of the Thirteenth Annual Meeting* (pp. 435–444). Berkeley: Berkeley Linguistics Society.

Slobin, D. I. (1990a). The development from child speaker to native speaker. In J. W. Stigler, G. Herdt, & R. A. Shweder (Eds.), *Cultural psychology: Essays on comparative human development* (pp. 233–256). Cambridge: Cambridge University Press.

Slobin, D. I. (1990b). *Factors of language typology in the crosslinguistic study of acquisition.* (Tech. Rep. No. 66). Berkeley: University of California, Institute of Cognitive Studies.

Slobin, D. I. (1991a). Learning to think for speaking: Native language, cognition, and rhetorical style. *Pragmatics, 1,* 7–26.

Slobin, D. I. (1991b). Passives and alternatives in children's narratives in English, Spanish, German, and Turkish. In B. Fox & P. Hopper (Eds.), *Voice.* Amsterdam: John Benjamins.

Toupin, C., & Dasinger, L. K. (1993). Using relative clauses. In R. A. Berman & D. I. Slobin (Eds.), *Different ways of relating events in narrative: A crosslinguistic developmental study.* Hillsdale, NJ: Lawrence Erlbaum Associates.

9

Representing Hierarchy: Constituent Structure for Discourse Databases

John W. Du Bois
University of California at Santa Barbara

Stephan Schuetze-Coburn
University of California at Los Angeles

1. INTRODUCTION

A major focus of current linguistic research is language in use. For linguists who come to this study with a long-standing interest in grammatical structure, the question that presents itself is: How do structure and use—or grammar and discourse—coexist and coevolve? Within this domain of inquiry are subsumed a host of specific research questions, having to do with, for example, how much new information a clause can hold, whether noun phrases in specific grammatical roles tend to correlate with specific discourse-pragmatic statuses, and so on.

But a new kind of problem immediately confronts the linguist who has so recently escaped the artificial world where isolated, often freakish, sentences are accompanied by neatly drawn structural diagrams, all carefully selected to exemplify isolated aspects of a theory fragment. In discourse, isolation is nowhere to be found. Grammar is just one of the things that is happening, coexisting not only with different kinds of features (semantic, pragmatic, phonological, etc.) but even with different dimensions of hierarchical structure (grammatical, prosodic, rhetorical, etc.), whose unit boundaries may or may not coincide. Even within the domain of grammar, the cohesive relationships exhibited across large distances mean that the sheer bulk of material encompassed within a grammatical structure becomes problematic. And the grammatical structures, whether large or small, are not cut to fit whatever theoretical point one is currently making. All of this raises questions both practical and theoretical about how to deal with linguistic material of such size, complexity, and intrinsic integrity. Can it be studied? Should one retreat to the neater, safer, more comfortable and more malleable enterprise of sentence solitaire? Or should one rather ignore hierarchical constituent structure altogether and approach discourse as a soup of loose features, which perhaps correlate with each other somehow?

Fortunately, there are ways, we believe, to take grammar in discourse seriously. Discourse-oriented linguists deserve the chance to address the fundamental questions about why grammars are as they are, which the grammarians' theories have left unexamined. If the study of discourse is to contribute to a general theory of language, the specific domains of grammar, prosody, and so on must be taken as integral parts of, rather than complementaries to, any truly general theory of discourse. Discourse research must embrace hierarchical grammatical structure, to the extent that it is actually present as a genuine phenomenon within speech and to the extent that it interacts with all the other features that are necessarily brought into relation to it in any actual token of language use.

This orientation has led us to ask how we can represent the grammatical phenomena contained in a stretch of discourse, in such a way as to allow them to be studied in relation to other phenomena copresent in the discourse. In this chapter we focus specifically on the problem of grammatical constituency. But it should be clear that we are equally interested in the other things going on at the same time in discourse and that many of the analytical techniques that we outline here can be extended to other dimensions of discourse. Representing grammatical constituency is just one thrust in a many-pronged program that seeks to probe semantic, pragmatic, sociocultural and even phonological aspects of discourse (Du Bois, 1985, 1987; Du Bois, Schuetze-Coburn, Cumming, & Paolino, this volume; Du Bois & Thompson, forthcoming; Schuetze-Coburn, 1987; Schuetze-Coburn, Shapley, & Weber, 1991).

2. CONTEXT, HIERARCHY, AND COMPUTATIONAL TOOLS

Discourse researchers typically must manage vast amounts of linguistic material in a systematic way. This material consists not only of great expanses of textual material,[1] but of the accompanying analyses in terms of relevant grammatical, semantic, pragmatic, cognitive, and interactional features, which in general must be coded and linked to specific elements in the texts.

---

[1] The term *text* as used here encompasses in principle the spoken interaction's total symbolic realization and is certainly not to be confused with words on the printed page. Although this paper is primarily concerned with properties represented in the auditory dimensions of the text (e.g., prosody), the principles outlined could be extended to other dimensions as well.

Obviously, any analysis of a large body of data exhibiting such complex interrelationships stands to benefit greatly from efficient computational tools. Yet the user who begins to explore the computer's possibilities in this area may at first be put off by an apparently rigid structure that bids to impose constraints on the organization of the data, in ways that do not adequately respond to the fluidity and richness of discourse.   Although powerful microcomputers have made computer-assisted processing of linguistic data a common practice, discourse researchers who are not programmers have in many cases felt themselves obliged to "make do" with word processors, flat file managers, and other computer programs not specifically designed to meet the challenges of linguistic structure.   Although specialized software for language research has been available on mainframes since the 1970s, only recently have text retrieval, interlinear text processing, and concordance-making programs been (re)written for personal computers. Software packages of this sort now stand to contribute much to the systematic study of language.[2] For example, a concordance program offers the analyst a powerful tool for accessing immediate context: It can find all the unique word and morpheme types in a body of texts and, for each type, present all its tokens with a specified amount of the preceding and following text.   This makes a linguistically sophisticated concordance program probably the most effective tool there is for exploring new data, especially if the language is previously unstudied or if the investigator is new to the language.[3] The concordance's flexible approach to text files, which can be easily updated—and then immediately reconcordanced—as the investigator's understanding of the language under study grows, cannot be matched by any existing database system.

But linguists accustomed to operating with the powerful concepts of *context* and *hierarchy* in syntactic and discourse studies are likely to find that most of the readily available computational tools require some modification if they are to rise to the challenge of handling the fully elaborated data relationships implied by these terms. Because "key-word-in-context" concordances typically measure their context simply in characters before and characters after the item in question (or in lines before and lines after), something more is needed if one is to have access to a concept such as *constituent*, so familiar and so powerful for linguistic analysis. Whereas a simple tally of word tokens, for

---

[2] Such programs available on microcomputers include KWIC-MAGIC (Kenneth Whistler, available from Dr. LST: Software, 545 33rd St., Richmond, CA 94804-1535, USA), IT and Shoebox (Summer Institute of Linguistics), WordCruncher (Electronic Text Corporation, Provo, UT), CLAN (CHILDES) (Brian MacWhinney, Psychology Dept., Carnegie-Mellon University, Pittsburgh, PA), the Oxford Concordance Program (Oxford University Press), SALT, and so on.

[3] Among the most linguistically sophisticated concordance programs available is KWIC-MAGIC, a very powerful and linguistically versatile discourse research tool developed by Kenneth Whistler for IBM-compatible microcomputers (see footnote 2).

example, may supply a general characterization of a text, without contextual information about the tokens' relation to the larger fabric of discourse, little more than a sketch can be achieved. A count of the nouns in a text may provide a rough indication of lexical density, but it is only when the relationship of noun phrases to each other and to other elements in the linguistic environment have been taken into account that one can start to draw richer conclusions about such issues as clausal complexity and syntactic relations or about their systematic information flow correlates.

If one could expand the concordance concept to allow reference to constituent structure, this would be a powerful tool. Promising developments in this direction have indeed begun to blossom in recent years, as evidenced in the elaboration of new tools for creating computerized "tree-banks," or syntactically analyzed corpora of discourse data. Among the most important such discourse-oriented projects are the TOSCA project reported in Aarts and van den Heuvel (1985) and Aarts and Oostdijk (1988),[4] the CLAWS project reported in Garside, Leech and Sampson (1987), and the spoken discourse-oriented[5] TESS project reported in Svartvik (1990a, 1990b, 1990c).

What is wanted is a tool that will allow the discourse analyst to represent structure not only in the grammatical dimension but also in the other dimensions that interact with grammar and that will allow the units represented to be coded for various features in diverse dimensions. If one can take a text, read it into a database, and assign particular feature values efficiently to individual constituents, it then becomes feasible to ask linguistically sophisticated questions regarding correlation of the text's structural units with its features in other discourse dimensions. To this end, we have adapted a commercially available relational database program in order to create a flexible framework for representing facts about context and hierarchy in explicit relationship to other discourse features. As we have from the outset sought to balance the demands of keeping track of syntactic hierarchy with those of keeping track of a broad array of discourse-pragmatic and semantic features, our proposals are not so much directed toward parsing per se as toward illustrating the benefits that can be derived from an effective computer-

---

[4] The LDB/TOSCA program for creating and managing syntactically analyzed discourse databases is available for IBM-compatible microcomputers (as well as mainframe and Unix computers) from: Prof. Jan Aarts, Department of Language and Speech, University of Nijmegen, Nijmegen, The Netherlands.

[5] The goals of syntactic text-base construction and automatic parsing are even more formidable for spoken discourse than for written. With notable exceptions such as Svartvik's TESS project (1990a), it is written discourse alone that is studied by most parsing projects. One challenge that traditional parsing confronts especially in spoken discourse concerns the dichotomy between "grammatical" and "ungrammatical" utterances—a distinction that tends to blur in spoken discourse but is generally necessary to make a grammar-parser operational (see Sampson, 1987a, p. 222).

aided strategy for syntactically aware discourse research. Given that we were concerned to recognize the hierarchical nature of discourse without transforming it into a computational problem, we have heeded the maxim, "design complexity breeds coder perplexity"[6] and hence put a high value on simplicity.

3. TREES, BRACKETS, AND CONVERSATION

A means of representing hierarchical structure is an integral feature of any syntactic theory. Often, the representational conventions function not only to facilitate visually the comprehension of a given structure but also to constrain the theory itself. The best known of these conventions is the phrase-marker, or tree diagram. Figure 9.1 shows a standard tree diagram of a brief conversational exchange between two speakers.[7]

Alongside most of these representational systems, notational variants have been developed that permit the linguist to conveniently convey a hierarchical structure, or any portion thereof, in a completely linear fashion. One such system is labeled bracketing. At first, its use was perhaps most often motivated by typographical convenience, at the behest of journal editors concerned about the high cost of printing diagrams. But with increasing exploitation of computers in linguistic research, the importance of linear means for representing constituency has grown substantially, and its appeal has extended beyond the practical requirements of publishing. Currently, little software exists that will allow easy manipulation of the graphic representations that so aptly depict hierarchical relationships on paper.[8] On the other hand, pure labeled bracketing—although workable in theory—cannot be considered an attractive option for the discourse analyst for a variety of reasons. Even syntacticians and computational linguists often find it too unwieldy to keep straight: Without an automatic bracket-balancing mechanism, one can suffer

---

[6] A common complaint about the manual tagging phases of grammatically oriented corpus projects focuses on the "unreliability" of such coding (e.g., Keulen, 1986, p. 133). Whereas placing simultaneous demands for high consistency and high productivity on coders can indeed lead to difficulty, system design can make all the difference: Efficiency and clarity in the interface are just as important as computational practicality. A carefully planned coding system, crafted with the limitations of manual coding in mind—for example, avoiding category tags consisting of short strings of arbitrary, non-mnemonic alphanumeric sequences—can function highly reliably (see Du Bois & Thompson, forthcoming; Du Bois, Cumming, & Schuetze-Coburn, 1988).

[7] This and all other examples in this chapter are taken from natural conversations that we and our associates have recorded and transcribed. The examples are presented here in a fairly broad transcription for ease of reading; narrow transcriptions for most of the English examples can be found in Du Bois, Schuetze-Coburn, Cumming, & Paolino (1991).

[8] But see the displays of Aarts and van den Heuvel (1985) and Sampson (1987b).

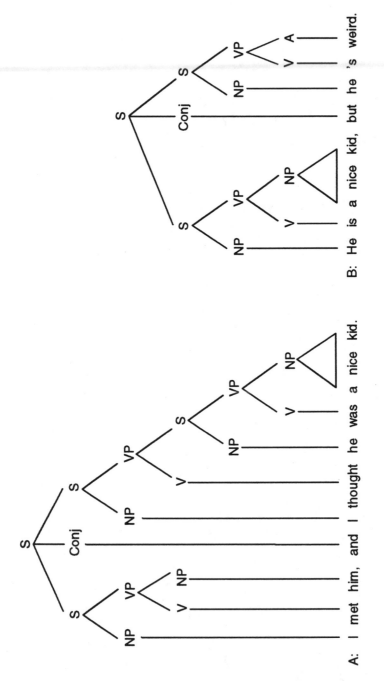

FIG. 9.1. Tree diagram of constituency in a simple conversational exchange.

endless frustration in trying to match up the pairs.   More importantly, the structure which is so effectively displayed in Fig. 9.1, when reduced linearly to bracketing, becomes virtually unreadable.

(1) ((Forces))

A: $[_S[_S[_{NP}$I$]$ $[_{VP}[_V$met$]$ $[_{NP}$him,$]]]$ $[_C$and$]$ $[_S[_{NP}$I$]$ $[_{VP}[_V$thought$]$ $[_S[_{NP}$he$]$ $[_{VP}[_V$was$]$ $[_{NP}$a nice kid.$]]]]]]$

B: $[_S[_S[_{NP}$He$]$ $[_{VP}[_V$is$]$ $[_{NP}$a nice kid,$]]]$ $[_C$but$]$ $[_S[_{NP}$he$]$ $[_{VP}[_V$'s$]$ $[_{ADJ}$weird.$]]]]$

This is true whether the brackets are labeled, as in (1), or unlabeled, as in (2):

(2) ((Forces))

A: [[[I] [[met] [him]]] [and] [[I] [[thought] [[he] [[was] [a nice kid.]]]]]]

B: [[[He] [[is] [a nice kid]]] [but] [[he] [['s] [weird.]]]]

And this conversational exchange is about as simple as they come. Natural conversations abound in exchanges that look far more intimidating and confusing in a traditional bracket notation; imagine a whole free-wheeling multiparty conversation represented in this way.   There are just too many symbols introduced into the text, in either version of bracketing, for the analyst to absorb without suffering visual overload.[9] To be sure, no system can avoid a certain amount of conflict between aesthetics (what is "readable" by the human analyst) and mechanics (what is computationally "required" for the analysis). But when the desired coding begins to compete with the original text for space on the page, it becomes prudent to keep one's main text line uncluttered, while placing most of the linguistic information relating to individual elements of the text in some ancillary location (e.g., in a database field).

Another concern is that in exploratory research, of the kind involved in many studies of discourse, labeled bracketing may force a degree of syntactic explicitness that is methodologically premature.   Requiring a complete and exhaustive syntactic analysis—prior to the overall analysis—can lead to unresolvable problems.   For example, Keulen encountered a number of unexpected grammatical structures that in the end had to be labeled "unidentifiable" (1986, p. 147).

---

[9] Representations used in corpus linguistics are not immune to such "verbose" proliferations, which can get to be a problem when category or feature labels ("tags") are placed directly in the main line of text. One way around this is to use a multiline format ("interlinear" glossing or tagging); another is to use separate fields in one's database. For the other side to this question, see Edwards (this volume).

Obviously, constituency notions cannot be imported wholesale from sentence-based syntactic models into the domain of discourse: Both the data and the goals of the theoretical syntactician differ markedly from those of the analyst of spoken discourse (see Svartvik, 1990a). Syntactic theories generally attempt to describe some aspects of a (potentially) infinite set of formal constructs with clearly defined initial and terminal points that usually lack any explicit context—commonly referred to as sentences. Although for some discourse analysts the clause plays an important role in syntactic analysis of discourse data, in actual conversation this unit does not have boundaries as neatly and abruptly delineated as the syntactician's isolated sentence.[10] Nor is it assured that everything in the stream of spoken discourse will be assignable as part of any one clause. The syntactician who parses a linguistic string assumes as a starting point a complete, grammatical sentence, be it simple or complex. In fact, generative models are designed so that technically they will not permit the parsing of "deviant" strings, which are simply filtered out or rejected. In discourse, however, one encounters many constructions where the syntax is not so compliant. A particular constituent might appear to belong, for example, to more than one clause (in literary terms, *apo koinou*) or to no clause at all (depending on how one defines *clause*, of course). Moreover, the syntax of a text being produced is in some sense in a state of flux: With the sequential addition of new lexical material, the previously "fixed" structures must often be dynamically reevaluated by speech event participants.

One well-known response to such difficulties has been simply to turn away from them. But the discourse analyst, recognizing the indeterminacy in language, does no editing to clean up fuzzy boundaries, nor filtering to evade challenging cases (Sampson, 1987b, p. 96). Corpus-oriented researchers are committed to "total accountability" (Svartvik & Quirk, 1980, p. 9) to the entire body of data. This simple commitment makes for a profound difference in outlook and powerfully shapes the resulting linguistic theories.

4. A DISCOURSE APPROACH TO REPRESENTING HIERARCHY

In discourse, there are at least three major dimensions or layers within which language is hierarchically structured: turn structure, prosodic structure, and grammatical structure. (Other viable dimensions, such as rhetorical and poetic structure, are not dealt with here.) Turns are crucial units in discourse (see Sacks, Schegloff, & Jefferson, 1974). Their representation in the system

---

[10] Chafe (1979, p. 162) and Svartvik, Eeg-Olofsson, Forsheden, Oreström, and Thavenius (1982, p. 73) report on the difficulty of determining sentence boundaries in narrative and conversation consistently.

described here is straightforward and is treated here mainly in conjunction with structure in other dimensions. We focus now on the intonation unit (within the prosodic dimension) and the word, the group, and the clause (within the grammatical dimension).[11]

4.1. The Intonation Unit

The intonation unit, defined roughly as a stretch of speech bounded by a single coherent intonation contour, is coming to be seen by many discourse researchers as the primary prosodic unit of spoken discourse (Chafe, 1980; see Halliday, 1967, and Crystal, 1969, on the similar unit "tone group"). This is especially true of research on information flow (Chafe, 1987, this volume), but the role of the intonation unit in structuring the ongoing conversational interaction is also beginning to be recognized (Ford & Thompson, forthcoming). Oreström (1983), Altenberg (1987), Schuetze-Coburn, Shapley, and Weber (1990), and others have documented correlations between intonational units and grammatical units. Svartvik et al. (1982, pp. 70–73) argue for considering the prosodic, as opposed to the syntactic, dimension when choosing the basic linguistic unit of analysis for spoken language. The fundamental role of intonation units means that for many researchers their identification has become a critical part of the basic transcription process (for criteria, see Cruttenden, 1986, pp. 35–45, and Du Bois, Schuetze-Coburn, Cumming, & Paolino, 1991). Intonation units are often prominently foregrounded, with each set off on a separate line of the transcript. In our own work, we have found that the analysis of spoken discourse into intonation units provides a solid foundation for all subsequent analysis, whether prosodic, grammatical, or interactional. Although it is possible to represent grammatical hierarchy while disregarding intonation, close attention to intonation unit structure actually helps, rather than hinders, the representation of syntactic structure.

Finally—and most significantly for the problem of representing hierarchy—intonation units, in this analysis, are fairly straightforwardly discrete and

---

[11] There is no special theoretical significance attached to this number of divisions; it is sufficient to illustrate our approach to representing constituency. Additional levels are in fact implemented in the Discourse Profiles program, such as the morpheme and the turn levels (not treated extensively in this article).

sequential in nature.[12] This fact, coupled with their relatively restrained variability in size, makes them an ideal unit for the analysis of indefinitely extended units such as conversations. Clauses, in contrast, are not strictly sequential and show considerable variability in length. Also, intonation units lend themselves well to the representation of interactionally crucial features such as turn-taking structure and overlaps, whereas clauses are less accommodating, as is amply exhibited in the examples to come.

4.2. Concurrent Hierarchies: Coexistence of Grammar, Prosody, and Interaction

One challenge that spoken discourse presents is the coexistence of the distinct yet partially overlapping dimensions of grammatical, prosodic, and interactional hierarchical structures. The clause, the intonation unit, and the turn are all simultaneously realized through the same act of speaking. The clause and the intonation unit are frequently coextensive, as many of the examples in this chapter illustrate, but this is by no means consistently the case. The two units are independent in principle and in practice; often a single clause contains more than one intonation unit, and conversely, a single intonation unit may contain more than one clause (especially embedded clauses). Similarly, a turn may consist of several intonation units or several clauses, whereas conversely it is not uncommon for a single clause to be realized by two speakers in successive (cooperative) turns. Because each dimension has its own hierarchical structure that is in some degree independent of the others', the result is a set of "concurrent hierarchies" (Sperberg-McQueen & Burnard, 1990, pp. 20ff), in which no single hierarchy can subsume as constituents all the elements from the various coexisting systems.

One way to respond to such multiple layers of structuring is to focus on one of them to the exclusion of the others. But one of the most interesting questions about units of a given layer is: What is their relation to units in other layers? Taking the perspective of the clause as a unit in discourse, one can ask when it gets realized in one intonation unit and when in two (or more). And from the intonation-unit perspective, one can ask what consistencies there are in the types of grammatical structure each unit contains (Altenberg, 1987). Given that in discourse all dimensions of language are copresent and must be

---

[12] Groupings of intonation units into larger rhythmical units may also be recognized: for example, the intonational schemata associated with "lists" and "alternative questions" (see Selting, 1987, on rhythmically coherent units; Couper-Kuhlen, 1986, on subordinate tone groups) or with declination units (Schuetze-Coburn et al., 1991). These types of structural complexity, though not specifically discussed in the present chapter, are readily accommodated in our system by means of additional notations along the same lines.

addressed simultaneously, it is important to represent grammatical, prosodic, and turn-taking constituencies in such a way that research questions can be framed profitably from any of these vantage points.

Consider the following example:[13]

(3) ((Hypochondria))

    K: He's only had,

        since since we've been married,

        ... cancer,

    D: @@ [@@]

    K: [@@]@@

        ... leukemia,

        ... bronchitis,

        ... uh,

        .. tuberculosis,

As noted, each line represents a separate intonation unit. Speaker K has emphasized the name of each disease in the list by preceding it with a slight pause and by giving it (in general) a rising "continuing" intonation contour.[14] The result is that this text segment comprises seven intonation units (the two lines of laughter, represented above by the @ symbols, are ignored for the moment), but only two clauses (as evidenced by the two verb complexes *had* and *'ve been married*). In fact, the constituents of the first line *He's only had*, taken together with each of the afflictions listed, *cancer, leukemia, bronchitis*, and *tuberculosis*, plus the vocalized hesitation *uh* (i.e., six intonation units), form just a single clause. Although it is interesting to focus on the internal constituency of the intonation units in this passage and note that several of these consist of only a single noun phrase, it is equally important to be able to recognize the relationship between the prosodic and syntactic layers from another perspective. Focusing on the clause layer of analysis, the syntactic unit in question extends over several intonation units. On the other hand, taking interaction into focus, speaker K's clause spans across the interjection of a laugh by speaker D; this is only one of the many possible relationships between clause and turn (or backchannel).

---

[13] Prosodic features represented in the examples include pause (...), continuing contour (,), final contour (.), truncated intonation unit (--), truncated word (-), speech overlap ([ ]), and laughter (@). See Du Bois et al. (this volume) for a full discussion of the transcription system.

[14] One instance of a narrow transcription feature, "short pause" (..), has been included in the example to make the point more clear. Note that the last intonation unit is also preceded by the "filled pause" *uh*.

As noted earlier, the opposite association between clausal and intonational dimensions may hold as well. Consider the following example:

(4) ((Ranch))

    R: a reining pattern is,

       a pattern where you do sliding stops,

       spins,

       ... lead changes,

       I know you probably don't know what that is.

Here, the last intonation unit is composed of three clauses (as indicated by the three verb complexes *know*, *don't know*, and *is*). From the syntactic viewpoint, this intonation unit contains a sequence of three clauses (albeit of different types) without a significant prosodic break between them. Such phenomena are frequent in discourse and worthy of attention.

The basic systematic relationship among the whole conversational "text" and its turns, intonation units, groups, and words is expressed in abstract terms in Fig. 9.2. The text is divided into turns (Turn 1, Turn 2, etc.) and also into intonation units (Intonation Unit 1, Intonation Unit 2, etc.). The intonation units are each divided into groups, which are in turn divided into words (and finally, if appropriate, into morphemes).

An alternative, perhaps more familiar perspective would take as its primary orientation the clause. Figure 9.3 shows the text as composed of clauses, which are divided into groups, which (as already stated) are themselves ultimately divided into words. (Notice that by convention, group number assignment is strictly determined by the intonation unit sequence, as this is the primary unit in the indexing scheme. But it is straightforward to represent in the database the actual placement of the clause boundary with respect to those groups.) Figure 9.3 also illustrates the overlapping of intonation unit constituency with clausal constituency, which coexist as concurrent hierarchies in a fairly straightforward manner.

The simultaneous structuring of the text in terms of concurrent prosodic and grammatical hierarchies is schematized in abstract terms in Fig. 9.4. Each discourse text is segmented, in the prosodic dimension, into a set of intonation units; in the grammatical dimension, into a set of clauses; and in the interactional dimension, into a set of turns. Any of these units can be further segmented, ultimately into its component groups, words, and morphemes.

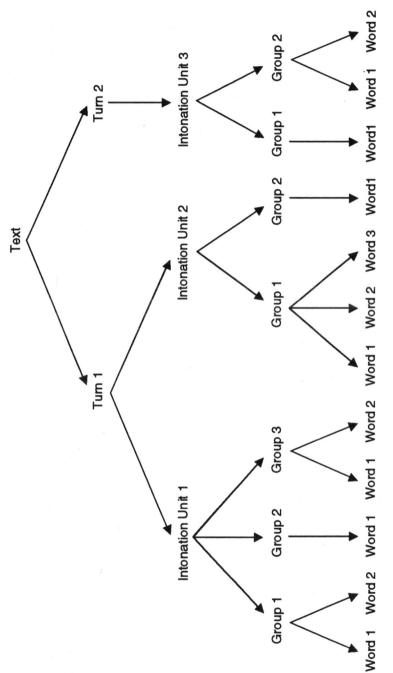

FIG. 9.2. Some constituency relationships in discourse (intonation unit focus).

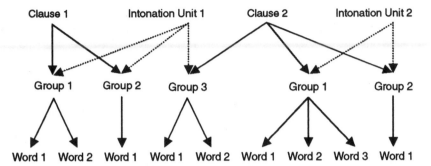

FIG. 9.3. Overlapping constituency relationships: Clause vs. intonation unit focus.

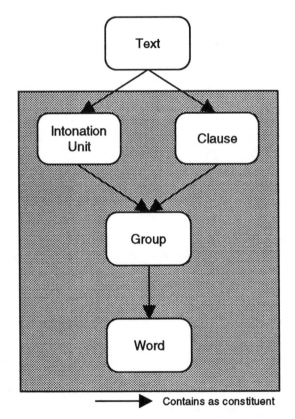

FIG. 9.4. Some constituency relationships in discourse

4.3. The Word

The word as a level of grammatical structure is one for which the standard orthographic conventions of a language such as English provide a nearly adequate representation, in the great majority of cases. Words are generally bounded by spaces (except that a punctuation symbol such as a comma or period may intervene between the word and one of its bounding spaces). Using spaces to segment a transcription into a series of words allows one to attach to each of them a notation specifying its relevant features at the word level: grammatical category, semantic class, lemma or base form, inflection, and so on. Thus, in the following example,

(5) ((Forces))

    A: He is a nice kid,

the words *he*, *is*, *a*, *nice*, and *kid* can be individually specified in the database for whatever features the researcher is interested in.[15]

But some adjustments must be made to the standard English conventions if the word as a linguistic unit is to be exploited effectively in discourse research. If one has decided, for example, to indicate for each word whether it is a noun, verb, and so on, then the phonological reduction commonly known as contraction will cause some difficulties for using the space as a word boundary symbol. Consider example (6), which presents the continuation of (5). The speaker went on to use nearly the same grammatical construction a second time but with the word *is* contracted to give enclitic *'s*:

(6) ((Forces))

    A: He is a nice kid,

       but he's weird.

If one tries to use an automatic procedure that exploits the space character to recognize word boundaries, the result will be that in the first line *he* and *is* are identified as two separate units, whereas in the next line *he's* is identified as a single undifferentiated unit. Barring some additional notation, this makes it hard for the researcher to, for example, attach the appropriate grammatical

---

[15] Below the level of the word, morpheme boundaries can be indicated. This is especially important for languages whose morphology is more complex than that of English. To avoid ambiguity, a plus sign (+) can be used for this (see Table 9.1): for example, *I use+d to help Barney,*. Alternatively, the more widely used hyphen can be retained as a marker of morpheme boundaries (*I use-d to help Barney,*), as long as the investigator remembers to distinguish this use from the equally widespread use of hyphen for truncation of words, etc. (Usually the contexts for the two functions are sufficiently distinct to allow fairly straightforward automatic discrimination: Morpheme boundaries are word-internal and truncations are word-external.)

tags "pronoun" and "verb" to *he* and *'s,* respectively. But this problem can be rectified, for English, by simply writing the contraction with spaces surrounding it—in effect, as a separate word. Thus, example (6) would be rewritten as follows:

(7) ((Forces))

A: He is a nice kid,
    but he 's weird.

Phonological reduction of this type comes up frequently in spoken discourse and involves a variety of different forms:

(8) ((Ranch))

A: the horse is always wet,
    and it 's always moist,

(9) ((Ranch))

A: You do n't really realize you 're progressing.

Note that in example (9), the auxiliary verb *'re,* although phonologically closer to *you,* is grammatically closer to *progressing.* This bespeaks another advantage to separating contractions, which becomes clear when it comes time to represent phrase-level constituency.

Thus, if the symbol for a word unit boundary is to be a single space, some special attention must be given to the precise placement of the space character. Orthographic words containing a phonologically reduced lexeme (English *don't,* French pronoun plus auxiliary *l'a*) must in general be rewritten, separating the lexemes. Although this is a departure from modern standard orthography, there is precedent for this practice in some older editorial practices for English (e.g., *would n't* in some turn-of-the-century publications), and similar solutions have been adopted by other corpus-oriented computational linguists (Booth, 1987, p. 100; Garside, 1987, p. 31).

For a language like English, the set of contracted elements is finite and readily listable, allowing for easy automatic recognition: *'m* (*am*), *'s* (*is/has*), *'re* (*are*), *'ve* (*have*), *'d* (*had/would*), *'ll* (*will*), and *n't* (*not*). (The interpretation of *'s* as either *is* or *has* would often require human judgment; the same applies to the interpretation of *'d* as *had* or *would.* Note that when *'s* represents the genitive inflection it is not a contraction and hence should not be written as a separate word.)[16] Transcribers need not learn to write contractions

---

[16] It can of course be written as a separate morpheme, using an appropriate symbol such as a hyphen (-) or a plus (+) sign.

as separate words: Except for judgments regarding the genitive *'s*, an ordinary word processor can be used to implement a series of search-and-replace commands (easily incorporated into a macro in some word-processing programs) that will go through one's finished transcriptions and pull apart all the contractions.

A converse problem arises in the case of related words, such as compound lexemes, proper names, and so on, which the researcher may wish to treat as single words for coding purposes. There are at least three possible ways to deal with these items. One solution is to mark a proper name such as *New York* as one "word" by replacing the space character between *New* and *York* with an underscore (_). A second solution is to leave the words separated by a space in the usual way but link them during coding. That is, whatever coding is appropriate for *New York* as a whole is then marked just on the first of the two words, whereas the second word is simply assigned "ditto" codes to indicate that its coding is located on the previous word (see Blackwell, 1987, pp. 112f.). A third option is to do nothing special: All segments surrounded by spaces are counted as words, and all of these words are coded individually.

This last option, however, has the disadvantage of introducing duplicate, unnormalized coding; the first two methods are thus preferable. In a language like English, where multipart lexemes are quite common, the first option is less attractive in some respects, since inserting underscore characters would require significant attention on the part of the transcriber and so would likely reduce consistency of constituent handling. In a language like German, however, in which compounds are normally written as one orthographic word (either without spaces or hyphenated), the first strategy is just as practical for the few exceptional instances. Either way, using space consistently for grammatical words makes it easier not only to code word-level features but also to represent constituency at higher levels, as is seen in the following section.

4.4. The Phrase

At the next higher level, it is useful to recognize the existence of phrases of various sorts, which may be labeled "groups."[17]   Roughly, a group may consist of a noun phrase (minus any phrasal or clausal modifiers), a verb complex (including auxiliaries and most adjacent adverbs), or other nonclausal elements, such as predicate adjectives, prepositions, complementizers, and so

---

[17] The work of Halliday (1985) and the systemicists on groups shows some similarity to ours, but there are also significant differences in orientation, purpose, and analysis. We use the term *group* primarily for practical reasons, in order to avoid the inappropriate expectations that would be raised by, for example, using the term *verb phrase* to speak of the verb complex consisting of a finite verb and its auxiliaries, but no direct object.

forth.[18] An asterisk (*)[19] is used to mark the boundaries between such units, except at the beginning or end of a line, where the asterisk would be redundant, because the end of an intonation unit by convention indicates the end of a group as well. (The implications of this convention—that groups are not directly recognized across intonation unit boundaries—are addressed briefly below.) Each utterance is exhaustively divided into adjacent groups, which leads—temporarily—to a flattening of the hierarchical structure. Consider the following example:

(10) ((Ranch))

    A: I * had been practicing * this * with * my horse,
        for * a long time.

Here, the noun phrases *I, this, my horse,* and *a long time* are signaled as constituents by the asterisk boundary symbol.[20] Similarly, the verb complex *had been practicing*—composed of a finite verb with all its attendant auxiliaries—is signaled as a unit. Although the basic syntactic divisions of the utterance are thus indicated, this segmentation does not complete the list of phrasal constituents in 10. The prepositional phrases *with my horse* and *for a long time*, for instance, have not yet been identified, and some researchers may wish to recognize other constituents such as a verb phrase. But as will be seen in the section on indirect representation, such structures can be represented in the present framework at higher levels: within the database (via numerical indices assigned to groups) rather than in the main line of text.

Consider the following example:

(11) ((Depression))

    A: ... I * remember,
        ... I * used to help * Barney,
        and * I * 'd get * twenty-five cents * a week,

Here, group-level units delineated by asterisks include the noun phrases *twenty-five cents* and *a week* and the verb complexes *used to help* and *'d get.*

---

[18] An isolated nonverbal vocal noise such as a laugh or an audible inhalation may also form a group, depending on its position in the intonation unit and function in the discourse, and on the analytic goals of the researcher.

[19] Any symbol will do, as long as it is readily discriminable visually and computationally from other symbols in the transcript.

[20] This use of symbols bears an interesting resemblance to the "juncture" symbols of classical American structuralists. Needless to say, our orientation here is somewhat different.

This last example underscores the value of separating contractions as separate "words," since this makes it easier to recognize the coherency of the appropriate verb complex. Although such verb-complex groups can get quite long, as in the following example, this presents no particular difficulties for the notation.

(12) ((Door))

    A: ... I * could n't even begin to do * it.

The problem of representing phrase-level constituents gets a bit more complicated than what we have illustrated thus far. The analyst is faced with diverse intermediate levels of phrases between word and clause, including the case of prepositional phrases mentioned above. Noun phrases in particular present a formidable challenge because of the rich possibilities for recursion (e.g., noun phrases within noun phrases). But again, the relationships found at these intermediate phrasal levels can be captured within the database, simplifying the direct representation of the constituents while reducing the need for extraneous symbols in the main line of text.

4.5. The Clause

The next higher level of syntactic structure represented directly is the clause. As alluded to earlier, a prototypical clause consists of a single verb group and its dependents. (Clauses lacking verbs are discussed later.) There are two types of symbols used to indicate units at the clause level. The boundary between clauses is represented by the number sign (#), as introduced in example (13), which is a discourse-oriented version of example (7). Embedded clauses are enclosed in curly brackets ({}), as shown in (13) for the clausal complement of the verb *thought*.

(13) ((Forces))

    A: I * met * him, #
       and * I * thought * {he * was * a nice kid.} #
    B: He * is * a nice kid, #
       but * he * 's * weird. #

This way of displaying the basic constituent structure is simpler to produce, as well as easier to read, than the bracketing of example (2). The high degree of convergence between intonation units and clauses, which is obscured in (2), is made readily apparent in (13), where each line ends with a number sign. Thus, the system of display used here allows the main facts of syntactic constituency to be depicted without sacrificing the more or less iconic representation of turn-taking, intonation unit rhythm, and other prosodic features.[21]

In the case of multiple clausal embedding, sets of brackets are used to represent the complex dependency. In (14), for example, three embedded clauses occur.

(14) ((Door))

A: ... All * {I * do} * is * {say,
  {Why * do n't * we * eat * something * first.}} #

The first embedded clause is the relative clause *I do*. Its dependent status is thus indicated by the surrounding curly brackets. The second and third embedded clauses overlap to a large degree, which the placement of the brackets for these clauses reflects.[22] The clause *why don't we eat something first* is embedded in the clause *say why don't we eat something first*, which itself functions as a clausal complement of the copula *is*. Despite the complexity of this example, notational conventions for representing the basic structure have been kept to a minimum. Table 9.1 summarizes the morphosyntactic symbols used.

TABLE 9.1
Morphosyntactic boundary symbols

Symbol	Boundary
– or +	morpheme[23]
[space]	word
*	group/phrase
#	clause
{}	embedded clause

---

[21] It is interesting to note that whereas computer printouts of the London-Lund corpus of Spoken English displayed one prosodic unit per line (see Svartvik et al., 1982, p. 23), the final, printed version (Svartvik & Quirk, 1980) resorts to the more usual (and less iconic) style of displaying texts, that is, the prosodic units for each speaker turn form one continuous stream, wrapping from line to line, arbitrarily filling out the available space.

[22] In this example there is no confusion as to how the brackets match up. When more explicitness is required, the brackets should be numbered, for example:

A: ... All * {I * do} * is * {2 say,
  {3 Why * do n't * we * eat * something * first. 3}2} #

(The numeral *1* should be avoided in this labeling function, because it is easily confused with the letter *l*; numerals *2–9* do not share this potential for confusion.)

[23] Regarding morpheme boundary, see footnote 15.

An additional feature of the system—positive or negative, depending on one's point of view—is that it avoids many potentially premature specifications of structural detail. In particular, the higher-level relationships between clauses are not directly indicated in the main text line. Consider the following example:

(15) ((Ranch))

    A: If * you * think * about * it, #

       yeah, #

       if * it * rains * a lot, #

       the horse * is always * wet, #

       and * it * 's always * moist, #

       it * 's always * on * something moist, #

       ... Sure * it * 's going to be * softer. #

In this stretch of speech, each line ends in a number sign, as in (13), indicating here that each intonation unit corresponds to a clause. On the other hand, there is no direct sign of the elaborate interclausal relationships present in this passage, one interpretation of which is displayed in the tree diagram given as Fig. 9.5.

Figure 9.5 nicely points up the fact that in a relatively short expanse of spontaneous discourse, the hierarchical relationship between clauses can grow with each new intonation unit until the result becomes quite complex. And although fairly unwieldy when brought to encompass the entire section, the tree diagram nevertheless presents the entire constituent structure of the passage in an intelligible display. In contrast, the necessary linearization of Fig. 9.5, shown in (16) and (17), suffers a great loss of clarity.

(16) ((Ranch))

    A: $[_S[_S[_C$If$]$ $[_{NP}$you$]$ $[_{VP}[_V$think$]$ $[_{PP}[_P$about$]$ $[_{NP}$it,$]]]]$ $[_S[_{INT}$yeah,$]]$ $[_S[_S[_S[_C$if$]$ $[_{NP}$it$]$ $[_{VP}[_V$rains$]$ $[_{ADV}$a lot,$]]]$ $[_S[_S[_{NP}$the horse$]$ $[_{VP}[_V$is$]$ $[_{ADV}$always$]$ $[_{ADJ}$wet,$]]]$ $[_C$and$]$ $[_S[_S[_{NP}$it$]$ $[_{VP}[_V$'s$]$ $[_{ADV}$always$]$ $[_{ADJ}$moist,$]]]$ $[_S[_{NP}$it$]$ $[_{VP}[_V$'s$]$ $[_{ADV}$always$]$ $[_{PP}[_P$on$]$ $[_{NP}$something moist,$]]]]]]]]$ ... $[_S[_{ADV}$Sure$]$ $[_{NP}$it$]$ $[_{VP}[_V$'s going to be$]$ $[_{ADJ}$softer.$]]]]]$

(17) ((Ranch))

    A: [[[If] [you] [[think] [[about] [it,]]]] [[yeah,]] [[[[if] [it] [[rains] [a lot,]]] [[[the horse] [[is] [always] [wet,]]] [and] [[[it] [['s] [always] [moist,]]] [[it] [['s] [always] [[on] [something moist,]]]]]]]] ... [[Sure] [it] [['s going to be] [softer.]]]]]

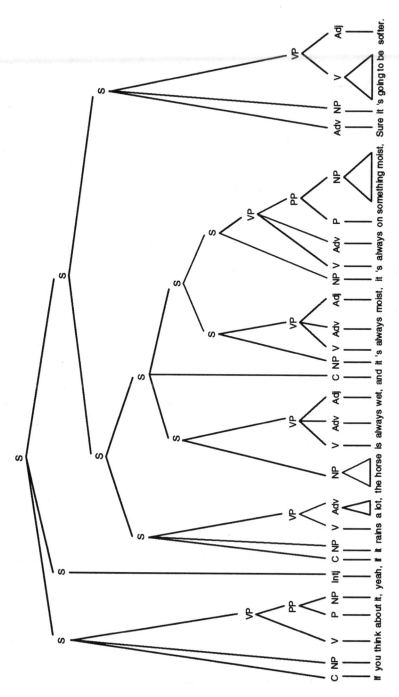

FIG. 9.5. Tree diagram of constituency in a stretch of discourse

Although a full representation of the hierarchical structure has been maintained in the bracketed versions, the nature of the clausal relationships has become visually indecipherable and thus practically unusable for the discourse analyst. Clearly, there is a balance to be struck between structural detail and comprehensibility, that is, how much structural information is directly integrated into the text. Placing group and clause boundaries within the text, and leaving other aspects of the structure to be noted elsewhere, seems to avoid the worst of the clutter. Once the asterisk, number sign, and curly bracket conventions become familiar, this kind of representation remains relatively transparent to the analyst.[24]

Naturally there are alternative ways to address the issue of precision versus simplicity in representations, using different notations and procedures. For some kinds of research, it may well be preferable, for example, to establish multiple distinct representations: one for surface phonetics, a separate one for phonological representation, a third for surface constituent structure, a fourth for "deep" constituent structure or semantic structure, and so on. But for discourse databases, there is much to be said for keeping things simple: taking a single unified representation as far as it can go in capturing the multiple layers of structure that come together in discourse.

But the representation of constituency here is not limited to a linear in-text display: A number of dependency relations are indicated in the database outside the main line of text. Most clausal dependencies constitute a level of detail that is perhaps best captured indirectly "behind the scenes" during later coding stages, as discussed below.

4.6. Relationships between Hierarchies

Although independent dimensions of hierarchical structure coexist in discourse, they are not completely at odds throughout a text. Although the syntactic and prosodic layers sometimes diverge—as when several intonation units constitute a single clause (3), or a single intonation unit contains several clauses (4)—more often they complement one another, as in (13) and (15).[25] In (15), each clause is coextensive with a single intonation unit, a fact that the representation readily displays.

Consider now the following, somewhat more complex example:

---

[24] The combination of asterisk and number sign (and curly brackets for embedded clauses) may not provide enough in-text structural detail for some purposes. In some cases, it may be necessary, for example, to indicate clause beginnings and clause endings distinctively. This could be done by extending the use of curly brackets ({ }) to mark the beginning and ending of all clauses and then additionally marking main clauses with a number sign (#) affixed to the right bracket that marks its end. There is a trade-off in simplicity and visual clarity, however.

[25] See also (8), (11), and (12), although clause boundaries are not marked in these earlier examples.

(18) ((Depression))

    A: ... She * just pulled * the cat * and * the kittens * out, #
        and * pulled * off * the bread * {that * was * dirty,} #
        and,
        ... we * served * the rest of it. #

Here there are a total of four clauses in a four-intonation-unit stretch.[26] The first clause and the first intonation unit coincide, whereas the last clause is composed of the third and fourth intonation units together. The remaining two clauses are contained in the second intonation unit. The relative clause *that was dirty* is embedded in the clause *and pulled off the bread that was dirty*. This dependency is captured by enclosing the relative clause in curly brackets and following the main clause with a number sign, showing how straightforward it is to incorporate clausal units into the framework of a prosodically segmented text.

Once the interactional dimension is added to the picture, this introduces a different kind of challenge for the reconciling of concurrent hierarchical structure. Although the examples considered so far have exhibited some complexity in the domain of syntax (ranging from simple one-clause intonation units to multiple embeddings), interactionally they have all been rather simple, with relatively uncomplicated turn-taking dynamics. Either the speech of only a single speaker has been presented, as in (7)–(12), (14)–(15), or (18), or the contribution by the second speaker has smoothly followed that of the first, as in (13). But in ordinary conversation one frequently encounters far more intricate turn sequences, as speakers do not always alternate speaking in such a simple fashion. Often the speech of two (or more) speakers will overlap to some degree, whether due to anticipation of the end of a turn or as the result of a multiparty interaction, as in the following example.

---

[26] One key issue that arises in example (18) involves the treatment of zero anaphora. Assuming that one wishes to be able to code for features such as grammatical role ("subject of intransitive," "subject of transitive," etc.), it is advisable to insert "null" groups in one's database during the coding (not transcribing) stage to act as placeholders to which these and other codes can be attached (e.g., for the subject of *pull* in line 2). This zero group can be assigned an arbitrary group index number of 91, to distinguish it from non-null groups, numbered 1, 2, 3, and so on (multiple zero groups in the same intonation unit would be numbered 91, 92, 93, and so on). Note that for English zero is posited only in the case of fully inflected verb forms, that is, where insertion of an actual overt pronoun or noun phrase as subject argument would result in an "acceptable" sentence. The location of the zero is determined by the potential location of such an overt pronoun. Needless to say, the simplicity and effectiveness of this approach for English will not necessarily be matched in other languages.

(19) ((Hypochondria))

    A: What * is * that. #

    B: He * 'll be * over * his leprosy * [soon.] #

    C: [Nothing,] #

       it * 's just * dry skin. #

In (19), speaker C's initial response (*Nothing*) to speaker A's question overlaps with the last word of speaker B's intervening utterance. (The overlap is indicated by pairs of square brackets that are aligned vertically on the left.) The nature of this overlap highlights the compatibility between prosodic and interactional dimensions. Again, the segmentation of a text into intonation units does not in general conflict with the representation of other linguistic layers, in this case the turn-taking structure of that text. Given a basic prosodic framework to build on, details of other dimensions can be accommodated easily, providing the analyst with a more comprehensive picture of the speech event, including turn-taking structures of much greater complexity than in (19).

Special considerations must be made in the syntactic dimension as well when interactionally complex stretches are involved. Whereas the representation of basic prosodic and interactional units in the present system is linear—intonation units are strictly sequential, and turns have been linearized, on paper at least, by indicating simultaneous speech with bracketed text portions arranged sequentially—the occurrence of clauses may be more complex, especially when utterances by more than one speaker must be taken into consideration. Even in simple cases where one speaker has the floor, back-channel utterances by other speakers commonly intervene.[27]   Consider the following example:

(20) ((Aesthetics))

    A: I * think * of * ... aesthetics,

       and,

    B: mhm, #

    A: uh,

    B: ... Hm.

       ... @ #

    A: ... creation * of * desire,

       for * one thing. #

---

[27] Determining whether a particular utterance constitutes a turn or backchannel is a complex interpretive issue that cannot be addressed here.

Speaker A's utterances in (20) constitute exactly one clause, which is distributed over five intonation units. Although speaker A retains the floor during this stretch, speaker B is not silent but overtly acknowledges that she is listening (among other things) by uttering *mhm* and *hm*. The most straightforward way to delimit clauses in such conversational exchanges, we have found, is—expressed in procedural terms—to temporarily follow only the utterances of one (current) speaker, skipping over any backchannels, turns or other utterances by other speakers in order to link up all the clause segments uttered by the speaker currently being tracked. The conventions for use and interpretation of clause boundary markers are framed with such a clause recognition procedure in mind. For example, in (20), the procedure begins with speaker A's first word and continues through just A's utterances until the clause completion marker (#) is reached, in the last line. Later, the procedure goes back through the utterances of speaker B in the same way—and then through each additional speaker in turn, looking for each one's clause boundary markers. This convention reflects the observation that *most* of the time in conversation, each speaker begins and eventually finishes his or her own clauses—but not necessarily without intervening backchannels, and even whole turns, produced by other speakers.

In many cases, the continuity of the current speaker's clauses must be pursued across more substantial interjections, amounting to a full clause or more. Consider the following example:

(21) ((Hypochondria))
    G: the worst [thing * {I * ever had},
    K: [@ He * 's * a medical miracle]. #
    G: was * brain] fever, #
        when * I * had proposed * to * her. #

Here, G's main clause, *the worst thing I ever had was brain fever* (incidentally containing the embedded *I ever had*), appears in two intonation units that are necessarily separated in the transcription by K's full-clause, overlapped interjection, *He's a medical miracle*. But because the clause-recognition procedure moves through K's clauses in a separate pass from G's clauses, the syntactic structure of the two speaker's utterances is readily captured simply by placing number signs after *miracle* and *fever*. Although this particular example involves overlap, the same kind of interjected clause-turn configuration can occur with material that is not overlapped at all.

(22) ((Lunch))
    R: when * he * was &

L: Oh really?

M: Hey.

R: & three. #

Such configurations[28] are quite frequent in conversation and tend to support the one-speaker-at-a-time clause recognition conventions adopted here.

Although in some cases it might seem tempting to rearrange the words of a transcription so as to make the clauses come out more neatly, this would be self-defeating: Simplicity in the clause representation would usually be gained only at the cost of complexity in the intonational and turn-taking representations. Moreover, the first commitment must be to maintaining the integrity of the transcription, where the temporal sequencing of turns has first claim on the space-time iconicity implicit in the vertical sequencing of text lines on the page (Du Bois, 1991). It is greatly preferable to let the turns and intonation units fall where they may on purely transcriptional grounds and to work within this framework to devise special conventions for tracking clause structure, than to undermine the integrity of the transcription itself by shuffling clauses around. And in the end, it is surprisingly straightforward to overlay a representation of syntactic structure on a transcription whose basic outlines are determined by intonational and turn-taking considerations.

Another syntactic issue raised by highly interactional speech regards the nature of clauses. Although a prototypical clause consists of a verb plus its dependents, in interactional contexts one finds some units that, despite their lacking a verb, are nevertheless best treated as clauses. Three types of verbless clauses are common in spoken discourse: ellipses (reduced or partial clauses, typically completable on the basis of discourse context, such as the answer to a question); repairs (utterances repaired or abandoned); and interjections, exclamations, and other regulatory utterances.

The ellipsis type is exemplified in (19). In this passage, speaker C answers speaker A's question *What is that* by saying *Nothing*. Because it lacks constituency in any other clause and in effect functions as a clause, the single noun phrase *Nothing* itself is recognized as a clause.

Consider the following example, which contains several instances of repair:

(23) ((Forces))

A: But,

[the thing * ab-] -- #

B: [The special] forces. #

---

[28] The & in this example indicates the continuation of an intonation unit across an interjection by another speaker or speakers (see Du Bois et al., this volume).

A: Yeah. #
  ... [But * the thing * about * him] -- #
B: [This place * is getting] * weird. #
A: ... The thing * about * him * is,
  {he * ca n't spell.} #

In this exchange, speaker A's intended utterance is restarted twice after interruption by speaker B and finally completed on the third try (*The thing about him is*). Each restart of the clause is treated as a separate clause, and marked with the number sign.

The exchange in (23) also shows how interjections and regulatory (interpersonal) utterances can fulfill the role of clauses. Speaker B's first utterance (*The special forces.*) is an interjectional noun phrase that exhibits no obvious links (e.g., grammatical dependency) to any neighboring clause. Speaker A's direct regulatory or interpersonal response *Yeah* likewise does not function as an argument of any (verb-centered) clause. Thus, both are treated as independent clauses.

4.7. Indirect Representation of Constituents

In the preceding sections, several cases arose where constituents that ought to be accessible to the discourse analyst were not delimited as constituents in the main line of text—seemingly a case of missing constituent markers. But representing the hierarchical structure of texts in a fashion that is both computer manipulable and readily interpretable to the human analyst calls for a combination of devices. No one strategy—not tree diagrams nor labeled bracketing nor morphosyntactic tags alone—can in our view satisfactorily achieve both aims. Thus, whereas most basic syntactic boundaries (clauses, words, basic-level phrases) are here represented directly in the main text line, the database component is also exploited for purposes of keeping track of additional hierarchical structure. Because every group in the discourse database is automatically assigned a unique numerical index (based on the transcription title, intonation unit number within the text, and group number within the intonation unit), any group can be linked to any other by means of this index. This can be used to indirectly represent hierarchical structure beyond what is represented directly in the main text line.

For example, the constituency of prepositional phrases in English, such as *with my horse* and *for a long time* in (10) or *on something moist* in (15), is not directly represented, because prepositions (*with, for, on*) and prepositional objects (*my horse, a long time, something moist*) are always assigned to separate groups. But in the database, one of the items of information attached to each preposition is the location of its object. This method of indirect representation (through numerical indices) is needed in any case[29] for discontinuous constituents, for example, the English verb particle, which may or may not be adjacent to its verb group. Example (18) illustrates the treatment of these constituents. The particle in *pull...out* (in the first intonation unit) is separated from its verb, whereas in *pull off* (in the next intonation unit) the particle is adjacent to its verb. Such distributional facts motivate consistently treating verb particles as groups separate from their associated verbs, no matter where they occur. In many cases the particles will be grouped separately of necessity (as in the first instance); and a consistent treatment of such a word class is preferable if one is to be able to study the whole set of instances as a class. This means that the constituency of the verb-particle construction is not directly represented in the main line of text; however, once the database is called into play the complete structure of the verb complex becomes accessible. The particle *out* is tagged with the information that its associated verb is the (uniquely indexed) group *just pulled*, thus explicitly allowing for the automatic reconstitution of the verb complex *pulled out*. At the same time, additional information such as the nature of a particle's relationship to its verb can be represented by attaching appropriate codes to it in a database field. Similarly, in cases of "inversion," the nonadjacent parts of the verb complex can be related to each other through indexing. Thus, the constituency of the nonadjacent elements *don't* and *eat* in (14) is not captured directly in the text line but, rather, indirectly in the database.

At the heart of the group coding method are the conventions that each intonation unit must consist of at least one group, and each intonation unit boundary implies a group boundary. These two principles, together with the treatment of the intonation unit as the fundamental unit in discourse, provide the characteristic shape to syntactic representation that is evident in the cited examples. But despite the seeming rigidity of these principles, even the main text line taken alone typically gives a fairly good approximation to the syntactic facts in spoken discourse. For example, group boundaries are for the most part coextensive with actual constituent boundaries. Informal counts in an English and a German text showed that, in both cases, about 90% of the time, a noun phrase was contained within exactly one group. Where the two are not coextensive, the direct marking of groups is supplemented by indirect means, as described earlier. And in those very rare cases where a single group-level constituent (e.g., a noun phrase) is distributed across an intonation unit boundary, the "split" constituent can be marked via indexing, as with other indirectly represented constituents.

---

[29] Is "independently motivated," some would say.

5. ALTERNATE ANALYSES FOR OTHER LANGUAGES

Whereas the discussion up to now has dealt exclusively with English examples, our orientation is by no means restricted to this language. For other languages, the user can make use of several options that are sensitive to the particulars of the grammar in question. Details of grammatical classes and category delimitation are certainly likely to differ from one language to the next. Clause boundary identification, word class features, word-internal structure, and the constitution of group-level constituents can all be tailored to the grammatical description of an individual language, as well as to the specific theoretical and research orientations of the investigator, while still keeping the basic outlines of the present analytical framework relatively constant.

In German, for instance, the representation of prepositional phrases requires special consideration. Recall that for English each prepositional phrase is counted as two groups: a preposition group plus a noun phrase group. But the driving motivation behind this choice, the dual nature of prepositions (see (18)), plays a relatively minor role in German. An alternative analysis for German (following the valency grammar of Heidolph, Flämig, & Motsch, 1984) treats dependent phrases headed by both nominals and prepositions as basic-level arguments: Prepositions are not separated from, but are grouped together with, their associated noun phrases.

Several factors motivate this approach. First, prepositional-phrase arguments of verbs, adjectives, and nouns bear a relationship similar to nominal arguments with oblique case marking. Second, because German has "prepositional adverbs" that stand in paradigmatic opposition to preposition-plus-pronoun sequences (e.g., *davon* 'of it/him/her' vs. *von ihm/von ihr* 'of him/of her'), a uniform treatment should recognize that prepositional phrases are parallel to this. The frequently obligatory phonological reduction of preposition and article (which in the spoken language extends to most simplex prepositions) provides an additional motivation for handling prepositional phrases as one group. (However, the orthographic considerations are in some sense secondary. As illustrated earlier for English pronoun-auxiliary and auxiliary-negative contractions, conventional spellings can be adjusted if need be.)

Consider the following example:

(24) ((Botschafter))

    A: .. das * is' * ... die Frau * vom   Botschaft- --
        that is   the wife   of.the ambassad-

      vom   deutschen Botschafter,
      of.the German ambassador

B: unhhunh, #
unhhunh

A: ... die Tochter * meiner Freundin, #
the daughter of.my friend.FEM

Here, the prepositional phrase *vom deutschen Botschafter* 'of the German ambassador' is regarded as a single group, reflecting a status parallel to the genitive noun phrase *meiner Freundin* 'of my friend' in A's next intonation unit. The internal constituency of the prepositional phrase is then indicated indirectly by specific coding linked to the group. Thus, internal constituency, as well as group and clause relations, may be indicated indirectly through coding.

An additional example of the variability that is possible across languages is illustrated in (25) and (26). In the treatment of English texts, adverbs adjacent to the verb group are normally grouped together with it, as in (12) and (15). But in German, two independent considerations argue for a segmentation where adjacent adverbs are kept separate from the verb. The problem of adverb class assignment provides the first motivation for placing the group boundaries differently. Consider the grouping of adverbs in example (25):

(25) ((Visum))

A: ...(1.0) nee, #
no

ich * mußte * natürlich * noch * dahin * fahren,
I had.to naturally still there drive

den letzten Tag, #
the last day

... aber * das * war * eigentlich * auch * 'n bißchen * unsre Schuld, #
but that was actually also a bit our fault

Here, *natürlich* 'naturally', *noch* 'still', *eigentlich* 'actually', *auch* 'also', and *'n bißchen* 'a bit' all form independent units at the group level, leaving the adjacent finite verbs *mußte* 'had to' and *war* 'was' in their own groups. Although some of these adverbs might ideally be grouped either with each other or with their associated lexical verbs, depending on scope and function, the difficulty of determining the subclass of every adverb reliably at the time group boundaries are set would place undue demands on the human analyst, which could easily lead to inconsistencies at the group level. Such fine distinctions are best reserved for later analysis, during the coding phase, for example, where the attention devoted to each individual group can vary as needed and where coding decisions can easily be reversed if need be.

A second argument for not placing adverbs in an adjacent verb group involves clause type distinctions. As accounts of word order in the German clause generally center around the verb (e.g., clauses are described as being verb first, verb second, or verb last), it is advantageous to keep the finite verb completely separate from other clausal elements so that its exact position in the clause can be determined easily. Because in (25) the finite verbs would both be group-initial, no problems would surface in grouping the adverbs with the verb. But this is not always the case. Consider the following example:

(26) ((Visum))

    A: ... [{oh} * dachten] * wir, #
           oh   thought we

    B: [oh je,] #
          oh no

    A: jetzt * rufen * wir * die * mal * an *ne, #
       now   call   we   them once up ok

In the third intonation unit, the adverb *jetzt* 'now' precedes the finite verb. Were it grouped together with *rufen* 'call', the first group in the clause would be a verb group, an undesirable result, as this is a clear case of a verb-second clause. By keeping the adverb separate, the position of the verb in the clause can thus be referenced without having to examine the internal structure of the larger verb complex.

The German examples illustrate only a few of the different treatments of linguistic complexity that are possible within the present framework, whose flexibility ensures that a variety of vantage points can be accommodated. Although the discourse analyst must commit to an exhaustive and unique segmentation of constituents into groups during the final stages of text preparation, there is room in the coding of the groups themselves to accommodate the particular research goals and analytical preferences of the investigator and the specific requirements of the language and the data.

6. THE DISCOURSE PROFILES DATABASE SYSTEM

Once a speech event representation has been segmented into prosodic and interactional units (during the transcription process), and then into morphosyntactic units (during the morphosyntactic analysis, or text mark-up, process), it is ready to be inserted (i.e., imported) into a discourse database. Once in the database, each turn, intonation unit, clause, group, word, and morpheme will be accessible for coding, after which questions can be asked about any combination of features, from almost any perspective. (It is equally possible to use the morphosyntactically marked texts directly as files that can be concordanced, which offers advantages of its own; but that is beyond the scope of this chapter.) Figure 9.6 outlines schematically the full extent of a database architecture designed for studying what we call "discourse profiles," which can be broadly characterized as the total network of recurrent cooccurrences exhibited by a linguistic element across all domains (e.g., linguistic form, prosody, grammar, semantics, pragmatics, and other domains) in a body of discourse. There are two basic steps involved in entering a text into the database: importing and coding. We give only the briefest overview here, to suggest how the system described can be put to use in discourse research.

For importing discourse data from an ordinary word-processing file, we have written a program (using the database manager Paradox) called "Discourse Profiles."[30] This program takes an ordinary text file (e.g., a transcription of a conversation to which syntactic symbols described in this chapter have been added) and automatically transforms it into database file format. During this process, the program goes through the text file and, based on the location of the symbols described earlier, identifies every intonation unit, group, word, morpheme, turn, and clause. Concurrently, it places each unit into a separate record and assigns it a unique index, based on the text title, intonation unit number within the text, group number within the intonation unit, word number within the group, and morpheme number within the word. (Turns and clauses are defined and indexed automatically in a slightly different way, in terms of their component units.) This unique index allows the researcher to find, or make reference to, any basic constituent in the entire discourse database. The whole process is automated and takes a few minutes for a moderate-sized text (e.g., several hundred intonation units).

---

[30] For those who would rather use an existing program than develop their own, the Discourse Profiles program is available from John Du Bois, Linguistics Department, University of California, Santa Barbara, CA 93106, USA. Discourse Profiles must be used in conjunction with Paradox, a relational database program for IBM-compatible personal computers (available from Borland International, Scotts Valley, CA).

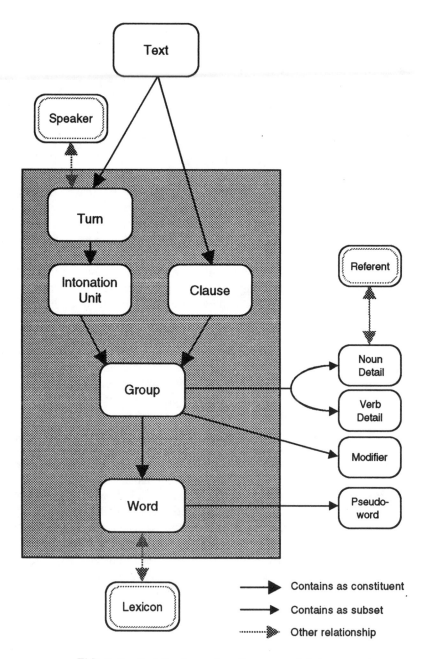

FIG. 9.6. Architecture of a discourse database.

This sets the stage for inquiry on whatever topic the discourse researcher wishes to pursue. For example, some would like to know how certain syntactic structures correlate with intonational structures or how grammatical roles correlate with specific discourse-pragmatic functions. How often does a clause contain two noun phrases, each expressing new information? How often is the direct object of a verb of perception used to introduce a human referent modified by an attributive adjective? To what extent do prosodic and syntactic boundaries align with turn boundaries? Now that the hierarchical structure of the text in multiple dimensions has been represented, questions like these (and many others) can be answered, with a little coding and querying.

In our own research on information flow, for example, we specify for each noun group its semantic class, grammatical role, discourse referentiality, identifiability, activation state, and so on. This makes it possible to ask a practically unlimited variety of questions regarding correlations of information flow features with grammatical role, intonation unit size, turn position, and so forth. (For discussion of an extensive system of grammatical and discourse-pragmatic codes that can be attached to any of the unique constituents identified in the importing stage just described, see Du Bois, Cumming, & Schuetze-Coburn, 1988, and Du Bois & Thompson, forthcoming.)

For example, consider how the following text (a slightly extended version of (3)) would be imported and coded using the Discourse Profiles system. First, the transcription is marked up with asterisks, number signs, curly brackets, and so on, using an ordinary word processing program:

(27) ((Hypochondria))

    K: ... Greg * 's never had * a- * a cold,
        or * the flu, #
        He * 's only had,
        {since * since * we * 've been married,}
        ... cancer,
    D: @ @ [@ @] #
    K: [@ @] @ @
        ... leukemia,
        ... bronchitis,
        ... uh,
        .. tuberculosis, #
        @ @ @ @
        and * he * 's recovered * from * all of them. #
        That * 's * {what * 's * [so amazing.]} #
    G: [Nasal polyps,] #

Once the transcription has been marked up in this way to show grammatical constituency, the next step is to "import" the text into the database. The database program automatically segments the text, attaches the correct speaker label, and assigns the appropriate index. For example, HYPO.60.1 indicates "the first group of the 60th intonation unit of the text Hypochondria." The analyst is then free to attach any desired codes to the text, at any level in any layer. For example, at the (noun) group level in the syntactic layer, the analyst might code for grammatical category (CAT), referent identifiability (ID), and concept activation state (ACT) (see Table 9.2 for a list of codes).

Once this coding is done, the database file will look as follows:

INDEX	SPKR	TEXT	CAT	ID	ACT
HYPO.60.1	K	... Greg	N	I	G
HYPO.60.2	K	's never had	V		
HYPO.60.3	K	a-	N	*	*
HYPO.60.4	K	a cold,	N	N	N
HYPO.61.1	K	or	L		
HYPO.61.2	K	the flu, #	N	N	N
HYPO.62.1	K	He	N	I	G
HYPO.62.2	K	's only had,	V		
HYPO.63.1	K	{since	L		
HYPO.63.2	K	since	L		
HYPO.63.3	K	we	N	I	G
HYPO.63.4	K	've been married,}	V		
HYPO.64.1	K	... cancer,	N	N	N
HYPO.65.1	D	@@[@@] #	Y		
HYPO.66.1	K	[@@]@@	Y		
HYPO.67.1	K	... leukemia,	N	N	N
HYPO.68.1	K	... bronchitis,	N	N	N
HYPO.69.1	K	... uh,	F		
HYPO.70.1	K	.. tuberculosis, #	N	N	N
HYPO.71.1	K	@@@@	Y		
HYPO.72.1	K	and	L		
HYPO.72.2	K	he	N	I	G
HYPO.72.3	K	's recovered	V		
HYPO.72.4	K	from	P		
HYPO.72.5	K	all of them. #	N	I	G
HYPO.73.1	K	That	N	I	G
HYPO.73.2	K	's	V		
HYPO.73.3	K	{what	N	*	*
HYPO.73.4	K	's	V		
HYPO.73.5	K	[so amazing.]} #	J		
HYPO.74.1	G	[Nasal polyps,] #	N	N	N

TABLE 9.2

Selected Group-Level Codes for a Discourse Database

Category		Identifiability		Activation State	
N	noun	I	identifiable	G	given
V	verb	N	nonidentifiable	A	accessible
A	adverb	*	inapplicable	N	new
J	adjective			*	inapplicable
P	preposition				
T	particle				
L	linker				
C	complementizer				
I	interactional				
F	filled pause				
Y	nonlinguistic				
*	inapplicable				

The resulting discourse database can then be queried in a tremendous variety of ways, to yield answers in the form of selected lists, sorted data, correlations, counts, statistical tests, and graphs, all within moments of formulating the question. But this example gives only the briefest hint of what is possible. This system was designed from the outset to be amenable to a variety of different research purposes. According to the interests of the researcher, codes for morphosyntactic form can be correlated with semantic, pragmatic, prosodic, interactional, and other features. And the same general principles for representing hierarchy can be extended to additional layers and higher levels of discourse structure as well.

7. CONCLUSIONS

In this chapter, we have sought to introduce a system for the representation of syntactic constituent structure as it appears in conversational discourse. This system of constituency analysis is specifically designed to allow researchers to use computers to ask questions about hierarchical structures exhibited in discourse, encompassing clauses, phrases, words, morphemes, intonation units, turns, and other units, whether these are being investigated in their own right or in relation to other aspects of discourse. The principles outlined here can be extended to the analysis and representation of additional dimensions of hierarchy, including higher-level discourse units such as episodes. We have sought to show how the potential for discourse research can be broadened and deepened by introducing a simple yet relatively sophisticated system for building constituency representation into computational procedures for text analysis, allowing researchers access via both computer and the naked eye to concurrent and interrelated grammatical, prosodic, and turn-taking structures and features within a single unified discourse database. We believe it is important for discourse researchers to be able to work both visually and computationally with full transcriptions of conversational discourse without having to neglect either the grammatical structure or the prosodic and interactional features that shed so much light on the sociocognitive processes that give rise to (among other things) that grammatical structure.

This constituency representation system is to a large degree independent of the specific shape of our own research and thus can be exploited by other discourse researchers for inquiry into questions that are of particular interest to them. If discourse is the domain where all linguistic dimensions coexist and coevolve, our tools must let us see this.

ACKNOWLEDGEMENTS

This chapter was based upon research supported by the National Science Foundation under grant #IST85-19924, "Information Transfer Constraints and Strategies in Natural Language Communication." The system presented here derives in part from research carried out in conjunction with Susanna Cumming (Du Bois, Cumming, & Schuetze-Coburn, 1988). The writing reflects equal contributions by its authors; the ordering of names is alphabetical. We thank Jane Edwards for comments on an earlier version of this chapter, and Ken Whistler for his observations on the distinctive research roles of text-file concordances and relational databases.

REFERENCES

Aarts, J., & Oostdijk, N. (1988). Corpus-related research at Nijmegen University. In Merja Kytö, Ossi Ihalainen, & Matti Rissanen (Eds.), *Corpus linguistics, hard and soft* (pp. 1–14). Amsterdam: Rodopi.

Aarts, J., & van den Heuvel, T. (1985). Computational tools for the syntactic analysis of corpora. *Linguistics, 23,* 303–335.

Altenberg, B. (1987). *Prosodic patterns in spoken English: Studies in the correlation between prosody and grammar for text-to-speech conversion* (Lund Studies in English 76). Lund, Sweden: Lund University Press.

Blackwell, S. (1987). Syntax versus orthography: Problems in the automatic parsing of idioms. In R. Garside, G. Leech, & G. Sampson (Eds.), *The computational analysis of English: A corpus-based approach* (pp. 110–119). New York: Longman.

Booth, B. (1987). Text input and pre-processing: Dealing with the orthographic form of texts. In R. Garside, G. Leech, & G. Sampson (Eds.), *The computational analysis of English: A corpus-based approach* (pp. 97–109). New York: Longman.

Chafe, W. L. (1979). The flow of thought and the flow of language. In T. Givón (Ed.), *Discourse and syntax* (pp. 159–181). New York: Academic Press.

Chafe, W. L. (1980). The deployment of consciousness in the production of a narrative. In W. L. Chafe (Ed.), *The pear stories: Cognitive, cultural and linguistic aspects of narrative production* (pp. 9–50). Norwood, NJ: Ablex.

Chafe, W. L. (1987). Cognitive constraints on information flow. In R. Tomlin (Ed.), *Coherence and grounding in discourse* (pp. 21–51). Amsterdam: John Benjamins.

Couper-Kuhlen, E. (1986). *An introduction to English prosody.* London: Edward Arnold.

Cruttenden, A. (1986). *Intonation.* Cambridge: Cambridge University Press.

Crystal, D. (1969). *Prosodic systems and intonation in English.* London: Cambridge University Press.

Du Bois, J. W. (1985). Competing motivations. In J. Haiman (Ed.), *Iconicity in syntax* (pp. 343–65). Amsterdam: John Benjamins.

Du Bois, J. W. (1987). The discourse basis of ergativity. *Language, 63,* 805–855.

Du Bois, J. W. (1991). Transcription design principles for spoken discourse research. *Pragmatics, 1,* 71–106.

Du Bois, J. W., Cumming, S., & Schuetze-Coburn, S. (1988). *Discourse profiles coding manual.* Unpublished manuscript, University of California, Santa Barbara.

Du Bois, J. W., & Thompson, S. A. (forthcoming). *Dimensions of a theory of information flow.* Unpublished manuscript, University of California, Santa Barbara.

Du Bois, J. W., Schuetze-Coburn, S., Cumming, S., & Paolino, D. (1991). *Discourse transcription.* Unpublished manuscript, University of California, Santa Barbara.

Ford, C. & Thompson, S. A. (forthcoming). *Interactional units in conversation: Syntactic, intonational, and pragmatic resources for the projection of turn completion.* Unpublished manuscript, University of California, Santa Barbara.

Garside, R. (1987). The CLAWS word-tagging system. In R. Garside, G. Leech, & G. Sampson (Eds.), *The computational analysis of English: A corpus-based approach* (pp. 30–41). New York: Longman.

Garside, R., Leech, G., & Sampson, G. (Eds.). (1987). *The computational analysis of English: A corpus-based approach.* New York: Longman.

Halliday, M. A. K. (1967). Notes on transitivity and theme in English, Part 2. *Journal of Linguistics, 3,* 199–244.

Halliday, M. A. K. (1985). *An introduction to functional grammar.* London: Edward Arnold.

Heidolph, K. E., Flämig, W., & Motsch, W. (1984). *Grundzüge einer deutschen Grammatik.* Berlin: Akademie-Verlag.

Keulen, F. (1986). The Dutch Computer Corpus Pilot Project: Some experiences with a semi-automatic analysis of Contemporary English. In J. Aarts & W. Meijs (Eds.), *Corpus linguistics II: New studies in the analysis and exploitation of computer corpora* (pp. 127–161). Amsterdam: Rodopi.

Oreström, B. (1983). *Turn-taking in English conversation* (Lund Studies in English 66). Lund, Sweden: Lund University Press.

Sacks, H., Schegloff, E. A., & Jefferson, G. (1974). A simplest systematics for the organization of turn-taking. *Language*, 50, 696–735.

Sampson, G. (1987a). Evidence against the "grammatical"/"ungrammatical" distinction. In W. Meijs (Ed.), *Corpus linguistics and beyond* (pp. 219–226). Amsterdam: Rodopi.

Sampson, G. (1987b). The grammatical database and parsing scheme. In R. Garside, G. Leech, & G. Sampson (Eds.), *The computational analysis of English: A corpus-based approach* (pp. 82–96). New York: Longman.

Schuetze-Coburn, S. (1987). *Topic management and the lexicon: A discourse profile of three-argument verbs in German.* Unpublished Masters thesis, Department of Linguistics, University of California, Los Angeles.

Schuetze-Coburn, S., Shapley, M., & Weber, E. G. (1990, July). *Prosodic units in ordinary American English conversation.* Paper presented at the International Pragmatics Conference, Barcelona, Spain.

Schuetze-Coburn, S., Shapley, M., & Weber, E. G. (1991). Units of intonation in discourse: A comparison of acoustic and auditory analyses. *Language and Speech*, 34, 207–234.

Selting, M. (1987). Descriptive categories for the auditive analysis of intonation in conversation. *Journal of Pragmatics*, 11, 777–791.

Sperberg-McQueen, C. M. & Burnard, L. (1990). *Guidelines for the encoding and interchange of machine-readable texts* (Document No. TEI P1). Text Encoding Initiative.

Svartvik, J. (Ed.). (1990a). *The London–Lund corpus of spoken English: Description and research.* Lund, Sweden: Lund University Press.

Svartvik, J. (1990b). Tagging and parsing on the TESS project. In J. Svartvik (Ed.), *The London–Lund corpus of spoken English: Description and research* (pp. 87–106). Lund, Sweden: Lund University Press.

Svartvik, J. (1990c). The TESS project. In J. Svartvik (Ed.), *The London–Lund corpus of spoken English: Description and research* (pp. 63–86). Lund, Sweden: Lund University Press.

Svartvik, J., Eeg-Olofsson, M., Forsheden, O., Oreström, B., & Thavenius, C. (1982). *Survey of spoken English: Report on research 1975–81* (Lund studies in English 63). Lund, Sweden: C. W. K. Gleerup.

Svartvik, J. & Quirk, R. (Eds.). (1980). *A corpus of English conversation* (Lund studies in English 56). Lund, Sweden: C. W. K. Gleerup.

III RESOURCES

10

Survey of Electronic Corpora and Related Resources for Language Researchers

Jane A. Edwards
University of California at Berkeley

CONTENTS

1. INTRODUCTION

Corpora and textbanks of natural language sentences or utterances are becoming increasingly widely used in linguistics, lexicography, and computer science research, in part due to facilitatory technological advances but also due to a broadening of focus in these three fields to include a greater interest in produced language (vs. introspective knowledge), structured interdependencies involving larger stretches of text (vs. individual utterances or sentences), and contrasts across language varieties, genres, and modalities (e.g., British vs. American English; narratives vs. interviews; spoken vs. written language). For further discussion, see Chafe (1992), Church (1991), Fillmore (1992), Francis (1982), Halliday (1992) Leech (1991, 1992), Sinclair (1992), and Svartvik (1992a).

It is significant that a corpus often contains utterances or sentences which would seem implausible from introspection but are perfectly natural and acceptable in context (such as "It'll've been going to've been being tested every day for about a fortnight soon!" from Halliday, 1992), and conversely, that sentences invented to illustrate grammatical points may seem implausible as actual utterances because they violate discourse constraints or expectations reflected in definiteness of referents, aspectual perspectives taken on events, or other properties (see Chafe, 1992, for examples and discussion). Corpus-based approaches can bring to light aspects of linguistic structure and process which are not illuminated in introspectively generated data or psycholinguistic experiments and are needed for comprehensive understanding of language phenomena (see Chafe, 1992; Leech, 1991, 1992; Svartvik, 1992a concerning the particular contributions of different approaches).

In lexicography, corpora and textbanks enable a more efficient exhaustive cataloging of word senses and collocations than is possible with introspection alone (see Kjellmer, 1984; Sinclair, 1982; Sinclair & Kirby, 1990). In addition, they enable systematic attention to contrasts between spoken and written uses of words, contrasts in meaning as a function of position in the utterance or prosodic features, and the relative frequencies of word senses (see Altenberg, 1990, for a comparison of corpus-based dictionaries).

Corpora of increasing size are also being used in probabilistic sense disambiguation, speech recognition, automatic syntactic analysis, automatic assignment of intonation to written texts, and other types of models and applications (to name but a few: Bachenko & Fitzpatrick, 1990; Bindi, Calzolari, Monachini, & Pirrelli, 1991; Brill, Magerman, Marcus, & Santorini, 1990; Church & Hanks, 1990; Hindle & Rooth, 1991; Knowles & Lawrence, 1987; Leech & Garside, 1991; Liberman, 1989; Morris & Hirst, 1991; Sampson, 1992, Svartvik, 1990).

Where one million words was once considered large, some of the projects summarized below seek to gather 100 million words. For written language, this is facilitated by the increasing availability of text already on computer media (such as from typesetter tapes). Spoken language is less frequently available in this way, and therefore must be specially gathered and prepared for electronic use. In both cases, data sharing and reuse is increasingly important both within and across disciplinary boundaries, and a single (large) corpus community seems to be emerging.

This survey is intended in a modest way to help with this development. Its focus is electronic corpora and textbanks, and related information of primary interest to linguistic, computer science, and humanities research. The information summarized here was garnered from standard published sources and the email discussion lists described below. For accuracy, the wording of the individual descriptions is as close as possible to the original source, which is typically the person cited as the contact person in the entry. In addition, the descriptions of completed corpora owe a debt to the following: Chafe, Du Bois, and Thompson (1992); Svartvik (1990), Taylor, Leech and Fligelstone (1989), and the catalogs of the Oxford Text Archive, the ICAME archive, and the Georgetown University archives project, all described below.

What is unique to the current survey is its inclusion of a number of projects and corpora that have sprung up during the past two years, a heavier representation of projects in computational linguistics than in available surveys to date, and the inclusion of electronic discussion lists and public lists of email addresses, few of which were available at the time of the earlier surveys.

The first version of this compilation was completed in 1991, and was updated and expanded to include new developments through October 1992. Although I have attempted to make this survey as complete as possible, this is a rapidly growing area. Any update of this survey will be submitted to the ICAME fileserver (see below), possibly for access via anonymous ftp (file transfer software available on many mainframes).

Concerning corpora developed before computers, readers are referred to Francis (1992). Lexicographical resources are treated here only briefly, in Sections 5H and 5I. For further information, readers are referred to Altenberg (1990), Atkins, Clear, and Ostler (1992), Boguraev and Briscoe (1988), Gellerstam (1988), Sinclair (1987), Sinclair and Kirby (1990), and Walker (1992).

The materials survey below are organized with respect to five main headings:

- information sources (associations, email addresses and discussion lists);
- encoding standards;
- data sources (archives and repositories, surveys of electronic language data);
- descriptions of selected corpora and textbanks; and
- bibliographies of related research.

The Appendix contains Susan Hockey's summary of resources relevant to humanities computing.

2. INFORMATION SOURCES

A. Centers and Associations

The following organizations encourage corpus-related research and the exchange of corpus-related information by publishing journals, sponsoring conferences and workshops, and various other professional activities. (Organizations concerned with the gathering and distribution of electronic data are summarized under "Data Sources," later in this chapter.)

   1. **The Norwegian Computing Centre for the Humanities (NCCH)** was established in 1972 as a center for research and development to help individual researchers and academic institutions in the use of computers in the humanities. To this end, it develops computing methods and software for application in humanistic research and provides information and teaching services to demonstrate how computer technology can be utilized in the field. This work is carried out in cooperation with humanities research institutions and the Norwegian universities' computing departments. NCCH houses the ICAME archive (described later), which contains the most widely used linguistic corpora of English, and distributes these data at low cost to researchers. Its ICAME CD-ROM contains the Brown Corpus (written American English), the LOB Corpus (written British English), the London–Lund Corpus (spoken British English), the Helsinki Corpus (diachronic English) and the Kolhapur Corpus (Indian English), and costs roughly $500 US. Further information on the CD-ROM can be obtained by emailing the message "send icame info.cd" to fileserv@nora.hd.uib.no, or via anonymous ftp to nora.hd.uib.no (129.177.24.42) (filename: pub/icame/info.cd). NCCH sponsors the electronic bulletin board, "CORPORA" (described below), and serves as a clearinghouse for information concerning corpora, corpus availability, and corpus research. For more information: NCCH, Humanistisk Datasenter, Harald Haarfagres gt. 31, N–5007 Bergen, Norway; Tel: +47 (5) 212954; FAX: +47 (5) 322656; email: adm@nora.hd.uib.no or knut@x400.hd.uib.no.

   2. **The Computers in Teaching Initiative Centre for Textual Studies (CTI)** was established in 1990 to promote and support the use of computers in teaching literature, linguistics and related disciplines in all British universities. Begun under the direction of Susan Hockey, the CTI produces a newsletter, called *Computers in Literature*, and a software guide and holds periodic

training workshops concerned with the use of computers in humanities training and research. It also sponsors the Humanities Bulletin Board (HUMBUL) described in a later section. For more information: CTI Centre for Textual Studies, University of Oxford Computing Services, 13 Banbury Road, Oxford, OX2 6NN, UK; Tel: +44 (865) 273 221; FAX: +44 (865) 273 275; email: ctitext@vax.oxford.ac.uk.

3. **The Center for Electronic Texts in the Humanities (CETH),** directed by Susan Hockey, was established in 1991 by Rutgers and Princeton Universities with external support from the Mellon Foundation and the National Endowment for the Humanities. It is intended to become a national focus of interest in the United States for those who are involved in the creation, dissemination and use of electronic texts in the humanities, and it will act as a national node on an international network of centers and projects which are actively involved in the handling of electronic texts. Developed from the international inventory of machine-readable texts which was begun at Rutgers in 1983 and is held on RLIN, the Center is now reviewing the records in the inventory and continues to catalog new texts. The acquisition and dissemination of text files to the community is another important activity, concentrating on a selection of good quality texts which can be made available over Internet with suitable retrieval software and with appropriate copyright permission. The Center also acts as a clearinghouse on information related to electronic texts, directing inquirers to other sources of information. Susan Hockey's useful list of resources for humanities computing is included below in the Appendix. For further information: Center for Electronic Texts in the Humanities, 169 College Avenue, New Brunswick, NJ 08903, USA; email ceth@zodiac.rutgers.edu or ceth@zodiac.bitnet or hockey@zodiac.bitnet; Tel: +1 (908) 932-1384; FAX: +1 (908) 932-1386.

4. **The Association for Computers and the Humanities (ACH)** is an international organization devoted to computer-aided research in literature and language studies, history, philosophy, anthropology, and related social sciences, especially research involving the manipulation and analysis of textual materials. The ACH encourages development and dissemination of significant textual and linguistic resources and software for scholarly research. Its official journal, *Computers and the Humanities,* is published six times a year. It also publishes *Bits and Bytes Review,* a review of software in the humanities and social sciences, nine times each year. Jointly with the ALLC (see next entry), it sponsors an annual meeting held in North America in odd-numbered years and in Europe in even-numbered years, which brings together scholars from around the world to report on research activities and software and hardware developments in the field. ACH initiated the Text Encoding Initiative (TEI),

an international effort to develop guidelines for the encoding of machine-readable literary and linguistic data.   The ACH also sponsors the Rutgers/Princeton National Text Archive, the HUMANIST Electronic Discussion Group, and the LN Electronic Bulletin Board for Natural Language Studies in French and English.   For further information: Joseph Rudman, Association for Computers and the Humanities, Department of English, Carnegie-Mellon   University,   Pittsburgh,   PA   15213,   USA;   email: rudman@cmphys.bitnet.

5. **The Association for Literary and Linguistic Computing (ALLC)** has representatives in over 30 countries, including advisors in the following areas: Machine Translation, Computer-Assisted Learning, Lexicography, Software, Structured Databases.   Its journal, *Literary and Linguistic Computing*, is published four times per year, containing papers on all aspects of computing applied to literature and language, ranging from computing techniques to results of research projects.   To join ALLC and obtain the journal: Journals Marketing, Oxford University Press, Pinkhill House, Southfield Road, Eynsham, Oxford, OX8 1JJ, UK, or Journals Marketing, Oxford University Press, 2001 Evans Road, Cary, NC 27513, USA.

6. **The Association for Computational Linguistics (ACL)** promotes research on computational linguistics and natural language processing.   It publishes the journal *Computational Linguistics* and sponsors annual meetings (usually in North America), biennial European meetings, and biennial meetings on applied natural language processing, and supports the international conferences on Computational Linguistics (COLING). Proceedings of past meetings are available through the ACL Office.   The ACL also sponsors the Text Encoding Initiative (TEI), for standardizing the encoding and interchange of machine-readable text, and two data collection initiatives—the Data Collection Initiative (DCI) and the European Corpus Initiative (ECI)—(described later, under Data Sources) to assemble massive text corpora in English and other languages, and make them available for scientific research at cost and without royalties.   Recently, the ACL established a series of Special Interest Groups (SIGs) on the Mathematics of Language, the Lexicon, Parsing, Generation, Computational Phonetics, and Multimedia Language Processing.   Others are likely.   The SIGs organize workshops, prepare bibliographies, and provide specialized communication channels.   For more information: Donald E. Walker (ACL), Bellcore, MRE 2A379, 445 South Street, Box 1910, Morristown, NJ 07960–1910, USA; FAX: +1 (201) 829–5981; email: walker@bellcore.com.

B. Electronic Mail Distribution Lists and Discussion Lists

Electronic distribution lists and discussion lists distribute messages contributed by subscribers to all other subscribers on that list. They are a good forum for queries and current information, are easy to join and unjoin, and often cost nothing beyond what the user's institution is already paying for email service.

1. **HUMBUL (Humanities Bulletin Board)** is a long-running service aimed at providing academics and interested parties with news and information on Humanities Computing. This service is an on-line bulletin board, edited by Stuart Lee at the CTI (described earlier) at Oxford University. Information is collected from all applicable electronic networks plus periodicals, leaflets, and also direct requests to the editor. At regular intervals, HUMBUL indicates its most recent acquisitions, and these can be accessed via ftp, telnet, or other means. To subscribe, send the following one-line command to listserv@UKACRL.bitnet:

SUB HUMBUL <John Doe>

where <John Doe> is your name. If you do not then receive an automatic message saying you have been added to the list, send email to: humbul@vax.oxford.ac.uk.

2. Begun in 1992, **CORPORA** is an international email discussion list for information and questions about text corpora, such as availability, aspects of compiling and using corpora, software, tagging, parsing, bibliography, and related matters. To join the list, send a message to:

CORPORA-REQUEST@nora.hd.uib.no

To submit a contribution to the list, send it to:

CORPORA@nora.hd.uib.no

The list administrator is Knut Hofland, NCCH, Humanistisk Datasenter, Harald Haarfagres gt. 31, N-5007 Bergen, Norway; Tel: +47 (5) 212954; FAX: +47 (5) 322656; email: knut@x400.hd.uib.no.

3. **HUMANIST** is an international email discussion list for issues relating to the application of computers to scholarship in the humanities. This includes linguistics, comparative literature, philosophy, Biblical studies, and several other fields. Begun in 1987 under joint sponsorship of the ACH, the ALLC and the University of Toronto's Centre for Computing in the Humanities, it is

currently housed at Brown University and moderated by Elaine Brennan and Allen Renear. It has over 600 members in 24 countries. To subscribe, mail "SUB <your email address>" to listserv@brownvm.brown.edu; to post articles, mail them to humanist@brownvm.brown.edu. Articles submitted to HUMANIST are archived on a file server and can be searched remotely by means of one-line listserv commands.

4. **LINGUIST** is an international list intended as a place for discussion of issues of concern to the academic discipline of linguistics and related fields. It is moderated by Anthony Aristar (University of Western Australia) and Helen Dry (University of Texas at San Antonio). It explicitly welcomes discussion of any linguistic subfield. To subscribe to LINGUIST, send email to the LINGUIST listserver (listserv@TAMVM1.bitnet or listserv@TAMVM1.tamu.edu), containing the following one-line message:

SUBSCRIBE LINGUIST <Your Name>

for example, "subscribe linguist Jane Smith." To submit a posting to the list, mail it to linguist@TAMVM1.tamu.edu.

The LINGUIST fileserver may contain contributed files of interest to language researchers, such as the LSA or Georgetown lists of corpora, and linguists' email addresses and these are similarly obtainable by one-line commands. For more information, send the one-line command "help linguist" via email to linguist-request@TAMVM1.tamu.edu. For questions requiring human attention, send a message to: linguist-editors@TAMVM1.tamu.edu.

5. **LN, Langage Naturel**, is an international list for computational linguistics, sponsored by the Association for Computational Linguistics (ACL) and the Association for Computers and the Humanities (ACH). Its goal is to disseminate calls for papers; conference and seminar announcements; requests for software, corpora, and various types of data; project descriptions; and discussions on technical topics. The list is primarily French-speaking, but many items are circulated in English. The list is moderated by Jean Veronis (Vassar University) and Pierre Zweigenbaum (France). To subscribe to LN, send the following one-line message to listserv@FRMOP11.bitnet:

SUBSCRIBE LN your name

To post a message to the list as a whole, email it to LN@FRMOP11.bitnet. In case of problems, send a message to one of the editors: veronis@vassar.bitnet or zweig@FRSIM51.bitnet.

6. **PROSODY** is an international list with members representing a broad spectrum of approaches including linguistics, psycholinguistics, and computer science. It serves a vital function of disseminating information concerning available resources in a technologically rapidly expanding area. To subscribe, send: "subscribe prosody <your name>" to LISTSERV@msu.bitnet. Send postings to PROSODY@msu.bitnet. The list is managed by George Allen, Michigan State University (email: alleng@msu.bitnet) who also owns the list, "HYPERCARD."

7. **Comserve** is an electronic information service for professionals and students interested in human communication studies. It is located at Rensselaer Polytechnic Institute and coordinated by Timothy Stephen and Teresa Harrison, both of whom are professors in communication studies. Comserve keeps archives of bibliographies, course materials, job announcements, text transcripts, and other materials, with the author retaining the rights and the copyright. It coordinates a number of hotlines on communication, which can be subscribed to via the listserver. To subscribe to the Ethnomethodology hotline, send the following one-line message to comserve@rpiecs.bitnet:

Join Ethno Your_name

To obtain a long list of useful bibliographic information, send the following one-line message to comserve@rpiecs.bitnet:

send compunet biblio

Send materials to be posted to the net to ethno@rpiecs.bitnet and materials to be archived to support@rpiecs.bitnet;

8. **Applied linguistics lists**. From Ken Willing at Macquarie University, I learned of the following four lists and their listserver addresses:

TESL-L (Teaching English as a Second Language)
        Listserver address: listserv@cunyvm.bitnet

SLART-L (Second Language Acquisition Research and Teaching)
        Listserver address: listserv@psuvm.bitnet

MULTI-L (Language and Education in Multicultural Settings)
        Listserver address: listserv@barilvm.bitnet

LTEST-L (Language Testing Research and Practice)
        Listserver address: listserv@UCLACN1.bitnet

To subscribe, send a one-line email message to the indicated address, containing:

subscribe XXXXXX John Doe

where XXXXXX is the list-name (e.g. TESL-L), and John Doe is your name.

9. **FUNKNET**, headed by Talmy Givon and Paul Hopper, is a discussion list concerned with various aspects of human language, communication, cognition, socioculture, neuropsychology, and other facets of cognitive and communicative behavior, viewed from what might loosely be called the functionalist perspective, that is, language viewed as an instrument of communication, coding experience, an evolved neurobiological phenomenon, a sociocultural phenomenon, or a combination of these, with an emphasis on empirical language study, including especially corpus data.   For further information, contact Talmy Givon at:

funknet-request@oregon.uoregon.edu

10. **info-childes** and **info-psyling** are international email distribution lists, moderated by Julia Evans and Brian MacWhinney, Psychology Department, Carnegie Mellon University.   Info-childes circulates information concerning corpus-related child language research, and info-psyling circulates information on psycholinguistics.   To subscribe, send email to brian+@andrew.cmu.edu.

11. **ASLING-L** is a list for linguistic study of signed languages, including all linguistic areas, including syntax, acquisition, phonology, morphology, psycholinguistics, and cognition.   To subscribe, send:

SUB ASLING-L <your name>

to listserv@yalevm.bitnet.   The listowner is Christine Romano (cromano @uconnvm.bitnet).

12. **List of lists**.   A very lengthy list of Bitnet and Internet discussion lists (presently over one megabyte long) can be obtained via anonymous ftp to ftp.nisc.sri.com (192.33.33.22) in the directory netinfo as "interest-groups.Z" or by sending the following one-line message to mail-server@nisc.sri.com, making sure in advance that your system has sufficient space to receive it:

SEND NETINFO/INTEREST-GROUPS

A related list can be obtained by sending email to listserv@ndsuvm1.bitnet with the following one-line message:

    sendme interest package

For further information concerning electronic discussion lists, see the ARL Directory of Electronic Publications (below).

C. Email Addresses

There are now several periodically updated lists of email addresses for researchers engaged in language-related research. One of them is compiled by Norval Smith and associates at the University of Amsterdam and accessible for retrieval and modification via the name server linguists@alf.let.uva.nl. For information, send the word "HELP" as a one line-command to this address. To receive the full list of email addresses, send "list *" (with a space between *list* and *). For a list of FAX addresses, send "list fax."

The other main list is the one compiled by John Moyne for the Linguistic Society of America (LSA). It can be obtained electronically via anonymous ftp to csli.stanford.edu or by sending the following one-line message to the LINGUIST listserver, listserv@tamvm1.tamu.edu:

    GET LSA LST LINGUIST

It can be obtained in hard copy from: LSA, 1325 18th St. NW, Suite 211, Washington D.C. 20036, USA; email: moygc@cunyvm.bitnet or ZZLSA@GALLUA.bitnet.

3. TEXT ENCODING STANDARDS

The sources listed in this section are not exhaustive, but are useful starting points in part as clearinghouses for information on related projects in addition to their own proposals.

1. The **Text Encoding Initiative (TEI)** (Burnard, 1991; Hockey, 1991; Sperberg-McQueen & Burnard, 1992; Walker, 1992; Walker & Hockey, 1991) is an international and interdisciplinary project of the ALLC, ACH, and ACL in collaboration to define text encoding guidelines and establish a common interchange for machine-readable literary and linguistic data. Fifteen other scholarly organizations including the Linguistics Society of America are

represented on its advisory board. The project has received major funding from the National Endowment for the Humanities, the European Economic Community, and The Andrew W. Mellon Foundation and has a number of subcommittees specializing in particular aspects of this enormous task. This includes working groups on spoken language encoding, encoding for lexicons, and phonetic encoding.

TEI working papers and reports, including a copy of the *Guidelines for the Encoding and Interchange of Machine-readable Texts*, can be obtained in hard copy from Wendy Plotkin (U49127@UICVM.bitnet) or electronically from LISTSERV@UICVM.bitnet. For a list of available documents, send the following line to LISTSERV@UICVM.bitnet:

GET TEI-L FILELIST

For further information: C. Michael Sperberg-McQueen, Editor of TEI, Computer Center (M/C 135), University of Illinois at Chicago, Box 6998, Chicago, IL 60680, USA; Tel: +1 (312) 996-2477; FAX: +1 (312) 996-6834; email: u35395@uicvm.cc.uic.edu or u35395@uicvm.bitnet.

2. In 1989 in Kiel, Germany, the IPA Working Group on Suprasegmental Categories initiated an **IPA Number scheme** that facilitates transmission of data by code (if correspondents set up their systems to refer to the common IPA Number). Their proposal also includes encoding of suprasegmental categories (see Bruce, 1989, 1992; Bruce & Touati, 1990). For further information: Gosta Bruce, Professor of Phonetics, Lund University, Sweden; email: linglund@seldc52.bitnet, or John Esling, Linguistics Department, University of Victoria, British Columbia, Canada; email: VQPLOT@uvvm.bitnet.

3. The **Speech Assessment Methodology (SAM)** project is developing a prosodic labeling system to facilitate computer readable prosodic transcriptions, representation of prosodic properties in the lexicon, and tools for prosodic labelling. Their system is intended to be uncommitted with respect to prosodic theories, and is being developed in conjunction with the ASL (Architecture for Speech Language Systems) project. For more information: Dafydd Gibbon, Linguistik und Literaturwissenschaft, University of Bielefeld, P-8640, D-4800 Bielefeld 1; FAX +49 (521) 1065844; email: gibbon@LILI11.UNI-BIELEFELD.DE.

4. The **TOnes and Break Indices (TOBI)** is a prosodic labeling system (Silverman et al., 1992). In 1991 and 1992, Victor Zue (MIT) and Kim Silverman (Nynex), sponsored two prosodic transcription workshops for the development of a prosodic labelling system, to facilitate the sharing of corpora in a manner

compatible with WAVES(tm) format, and to accompany speech files and time-aligned analysis records for sets of utterances. TOBI focuses especially on word groupings and prominences, in a manner loosely tied to Pierrehumbert (1980) and Pierrehumbert and Hirschberg (1990). The description of the TOBI system, sample WAVES(tm) scripts and supporting materials will be announced on the Prosody discussion list, and made available via anonymous ftp at kiwi.nmt.edu (129.138.1.82), or cassette tape, with an invitation for feedback from potential users.

4. DATA SOURCES

A. Electronic Data Archives and Repositories

1. The **Oxford Text Archive (OTA)**, directed by Lou Burnard, is by far the largest archive of computerized language texts and corpora on this list. Its catalog lists nearly 2000 titles, including over 450 separate collections of written or spoken language in nearly three dozen languages. It is a deposit archive for textbanks from private scholarly research, and welcomes for inclusion collections of any specialization and in any format for reuse within the scholarly community. Its facilities are free and secure and provided as a service to the world's academic community. Access to the archive is possible by anonymous ftp, online, by tape (9-track; Density 800, 1600 or 6250 bpi; ASCII or EBCDIC; fixed, variable, or formatted), by diskette (MS-DOS or Macintosh; HD or DD; 3.5" or 5.25"), by cartridge (DC300, TAR format only), or over networks. Costs to users are kept low to enable wide access.

Its catalogue, now over 60 pages long, is available in hard copy from the address given below, or electronically, in either SGML (international mark-up standard for written texts) or non-SGML format. The catalog and some of its texts are available via anonymous ftp to black.ox.ac.uk (or 129.67.1.165).

For more information: Alan Morrison or Lou Burnard, Oxford Text Archive, Oxford University Computing Services, 13 Banbury Road, Oxford OX2 6NN, UK; Tel: +44 (865) 273238 [direct line] or 273200 [switchboard]; FAX: +44 (865) 273275; archive@vax.oxford.ac.uk.

2. The **International Computer Archive of Modern English (ICAME)** was established in 1977 with the aims of (a) collecting and distributing information on electronically available English language materials and on linguistic research involving these materials, (b) compiling an archive of English text corpora in machine-readable form, and (c) making material available to research institutions. Its holdings include the three most widely used electronic corpora of spoken and written language (the Brown, LOB, and

London–Lund corpora, described later) and several other large corpora, some with grammatical annotations, together with corpus-related software, and are distributed through the NCCH in Bergen, Norway (described earlier). The ICAME CD-ROM contains the Brown, LOB, London–Lund, Helsinki and Kolhapur corpora together with software and a summary of discussion lists, networks, surveys, and corpora, and is available for approximately $500 US. Their survey is independent of the current one and should be consulted as an important resource, as it may contain information not covered here, especially with respect to European projects. Further information concerning the CD-ROM can be obtained by sending the command "send icame info.cd" to fileserv@nora.hd.uib.no or via anonymous ftp to nora.hd.uib.no (129.177.24.42). Its catalog of holdings and related document files can be obtained via anonymous ftp to nora.hd.uib.no (129.177.24.42) or by fileserver commands sent to fileserv@nora.hd.uib.no. For more information regarding the fileserver, email the following command to fileserv@nora.hd.uib.no: send icame file.servers.

ICAME holds an annual conference (with some proceedings available from Rodopi Publishers, Amsterdam) and produces a journal once a year, edited by Stig Johansson at the University of Oslo, containing analyses of corpus data, surveys of archives, and book reviews.

For more information: ICAME, Norwegian Computing Centre for the Humanities, Harald Haarfagres gt. 31, N–5007 Bergen, Norway; Tel: +47 (5) 212954 or 212955 or 212956; FAX: +47 (5) 322656; email: adm@nora.hd.uib.no or knut@x400.hd.uib.no.

3. The **Child Language Exchange System (CHILDES)** (MacWhinney, 1991; MacWhinney & Snow, 1985) contains child language data in several languages, including a number of the major child language corpora in English. It also contains some corpora of adult language (e.g., the Cornell Corpus described later). Data contributions are welcomed and secure and are made available free of charge after contacting Brian MacWhinney to become a member of CHILDES (also free of charge). The data are accessible via anonymous ftp to poppy.psy.cmu.edu or CD-ROM or other magnetic media. The archive also offers a free software package (CLAN) for use on PCs, MACs and mainframes and manages the info-psyling and info-childes electronic discussion groups. For more information: Brian MacWhinney, Department of Psychology, Carnegie Mellon University, Pittsburgh, PA, 15213 USA; email: brian+@andrew.cmu.edu; Tel: +1 (412) 268-2782.

4. The **Center for Electronic Texts in the Humanities (CETH)** is described earlier.

5. The **Aboriginal Studies Electronic Data Archive,** housed by the Australian Institute of Aboriginal and Torres Strait Islander Studies (AIATSIS), includes over 150 Australian indigenous languages. It is available to researchers, subject to deposit and access conditions. The catalog of holdings is available by sending the following one-line message to listserv@tamvm1.tamu.bitnet:

get aboriginal-cat

For further information: Aboriginal Studies Electronic Data Archive, AIATSIS, GPO Box 553, Canberra, ACT 2601, Australia; Tel: +61 (6) 246 1170; FAX: +61 (6) 249 7310; email: aiatsis@peg.apc.org.

6. **Project Gutenberg** makes available literary works on electronic media. These are available via anonymous ftp from mrcnext.cso.uiuc.edu (or 128.174.73.105).   For more information: Michael Hart, email: hart@vmd.cso.uiuc.edu.

7. **Library of the Future** is a set of CD-ROMs sold by DAK Industries, containing the complete unabridged text of 453 novels, stories, plays and historical documents. For more information: DAK Industries, 8200 Remmet Ave., Canoga Park, CA, 91304, USA; Tel: +1 (800) 888–6703.

B. Surveys of Electronic Language Data

Three long lists (items #1 through 3 below) cover the major language research corpora in the common domain (plus a couple which are not). These lists are best obtained from their sources (given below) rather than in static printed sources, since some of them are updated periodically. Some further data sources may be found in Levelt, Mills, and Karmiloff (1981), though, it is difficult to know which of these may have become computerized in the meantime. Two sources for humanities texts beyond those included below are Raben and Gaunt (forthcoming) and, from the Appendix, Hughes (1987) and Lancashire and McCarty (1989).

1. The **OTA** catalogue, mentioned earlier, provides 60 pages of corpus descriptions.

2. The **University of Lancaster Survey** describes 56 language archive projects intended mainly for linguistic research. This includes non-English corpora and several varieties of English (Indian, Canadian, and Australian), some of which contain rich grammatical and semantic tags for individual words in the corpus. Taylor, Leech, and Fligelstone (1989) is available from

the HUMANIST file server by sending the following one-line command to listserv@brownvm.bitnet:

GET SURVEY CORPORA HUMANIST

or via anonymous ftp to NCCH at nora.hd.uib.no (129.177.24.42) (filename: pub/icame/survey.corpora). The parts concerning English texts are published in Taylor, Leech, and Fligelstone (1991).

3. The **Georgetown University Catalog of Projects in Electronic Text (CPET)**, begun in 1989, contains highly informative descriptions and access information for over 312 electronic corpus projects in 27 countries and is continually updated. It can be accessed via telnet to guvax3.georgetown.edu. For further information: Paul Mangiafico, Center for Text and Technology, Reiss Science Building, Room 238, Georgetown University, Washington, DC 20057, USA; Tel: +1 (202) 687-6096; pmangiafico@guvax.georgetown.edu.

4. The **Walker and Zampolli Survey of Written and Spoken Language in Machine-Readable Form** (in progress), directed by Don Walker (Bellcore, Morristown, NJ, USA; walker@bellcore.com) and Antonio Zampolli (Institute for Computational Linguistics, Pisa, Italy; glottolo@icnucevm.cnuce.cnr.it), is being conducted to provide a comprehensive inventory of such materials. It is sponsored by several associations discussed elsewhere in this chapter (including the ACH, the ACL and its Data Collection Initiative, the ALLC, the CETH, and the TEI), and also the Modern Language Association, the European Science Foundation, the Commission of the European Communities, the Network of European Reference Corpora, the Linguistic Data Consortium (LDC) among others. For more information about the textual component: Textual Data Survey, Center for Electronic Texts in the Humanities, 169 College Avenue, New Brunswick, NJ 08903, USA; FAX +1 (908) 932-1386; ceth@zodiac.rutgers.edu.

5. The list of **Electronic Texts in Philosophy** was compiled by Leslie Burkholder (CDEC, Carnegie Mellon University) in December 1991 for the American Philosophical Association. It can be obtained from the HUMANIST file server by sending an email message to brownvm.bitnet containing only the following line:

GET PHILOSFY ETEXTS HUMANIST

6. **List of Electronic Dictionaries**. In a posting to HUMANIST (Vol. 4, No. 1137. Thursday, 7 Mar 1991), Russ Wooldridge (wulfric@vm.epas.utoronto.ca)

listed 58 electronic dictionaries, mostly in English but also including several European languages and Hebrew, Greek, and Latin. This list is available from the HUMANIST file server.

7. The **Catalog of the University of Cambridge Literature and Linguistics Computing Centre** is a published catalog (see Dawson, 1977).

8. The **Linguistic Society of America List,** compiled in 1987 by Lise Menn, turned up numerous data sets but only relatively few of them on computer. For more information, contact the LSA office (at the address provided above concerning the list of linguists' email addresses).

9. The **Marchand list of CD-ROM projects** was compiled by James Marchand at the University of Illinois and is available via the Humanist fileserver by mailing the following one-line command to listserv@brownvm.bitnet:

GET CDROM PROJECTS HUMANIST

10. **ARL Directory of Electronic Publications**. Although many journals, newsletters and scholarly lists may be accessed free of charge through Bitnet, Internet and affiliated networks, it is not always simple to know what is available. Compiled and published by the Association of Research Libraries (ISBN #1057–1337), this directory provides access information to 500 scholarly lists, 30 journals, and 60 newsletters. It is available in either hard copy or on 3.5 inch diskette, at a cost of $20 to nonmembers of the ARL. For more information: Office of Scientific and Academic Publishing, Association of Research Libraries, 1527 New Hampshire Ave., NW, Washington, DC. 20036, USA; email: ARLHQ@umdc.umd.edu or ARLHQ@umdc.bitnet; FAX: 202–462-7849. The "Directory of Electronic Journals and Newsletters," compiled by Michael Strangelove in 1991, can be obtained at no charge by sending an email message to listserv@uottawa.bitnet containing the following two lines:

GET EJOURNL1 DIRECTRY
GET EJOURNL2 DIRECTRY

5. CORPORA AND TEXTBANKS

It is common to distinguish between corpora and textbanks. These differ in size and composition, and serve somewhat different analytic aims. Corpora are intended to be representative of some specified population or genre. Textbanks tend to be collections of available data with looser connection to each other, or focus on a restricted number of genres (including perhaps only one). Corpora are needed for large scale, systematic contrasts of, for example, language varieties, genres, and modalities (e.g., American vs. British English, informative vs. imaginative prose, or spoken vs. written language). Other research requires enormous amounts of data, even if from fewer genres, as for example, in lexicography, in order to detect words and collocations which occur only rarely. (For systematic discussion of corpus design, size, and sampling issues, see Atkins, Clear, & Ostler, 1992; Church, 1991; Carroll, Davies, & Richman, 1971; Fillmore, 1992; Francis, 1982; Kucera & Francis, 1967; Leech, 1991, 1992; Poplack, 1989; Sinclair, 1982, 1992; Walker, 1991.) A particularly interesting concept is that of a "monitor corpus," intended to be not finite or temporally bounded but rather gaining and losing texts over time in parallel with the fluidity of the language itself (Sinclair, 1982; 1992).

Listed below are collections of running prose, followed by some phonetic databases, lexical databases, and treebanks (that is, databases of bracketed and syntactically labeled structures, such as noun phrase, verb phrase, etc.). The survey is probably less exhaustive for the phonetic, lexical, and treebank sections than for the sections on corpora and textbanks of running prose, which were the dominant focus in compiling it.

A. Running Text: English Language

The three most widely used corpora to date are the Brown corpus, the Lancaster/Oslo-Bergen (LOB) corpus, and the London-Lund corpus. These are described first, followed by descriptions of 23 others that are well-known within one or another subdomain of corpus-based language research (i.e., linguistics, psycholinguistics, computational linguistics, lexicology and lexicography), ordered in thematically related clusters and roughly chronologically within each cluster.

1. The **Brown Corpus** (The Standard Corpus of Present-Day Edited American English) (Francis, 1982; Francis & Kucera, 1979, 1982; Kucera, 1992; Kucera & Francis, 1967) is a corpus of 1 million words of written American English printed in the year 1961. It was the first corpus to be put on computer medium and is the most analyzed corpus of English to date. It consists of 500 written American English texts of 2,000 words apiece, selected to represent diverse genres of written American language. There are two main sections: Informative Prose and Imaginative Prose. Genres represented include newspaper reportage, press editorials, memoirs, religion, science fiction, detective fiction, and romance novels (excluding drama and fiction with more than 50% dialog). This corpus of running text is available for

academic research for the cost of materials from both the Oxford Text Archive and the ICAME archive and is contained on the ICAME CD-ROM available through NCCH (see above).

A "tagged" version of the Brown Corpus (i.e., supplemented by labeling of individual words for 82 part-of-speech designations) was produced at Brown University during the period 1970–1978 with assistance from the TAGGIT program, written by B. B. Greene and G. M. Rubin (for additional details, see Francis, 1980; Garside, Leech, & Sampson, 1987; Svartvik, 1990). The tagged version is protected by its own copyright, and is available for $1000 to academic institutions. For more information: Text Research, 196 Bowen Street, Providence RI 02906, USA. FAX: +1 (401) 751–8958 or Nelson Francis or Henry Kucera, Department of Linguistics, Brown University, Providence RI 02906, USA; email: henry@brownvm.bitnet or henry_kucera@brown.edu.

For a parsed (as opposed to part-of-speech tagged) version of part of the Brown corpus, known as the **Gothenburg Corpus**, contact: Gudrun Magnusdottir, Sprakdata, University of Göteborg, S–412 98 Göteborg, Sweden. The **Susanne Corpus** (Surface and Underlying Structural Analyses of Naturalistic English), using more transparent codes, for easier research use is currently in preparation. For information: G. Sampson, Department of Linguistics and Phonetics, University of Leeds, Leeds LS2 9JT, UK.

2. The **Lancaster–Oslo/Bergen Corpus (LOB)** is 1 million words of written British English from 1961. It was compiled in the 1970's under the direction of Geoffrey Leech, University of Lancaster, and Stig Johansson, University of Oslo. It is the British counterpart of the Brown corpus, and contains 500 texts of roughly 2,000 words each. The texts range across the same types of published written language as those of the Brown corpus, and the number of texts of each type are almost identical to those of the Brown corpus. A tagged version of the LOB corpus was produced between 1978 and 1983, using the CLAWS1 automatic tagging system, which uses text-based probabilities. Garside, Leech, and Sampson (1987) and Leech and Garside (1991) provide details of their methods and a survey of methods for automatic tagging and parsing of language corpora more generally.

Both the tagged and untagged versions of the LOB corpus are available for academic use from the ICAME archive, and are contained on the ICAME CD-ROM described above. Their manuals (Johansson, Leech, & Goodluck, 1978, and Johansson, Atwell, Garside, & Leech, 1986, respectively) are also available from ICAME. A hand-parsed version of 45,000 words from the LOB is available as the **Lancaster–Leeds Treebank**; an automatically parsed version of 140,000 words from the LOB is available as the **Lancaster Parsed Corpus** (both described below, under "Treebanks"). A larger treebank is being prepared by Steve Fligelstone. For further information: Steve Fligelstone, UCREL, Linguistics Department, Bowland College, Lancaster University, Lancaster LA1 4XZ, UK; email: eia002@lancaster.ac.uk.

3. The **London-Lund Corpus (LLC)** is 500,000 words of spoken educated British English, collected during the 1960's and early 1970's from speakers of various ages, representing a range of discourse types. They were transcribed to include markings of tone unit boundaries, nucleus (points of pitch prominence), direction of nuclear tones, pauses, degrees of stress, and other features. The data were originally gathered as the spoken half of the Survey of English Usage, used in several major reference grammars of English (Leech & Svartvik, 1975; Quirk, Greenbaum, Leech, & Svartvik, 1972, 1985). The first 87 texts to be computerized are published in Svartvik and Quirk (1980). The remaining 13 texts have now been added to the computerized corpus. The full 100 texts can be obtained for academic use from the ICAME and OTA archives, and are contained on the ICAME CD-ROM (described above). They are available as either running text or supplemented by semantic and syntactic tags associated with all words in the texts. The manual for the LLC (Svartvik, 1992b) is distributed through ICAME/NCCH. A bibliography of 200 studies using this corpus is found in Svartvik (1990). A parsed version of a part of the data is described in that source.

4. The **Lancaster Spoken English Corpus (SEC)** (Knowles & Lawrence, 1987) consists of 52,000 words of contemporary spoken British English, gathered between 1984 and 1987, from radio broadcasts, university lectures and several other types of speech. It is available from the ICAME archive in orthographic and prosodic transcription, with word–class tags (generated by CLAWS2) and accompanying manual. For more information, contact NCCH or Peter Roach, Linguistics Department, Leeds University; email: p.j.roach@cmsl.leeds.ac.uk; or Gerry Knowles, Linguistics Department, Bowland College, Lancaster University, Lancaster LA1 4XZ, UK; email: eia008@central1.lancaster.ac.uk.

5. The **PIXI Corpora** consist of 450 naturally occurring conversations recorded in bookshops in England and Italy, for the purpose of cross-cultural comparisons of discourse structure. They are available in electronic form from the Oxford Text Archive, and in book form in Gavioli & Mansfield (1990), together with careful details of the data gathering, discourse contexts, analytic approach and bibliography of related publications. For further information, contact the Oxford Text Archive or Guy Aston (VK1A@ICINECA.bitnet).

6. The **Helsinki Corpus of Historical English** (Rissanen, 1992) is a textbank of 1.5 million written words from law, handbooks, science, trials, sermons, diaries, documents, plays, and private and official correspondence from periods at roughly 100-year intervals beginning in 850. It is used for variational study of the development of English. The manual for this corpus is Kytö (1991), distributed through ICAME/NCCH. For more information contact: Matti Rissanen, or Merja Kytö (mkyto@cc.helsinki.fi), Department of English, University of Helsinki, Porthania 311, 00100 Helsinki, Finland. A corpus of dialectal English is underway (Ihalainen, 1987). For information, contact Ossi Ihalainen at the same address. The Helsinki Corpus is contained on the ICAME CD-ROM (see above).

7. The **Macquarie (University) Corpus** (Peters, 1987) is nearing completion. It consists of 1 million words of Australian English and is intended to be comparable to the Brown Corpus. For more information: Pam Peters, David Blair, Peter Collins, or Alison Brierley, School of English and Linguistics, Macquarie University, 2109 New South Wales, Australia.

8. The **Kolhapur Corpus of Indian English** (Shastri, 1985, 1988) contains 1 million words of written Indian English from the year 1978. Its texts were selected from the same text categories as the Brown Corpus and is available from ICAME.

9. The **American Heritage Intermediate Corpus** (Carroll, Davies, & Richman, 1971) consists of over 5 million words of written American English from the most widely used books in grades 3 through 9. It was compiled as a database for the American Heritage School Dictionary.

10. The **Birmingham Collection of English Text (BCET)** (Renouf, 1984, 1987; Sinclair & Kirby, 1990), compiled from 1980–1985 by J. Sinclair, A. Renouf, and J. Clear, contains 20 million words of written (18.5) and spoken (1.5) language (mostly British) used in producing a series of Collins COBUILD reference and teaching works. It also contains 20 million words of speech from a public inquiry including the complete transcripts of the 18-month-long inquiry into the plan for constructing the Sizewell nuclear power station. It is intended to be representative of modern British English and therefore consists of samples of current and general usage (rather than technical use), from adult speakers without regional dialects, and excludes poetry and drama. For more information: A. J. Renouf, Research and Development Unit for English Language Studies, 50 Edgbaston Park Road, Birmingham B15 2RX, UK; Tel: +44 (21) 414 3935; FAX: +44 (21) 414 6203; email: renoufaj@bham.ac.uk.

11. The **Longman/Lancaster English Language Corpus** (Summers, 1991) consists of 30 million words of mainly British and American English texts. Begun in 1985, it contains varied stylistic levels and text types, and is intended for lexicographic and academic research.   For more information: Longman/Lancaster English Language Corpus, Longman Group Ltd., Longman House, Burnt Mill, Harlow, Essex CM20 2JE, UK.

12. The **Corpus of Spoken American English (CSAE)** (in progress), will be a database of one million words of spoken American English, encompassing a wide range of spoken language types (Chafe, Du Bois, & Thompson, 1992). The corpus will be disseminated as widely as possible in several formats, including a printed book and an interactive computer format that will allow simultaneous access to transcription and sound. The creation of the Corpus of Spoken American English will be coordinated with the ICE project (described next), of which the CSAE is the officially designated representative for the United States.   For information: Wallace Chafe, John Du Bois, or Sandra Thompson, Department of Linguistics, University of California, Santa Barbara, CA 93106, USA; Tel: +1 (805) 961-3776.

13. The **International Corpus of English (ICE)** (Greenbaum, 1988, 1990, 1992) (in progress), was begun in 1988 for the purpose of providing comparable data for comparative studies of national varieties of English internationally. Under the coordination of Sidney Greenbaum, Department of English, University College London, parallel corpora of spoken and written texts will be compiled for a number of regions, including the United States, Australia, the United Kingdom, Wales, Canada, New Zealand, India, East Africa, Nigeria, Jamaica and others, using uniform classification and encoding schemes. The American English component of this project is the CSAE, described above. Each regional corpus will contain one million running words, half from spoken and half from written language. The material in each regional corpus must date from no earlier than 1990 and no later than the end of 1993 and will come from speakers 18 years or older with education through the medium of English. In addition, there are plans for nonregional supplementary corpora of written translations into English, international spoken communication, and EFL (English as a foreign language) teaching texts (see Francis, 1989). The ICE data will ultimately be made available together with original sound recordings and possibly also digitized recordings for a concordance format.

14. The **British National Corpus (BNC)** (Quirk, 1992) (in progress) is to be an electronic corpus of 100 million words of contemporary spoken and written British English. Texts will represent a cross-section of a wide range of

styles of current written and spoken English. A uniform target encoding scheme will be defined, conforming to the international Standard Generalised Markup Language (SGML), in which all texts in the corpus will be stored and distributed. The corpus is to be automatically tagged with word-class labels to enhance its value for linguistic research. Special purpose tools developed for manipulation and processing of the corpus will be distributed together with it. The BNC is intended to provide the UK research and industrial communities with state-of-the-art corpus and lexical resources, as a solid basis for the development and exploitation of new products in the rapidly expanding field of natural language processing as applied to British English. These resources will be made widely available under appropriate licensing conditions and at minimum cost to the academic research community and also to the wider industrial research community. Begun in 1991, this 3-year project is managed by Jeremy Clear, with major participation from Oxford University Press (OUP), Longman Group UK Ltd, the British Library, and the Universities of Oxford and Lancaster. For more information: Jeremy Clear, Oxford University Press, Walton Street, Oxford OX2 6DP, UK; Tel: +44 (865) 56767; FAX: +44 (865) 56646; email: JHCLEAR@vax.oxford.ac.uk.

15. The **Bellcore Lexical Research Corpora** (Walker, 1987) were compiled to support corpus linguistics and computational lexicography research. They include textbases of 200 million words of newswire text (New York Times, Associated Press), 50 million words of magazine and journal articles, a collection of English machine-readable dictionaries and other machine-readable reference books, electronic-mail digests, and assorted smaller texts. For more information: Donald E. Walker, Language and Knowledge Resources Research, Bellcore, MRE 2A–379, 445 South Street, Morristown, NJ 07960–1910, USA; FAX: +1 (201) 829–5981; email: walker@bellcore.com.

16. Established in 1989, the **Association for Computational Linguistics Data Collection Initiative (ACL/DCI)** (Church & Liberman, 1991; Liberman, 1989; Walker, 1991, 1992) is an activity which collects machine readable text to support scientific and humanistic research, and distributes it at cost and without royalties. Its first CD-ROM, available for only $25, contains about 300 Mb of Wall Street Journal text, about 180 Mb of scientific abstracts, the full text of the 1979 edition of the Collins English Dictionary in the form of a typographer's tape, and some samples of tagged and parsed text from the Penn Treebank project. Its second CD-ROM will contain most or all of six years of the Hansard corpus, that is, Canadian parliamentary sessions, in bilingual French/English aligned format. For more information: Mark Liberman,

Department of Linguistics, University of Pennsylvania, Philadelphia, PA 19104, USA; FAX: +1 (215) 573-2091; email: myl@unagi.cis.upenn.edu.

17. The **European Corpus Initiative (ACL/ECI)** (in progress), which is patterned after the ACL/DCI, was established in 1992 to bring together existing materials in as many major European languages as possible, and to make these available in digital form and in a consistent format to the research community at cost and without royalties. The ECI welcomes contributions from all researchers and will distribute the data on CD-ROMs, the number depending on the ultimate size of the archive. For more information (to contribute or obtain data): Henry Thompson, HCRC, University of Edinburgh, 2 Buccleuch Place, Edinburgh, EH8 92W, Scotland; FAX: +44 (31) 650-4587; email: eucorp@cogsci.ed.ac.uk.

18. The **Cambridge Language Survey (CLS)** (in progress) is an international multilingual survey of language. Under sponsorship from industry and government sources, and in cooperation with other projects, the CLS is bringing together existing data from a variety of languages, starting with English, French, German, Dutch, Italian, Spanish and Japanese, with the intent to code this data semantically and to prepare concordances and multilingual corpora, parallel and aligned, for educational and such publishing uses as the preparation of multilingual dictionaries and other reference books. The data will be made as available as possible, perhaps including distribution via CD-ROM. For more information: Paul Procter, Cambridge University Press, Edinburgh Building, Shaftesbury Rd., Cambridge CB2 2RU, UK; Tel: +44 (223) 325052; FAX: +44 (223) 315052; email: psp10@phx.cam.ac.uk.

19. The DARPA-funded **Linguistic Data Consortium (LDC)** (in progress) was inaugurated in the Spring of 1992. Its formation was stimulated by the establishment of the Data Collection Initiative (DCI) of the Association for Computational Linguistics (ACL), but also strongly influenced by cooperative work in the speech community that led to the development of corpora consisting of digits and of acoustic-phonetic data pronounced by multiple speakers. The LDC is intended to develop and distribute large amounts of linguistic data (e.g., speech, text, lexicons, and grammars) to assist the development of speech- and text-processing systems. The data will include large quantities of raw and annotated (i.e., syntactically and/or semantically tagged) text and speech (billions of words of text and thousands of hours of speech), a large lexicon, and a broad coverage grammar of English. The data will also include whatever additional materials (including foreign language materials) the Consortium can obtain by exchange or on other reasonable terms. Data are to be provided on CD-ROM on a subscription basis to

universities and corporations.   Although the Consortium does not need exclusive rights to donated data, DARPA does intend to make its growing holdings available exclusively through the Consortium.   General membership fees will be set at affordable levels, and foreign members will be considered if access to foreign data can be assured. The Consortium may be established as a separate legal entity, such as a nonprofit corporation or other form of association.   For further information: Mark Liberman, Department of Linguistics, University of Pennsylvania, Philadelphia, PA 19104, USA; email: myl@unagi.cis.upenn.edu.

20. **American News Stories** consists of approximately 250,000 words of written American English consisting of Associated Press news stories in December 1979 (available from the Oxford Text Archive).

21. The Nijmegen **TOSCA Corpus** (Oostdijk, 1988) is a textbank of 75 works (1.5 million words) of educated written British English drawn from a variety of genres meant to be read rather than spoken (i.e., excluding poetry, plays and speeches), compiled for studies of linguistic variation.   For more information: Dr. Jan Aarts and Prof. C. Koster, Directors, The Nijmegen Research Group for Corpus Linguistics, Department of English, University of Nijmegen, Erasmusplein 1, NL–6525 HT Nijmegen, The Netherlands; Tel: +31 (80) 512836; email: cor_hvh@hnykun52.

22. The **Melbourne-Surrey Corpus** (Ahmad & Corbett, 1987) consists of 100,000 words of Australian newspaper texts and is available from ICAME.

23. The **Corpus of English-Canadian Writing**, is a textbank of 3 million words of Canadian English from magazines, books, and newspapers, gathered beginning in 1984, and representing a wide variety of genre categories in common with the LOB and Brown corpora, plus "Feminism" and "Computing."   For more information: Margery Fee, Strathy Language Unit, 207 Stuart Street, Room 316, Rideau Building, Queen's University, Kingston, Ontario, Canada K7L 3N6; email: feem@qucdn.bitnet.

24. The **Warwick Corpus** is approximately 2.5 million words of written British English (letters, fiction and other genres) compiled by J. M Gill for use in research aimed at the automatic generation of Braille by computer (available from the OTA).

25. The **Cornell corpus** (Hayes 1988; Hayes & Ahrens, 1988) is a 1.6 million word corpus, consisting of 1151 written or spoken British and American English texts, representing a wide variety of language types.   It was compiled in the 1980's for a study on lexical adaptation of parents to children. The spoken samples range from abortion debates to the Patty Hearst trial to

television situation comedies. It is available from the CHILDES archive (described above).

26. **NEXIS, LEXIS,** and **MEDIS** (owned by Mead Data Central) and **WESTLAW** (run by the West Corporation) are commercial archives. These are used by newswriters, lawyers, and doctors, but they tend to be very expensive. NEXIS contains newspapers (New York Times, Reuters, Business Week), newsletters, and other periodicals from the 1980s to the present and is used by columnists such as William Safire. LEXIS and WESTLAW contain legal codes and almost all legal decisions at the federal and state level in the United States and several European countries from far back to very current. MEDIS is a medical literature database.

B. Running Text: French Language

1. The **Oxford Text Archive (OTA)** has a number of literary holdings in the French language.

2. The **Hansard corpus** contains six years of Canadian Parliamentary sessions, in English/French bilingual aligned format, and is available from the ACL/DCI.

3. The **Ottawa-Hull Corpus of Spoken French** (Poplack, 1989) is 3.5 million words, compiled in 1985 to address issues of sociolinguistic variation and language contact. Respondents were selected from two contiguous cities on the border between Ontario and Quebec, in an unbiased manner to reflect a carefully balanced sampling grid of occupational, age, sex and other variables. To avoid Labov's "observer paradox," the data were recorded by trained community members. For more information: Shana Poplack, Linguistics Department, University of Ottawa, Ottawa, Ontario, Canada; email: sxpaf@uottawa.bitnet.

4. The **Trésor de la Langue Française (TLF)** (Treasury of the French Language) contains about 2,000 texts (150 million words) of a variety of types of written French—from novels and poetry to biology and mathematics—stretching from the 17th to the 20th centuries, the result of a cooperative project between the Centre National de la Recherche Scientifique and the University of Chicago. Access to the ARTFL database is organized through a consortium of user-institutions, in most cases universities and colleges, each of which pays an annual subscription fee. The data will soon also be available on CD-ROM together with access software for UNIX systems. For more information, contact: Mark Olsen, ARTFL Project, American and French Research on the

Treasury of the French Language, Department of Romance Languages, University of Chicago, 1050 East 59th Street, Chicago, IL 60637, USA; Tel: (312) 702–8488; email: artfl@artfl.uchicago.edu or mark@gide.uchicago.edu.

C. Running Text: German language

The **Mannheim Corpus** (Teubert, 1984) is a textbank of 8 million words of modern literary prose and nonfiction, available from the Oxford Text Archive and also from the Institut für Deutsche Sprache, University of Mannheim, Friedrich-Karl-Strasse-12, Postfach 5409, D–6800 Mannheim, Germany. The Institut für Deutsche Sprache also houses the **Bonner Zeitungskorpus**, a three million word collection of representative samples from German newspapers between 1949 and 1974, and the **Freiburger Corpus**, a textbank of one-half million words from 224 texts and documents, including discussions, interviews, speeches, reports, narrations, and documentary. The **LIMAS Corpus** of modern German is 1.1 million words, constructed by the same rules as the Brown Corpus. It is available from the Institut für Deutsche Sprache. It is also available together with software on HD floppies for 1000 DM from Gerd Willee, email: upk000@dbnrhrz1.bitnet or upk000@ibm.rhrz.uni–bonn. The **Pfeffer Spoken German Corpus**, collected in 1961, contains 400 12-minute spontaneous interviews covering 25 different topics, recorded in 60 locations in Germany (including both former East and West), Austria, and Switzerland. The speakers represent diverse demographic characteristics with regard to gender, age, education, and geography. For information: the Oxford Text Archive or Randall L. Jones, Department of German, 4096 JKHB, Brigham Young University, Provo, UT 84602, USA; Tel: +1 (801) 378–3513; email: jones@byuvm.bitnet. Finally, the **Ulm Textbank** is mainly a textbank of psychiatric interviews, together with a very powerful text retrieval and concordance package (Mergenthaler, 1985). For more information: Erhard Mergenthaler, University of Ulm, Germany; email: lu07@dmarum8.bitnet. The **Muenster Textbank** contains 94 million words of newspaper text. For more information, Lothar Lemnitzer, lothar@hendrix.uni-muenster.de.

D. Running Text: Italian Language

The **PIXI Corpora** are transcripts of service encounters in comparable bookshops in Italy and England and are available through the Oxford Text Archive (described in fuller detail above with the English Language Corpora). The **Pisa Corpus** consists of 3.5 million words of Italian. For more information: Antonio Zampolli, Istitute di Linguistica Computazionale, Via

Della Faggiola 32, University of Pisa, I–56100 Pisa, Italy; email: glottolo@icnucevm.bitnet.

E. Running Text: Other Languages

Besides English, French, German and Italian, electronic corpora are increasingly available also in other languages. The Oxford Text Archive contains a diverse sampling of languages, best surveyed in the OTA catalog itself. The resources listed in this section are from other locations. (See also the other entries under "Data Sources: Surveys" above.)

The Center for **Native (American) Languages of the Plains and the Southwest**, at University of Colorado, has electronic versions of the Dorsey Omaha-Ponca texts in its Siouan Archives, and has several dictionary projects (Winnebago, Siouan, and Lakhota).

For **Australian indigenous languages,** please see the entry for the AIATSIS Aboriginal Studies Electronic Data Archive under "Electronic Data Archives and Repositories" above.

For **Danish** there are two corpora of written Danish from fiction, newspapers and professional texts: the *DANWORD corpus* is 1.25 million words (see Maegaard and Ruus, 1987), housed at the University of Copenhagen; *DK87* and *DK88* are one million words apiece, from work published in 1987 and 1988, respectively, and are available from: Henning Bergenholtz, The Aarhus School of Business, Fuglesange Alle 4, DK–8210 Aarhus V.

Regarding **Estonian,** a corpus is in progress at the Laboratory of the Estonian Language, Tartu University, EE2400 Tartu, Estonia.

Regarding **Finnish** corpora, contact: Fred Karlsson, Department of General Linguistics, University of Helsinki, Hallituskatu 11, SF–00100 Helsinki, Finland; email: fkarlsso@ling.helsinki.fi

For **Spanish,** the *Archivo Digital de Manuscritos y Textos Españoles* is available on CD-ROM. For more information: Charles Faulhaber, Department of Spanish and Portuguese, University of California, Berkeley, CA 94720; Tel: +1 (510) 642–0471; email: cbf@athena.berkeley.edu.

Swedish language corpora are surveyed and summarized in Gellerstam (1992).

Regarding **Yugoslavian,** there is the *YU-CORPUS*. It consists of mainly contemporary fiction prose in Serbo-Croatian, with the main areas represented: Serbia, Croatia, Montenegro, and Bosnia-Hercegovina. The corpus consists of 15 files for a total of approximately 700,000 words. These files are available via anonymous ftp at aau.dk (129.142.17.240) in the directory /home/ftp/pub/slav. For more information: Henning Moerk, Slavisk Institut,

Aarhus Universitet, Ny Munkegade 116, 8000 Aarhus C, Denmark; Tel: +45 (86) 136555; FAX: +45 (86) 192155; email: slavhenn@aau.dk.

F. Language Acquisition

1. **Child Language Acquisition.** The main archive for child language data is the *Child Language Exchange System (CHILDES)*, described earlier.

The *Polytechnic of Wales Corpus* (Fawcett, 1980) compiled by R. Fawcett and M. Perkins between 1978 and 1984, consists of 100,000 words of children's English (ages 6 to 12), gathered in Pontypridd, South Wales. The data are from 120 children (balanced by age, sex, and socioeconomic status and screened to exclude those with strong Welsh or other second language influence), recorded at play and in interview with an adult. The computer files contain detailed grammatical tagging and have been fully hand-parsed using an extension of Systemic Functional Grammar developed by Fawcett which includes functional and formal categories. These are available from the ICAME Archive. The recorded tapes and four volumes of transcripts with intonation contours are available for the cost of materials from: Robin Fawcett, Department of Behavioral and Communication Studies, Polytechnic of Wales, Treforest, Cardiff CF 37 1DL, UK.

2. **Adult or Second Language Acquisition.** The *European Science Foundation Second Language Data Bank* (ESFSLDB) consists of longitudinal data obtained systematically over a 3-year period from adult migrant workers in five nations in Europe with a focus on language learning in the absence of formal instruction (see Perdue, 1984, in press). This very large database contains texts of interviews, narratives, role plays, picture descriptions, and other data gathered mostly on a roughly monthly basis from the same informants during the course of this time period. The informants were chosen to be comparable in terms of age, recency of arrival, level of education, and other factors, and represented 10 combinations of source language (Moroccan Arabic, Italian, Spanish, Finnish, and Punjabi) and target language (French, English, Dutch, German, Sweden). The data and Word Cruncher software are accessible for noncommercial research with signed agreement, available through file server (psyli@hnympi51.bitnet), tapes, diskettes, or CD-ROM. For more information: Kees v.d.Veer, Technical Group, Max-Planck-Institut fuer Psycholinguistik, Postbus 310, NL-6500 AH Nijmegen, The Netherlands; Tel: +31 (80) 521–911; email: kees@mpi.nl.

The *Montreal Corpus* was gathered for a project headed by Prof. K. Connors concerning the acquisition of French as a second language by anglophones and lusophones in Montreal. The data consist of three sets of interviews each from anglophones, lusophones, and a control group of French speakers. The corpus is available for research in magnetic form. For more information: Michel Lenoble, Litterature Comparee, Universite de Montreal, Montreal, Canada; email: lenoblem@umtlvr.bitnet.

G. Phonetic Databases

1. The **DARPA Speech Recognition Research Databases** consist of phonetic transcriptions of sentences read aloud by American adults from various parts of the country. These databases include both a speaker-independent (a few sentences from many speakers) and a speaker-dependent (a lot of speech from a few speakers) part—designed for use in training and testing both speaker-independent and speaker-dependent recognition systems. Digitized versions are also available. For more information see Fisher, Doddington, and Goudie-Marshall (1986), Lamel, Kassel, and Seneff (1986), and Price, Fisher, Bernstein, and Pallet (1988).

2. The **Phonetic Database** (PDB) at the University of Victoria consists of language files in MS-DOS format that run with Micro Speech Lab/KayLab hardware/software and illustrate speech sounds of some less frequently encountered languages. Each language has about 40–50 words and a few to several sentences of text encoded. It is intended to provide illustrative and archival samples of different languages from field data and lab recordings. Some languages represented are Egyptian Arabic, Cantonese, Modern Standard Chinese, Scots Gaelic, Inuktitut, Korean, Miriam, Ditidaht, Nyangumarta, Rutooro, Runyoro, Skagit, Spokane, Turkish, Umpila, Xhosa, Yoruba, Sinhala, and Japanese. Files are being converted to 20K sampled data for use with CSL (KayLab) and ASL programs (on the IBM). Concordance material is in written text format. For more information contact John Esling, Linguistics Department, University of Victoria, British Columbia, Canada; email: VQPLOT@UVVM.bitnet.

3. The **Multi-Language Speech Database** (in progress) is to be a large 10–language database of digitized speech recordings over the telephone. Plans are to gather five minutes of speech from each of 100 native speakers in each of 10 languages. This database is scheduled for completion in mid-1992, and will be made available to researchers at nominal cost together with software (developed for UNIX xwindows) to display and interactively modify the speech files, and signal processing functions that compute different parameters of the speech waveform. For more information: Ronald Cole, Center for Spoken Language Understanding, Oregon Graduate Institute of Science and

Technology, 19600 NW Von Neumann Dr., Beaverton, OR   97006–1999, USA; Tel: +1 (503) 690–1159; email: cole@cse.ogi.edu.

H. Electronic Dictionaries

1. See the **Wooldridge list** of machine-readable dictionaries mentioned under "Data Sources: Surveys."

2. The **Oxford Text Archive** (OTA) distributes several machine-readable dictionaries, including some in languages other than English. These are listed and described, together with illustrative examples of the more widely used, in the file ota/dicts/info, available via anonymous ftp from black.ox.ac.uk (or 129.67.1.165).

3. The second edition of the **Oxford English Dictionary** is available on CD-ROM from: Electronic Publishing Division, Oxford University Press, 200 Madison Avenue, New York NY 10016; Tel (212) 679–7300, ext. 7370; or Electronic Publishing Division, Oxford University Press, Walton Street, Oxford OX2 6DP; Tel: +44 (865) 267979; email OUPJSC@VAX.OXFORD.AC.UK.

4. **Le Robert Electronique** is the electronic version of the nine-volume English-French dictionary by Robert Grant, *De La Langue Française* (1985 edition). It is available on CD-ROM for $995 (U.S.) from Chadwyck-Healey Inc., 1101 King Street, Alexandria, VA 22314, USA; Tel: +1 (703) 683–4890 or +1 (800) 752–0515; FAX: +1 (703) 683–7589; or Chadwyck-Healey Ltd., Cambridge Place, Cambridge CB2 1NR, UK; Tel: +44 (223) 311479; FAX: +44 (223) 66440.

I. Lexical Databanks

As noted in the introduction, this sampling of resources is probably less complete than for the corpora and textbanks of running texts.   References relating to corpus-based lexicography include: Altenberg (1990), Atkins, Clear, and Ostler (1992), Boguraev and Briscoe (1988), Gellerstam (1988), Sinclair (1987, 1992), and Walker (1992).

1. The **MRC Psycholinguistic Database**, described in Coltheart (1981), consists of 150,837 entries from the Shorter OED with various forms of additional information (including part of speech, the British pronunciation, rating of concreteness, familiarity, and frequencies from Kucera–Francis and Thorndike–Lorge) for various subsets of words. It is available together with computer programs for efficient access, written in C for UNIX systems via anonymous ftp from laurel.ocs.mq.edu.au (or 137.111.3.11) as the file

pub/wrec/incoming/mrc.tar.Z (binary) or from the Oxford Text Archive (black.ox.ac.uk or 129.67.1.165) in the directory ota/dicts/1054. The Macintosh version has been produced by Philip Quinlan and is marketed by the Oxford University Press.

2. The DARPA-funded **Consortium for Lexical Research (CLR)** (under development). Begun in 1989 and modeled partly after large data projects such as the British National Corpus, the CLR is an organization for sharing lexical data and tools used to perform research on natural language dictionaries and lexicons, and for communicating the results of that research. It is intended to make available to the whole natural language processing community certain resources now held by only a few groups that have special relationships with companies or dictionary publishers. The CLR would as far as is practically possible accept contributions from any source, regardless of theoretical orientation, and make them available as widely as possible for research. It will be located at the Computing Research Laboratory, Box 30001, Las Cruces, New Mexico, USA, under the direction of Yorick Wilks and an ACL committee consisting of Roy Byrd, Ralph Grishman, Mark Liberman and Don Walker. An annual fee will be charged for membership. For information on participating in the CLR as a provider or consumer of data, tools, or services, or on joining the lexical information list: Natural Language Research, Consortium for Lexical Research, Computing Research Lab, New Mexico State University, Las Cruces, NM 88003, USA; Tel: +1 (505) 646–5466; FAX: +1 (505) 646–6218; email: lexical@nmsu.edu or lexical@nmsu.bitnet.

3. The **Centre for Lexical Information (CELEX)** has a relational database containing lexical data on present-day Dutch (400,000 word forms), English (150,000 word forms), and German (51,000 word forms) that it makes available to institutes and companies for language and speech research and for the development of language- and speech-oriented technological systems. It contains detailed information on orthography, phonology, morphology, and syntax, as well as word frequencies based on the COBUILD corpus (described above). New information on translation equivalency is currently being developed, along with additional syntactic and semantic subcategorizations to establish semantic links among the three databases. The CELEX user interface was specially designed to make it easy for nontechnical people to use the databases. Researchers from several countries can log onto CELEX remotely and use it interactively. Costs for noncommercial use are modest; for commercial use, somewhat more expensive. If the network connections are not sufficient, then CELEX can prepare the information you require and send it on tape. For more information: CELEX—Centre for Lexical Information,

University of Nijmegen, Wundtlaan 1, 6525 XD NIJMEGEN, The Netherlands; email: celex@celex.kun.nl or celex@hnympi52.bitnet.

4. **ACQUILEX** (Boguraev, Briscoe, Calzolari, Cater, Meijs, & Zampolli, 1988) is a project funded by the European Community to draw on and extend current work on extracting data from published machine-readable databases in multiple languages and formalizing the data to facilitate the algorithmic processing of language. It is described also in Walker (1992).

5. The **Cambridge Language Survey (CLS)** is described above under "English Language" Corpora.

6. **Japanese Electronic Dictionary Research Project** (in progress) is a corpus-based project described in Walker (1991). Details of the corpus itself were not mentioned in this source but will no doubt become widely known as the project continues.

J. Treebanks

These are databanks containing not only part of speech tags but also labeled constituent structures (e.g., noun phrase, adverbial phrase, coordinate clause). Some treebanks were mentioned briefly above in the descriptions of the Brown and LOB corpora (under "Running text: English Language"). Bracketed structures have also been added to some texts in the LLC (see Svartvik, 1990). For parsed child language data, see 5F above. For a discussion of treebanks and methods used in compiling them, see Leech & Garside (1991).

1. The **Lancaster–Leeds Treebank**, compiled by G. Sampson and G. N. Leech, is a treebank of hand-parsed phrase structure analyses of 45,000 words from the LOB (written British English) representing all 15 of the LOB categories of text types. For more information: Carol Lockhart, CCALAS Secretary, Department of Linguistics and Phonetics, University of Leeds, Leeds LS2 9JT, UK.

2. The **Lancaster Parsed Corpus** (Garside, Leech & Sampson, 1987) is a treebank of approximately 140,000 words from the LOB Corpus (written British English) from all 15 LOB text types. The sentences were all automatically parsed with the UCREL parsing systems, using statistics derived from the Lancaster-Leeds Treebank. It is available for limited distribution. For more information: UCREL Secretary, Department of Linguistics and Modern English Language, University of Lancaster, Lancaster LA1 4YT, UK.

3. The **Linguistic DataBase System** (LDB) (de Haan, 1987; Lancashire, 1991; van Halteren & Oostdijk, 1988; van Halteren & van den Heuvel, 1990)

was developed by the TOSCA group at Nijmegen University. It is a software package which is distributed together with "syntactic analysis trees" of all utterances from the 130,000-word Nijmegen Corpus of modern British English. The LDB was designed to be easy to use even for computing novices and is independent of both formalism and language, so it is possible to use it for any other kind of analyzed corpus. It can be used on VAX VMS systems, IBM PCs (AT preferred), and UNIX systems, and in 1991 cost about $60 US for academic institutions ($3000 US for others). It can be used to examine trees, search for utterances with given properties, and handle database-wide queries about constructs in the utterances. A fully functional demonstration version is available for any MS-DOS machine with hard disk. For more information: Hans van Halteren, TOSCA Group, Department of English, University of Nijmegen, P.O. Box 9103, 6500 HD Nijmegen, The Netherlands; Tel: +31 (80) 512836; email: cor_hvh@kunrc1.urc.kun.nl.

4. The **Penn Treebank** is a databank of labeled bracketed structures, for samples of written language (the Wall Street Journal) (98%) and spoken language (Mari Ostendorf's WBUR radio transcripts) (2%). For more information: The Penn Treebank Project, Department of Computer and Information Science, School of Engineering and Applied Science, University of Pennsylvania, Philadelphia, PA 19104, USA; email: khanr@unagi.cis.upenn.edu or maryann@unagi.cis.upenn.edu.

5. **Treebank of Written and Spoken American English** (in progress) (as mentioned in Walker, 1992) is to contain potentially millions of sentences together with part of speech tags, skeletal syntactic parsings and intonational boundaries for spoken language. The data themselves will be derived at least in part from the ACL/DCI collection and to be available through it. For more information: Mitch Marcus, Department of Linguistics, University of Pennsylvania, Philadelphia, PA, USA; email: mitch@linc.cis.upenn.edu.

K. Translation into English

1. English/French parallel texts are provided in the Hansards material of the ACL/DCI, already described.

2. English/Italian parallel texts are part of the Italian Reference Corpus in Pisa (see Bindi, Calzolari, Monachini, & Pirrelli, 1991).

3. Parallel texts in various combinations of languages are also one of the goals of the Cambridge Language Survey (CLS), described above under "English Language" Corpora.

4. English translations of Pravda 1986–1987 on a CD-ROM disk for IBM PC or compatible for $249 U.S. (Product #CD–1505, Description: PRAVDA) are available from: Bureau of Electronic Publishing, P. O. Box 779, Upper Montclair, NJ 07043, USA; Tech. Support: Tel: +1 (201) 746–3033; Orders: +1 (201) 857–4300; FAX: +1 (201) 857–3031.

6. LITERATURE PERTAINING TO ELECTRONIC CORPORA

As sources for further information and bibliographies in corpus linguistics, lexicography, computational linguistics, and humanities, there are: (1) the 200-work bibliography of research involving the London-Lund Corpus in Svartvik (1990, Chapter 1), (2) the Altenberg (1991) bibliography of corpus research on written and spoken language, which is available also via the ICAME fileserver (fileserv@nora.hd.uib.no), together with annual updates, and (3) Susan Hockey's survey of resources for computer-assisted research in literature and other humanities (included as the Appendix below).

ACKNOWLEDGEMENTS

This compilation is indebted to all of the sources cited above, but I wish to thank especially the following people, for their help in providing information, corrections, and suggestions concerning earlier versions: Lou Burnard, Helmut Feldweg, Stig Johansson, Knut Hofland, Henry Kucera, Laura Proctor, and Don Walker. As already noted, this survey has benefited from several other corpus surveys concerning the earlier corpora: Chafe et al. (1992), Taylor, Leech & Fligelstone (1989), the Georgetown University Catalog of Projects in Electronic Text, and the catalogs of the OTA and ICAME archives. Any errors that remain are my own.

Given the rapid growth in this area, I have no doubt inadvertently overlooked some relevant projects. To them, my apologies. Similarly, mention of any resource is not intended as endorsement.

This work was made possible financially by the Institute of Cognitive Studies, University of California at Berkeley, which, however, bears no responsibility for opinions expressed in these pages.

Finally, I wish to thank Susan Hockey for her generosity in contributing the materials in the Appendix.

REFERENCES

Ahmad, K., & Corbett, G. (1987). The Melbourne-Surrey Corpus, *ICAME Journal*, **11**, 39–43.

Altenberg, B. (1990). Spoken English and the dictionary. In J. Svartvik (Ed.), *The London-Lund Corpus of Spoken English: Description and Research* (pp. 177–191). Lund, Sweden: Lund University Press.

Altenberg, B. (1991). A bibliography of publications relating to English computer corpora. In S. Johansson & A. B. Stenström (Eds.), *English computer corpora: Selected papers and research guide*. New York: Mouton de Gruyter.

Atkins, B. H., Clear, J., & Ostler, N. (1992). Corpus design criteria. *Literary and Linguistic Computing*, **7**, 1–16.

Bachenko, J., & Fitzpatrick, E. (1990). A computational grammar of discourse-neutral prosodic phrasing in English. *Computational Linguistics*, **16**, 155–170.

Bindi, R., Calzolari, N., Monachini, M., & Pirrelli, V. (1991). Lexical knowledge acquisition from textual corpora: A multivariate statistic approach as an integration to traditional methodologies. In *Using Corpora: Proceedings of the Seventh Annual New OED Conference* (pp. 170–196). Waterloo, Ontario: UW Centre for the New OED and Text Research.

Brill, E., Magerman, D., Marcus, M., & Santorini, B. (1990). Deducing linguistic structure from the statistics of large corpora. *Proceedings of the DARPA Speech and Natural Language Workshop, June 1990* (pp. 275–282). Arlington, VA: Defense Advanced Research Projects Agency.

Boguraev, B., & Briscoe, T. (Eds.). (1988). *Computational lexicography for natural language processing*. London: Longman.

Boguraev, B., Briscoe, T., Calzolari, N., Cater, A., Meijs, W., & Zampolli, A. (1988). *Acquisition of lexical knowledge for natural language processing systems. Proposal for ESPRIT basic research activities*. Cambridge: Cambridge University Press.

Bruce, G. (1989). Report from the IPA Working Group on Suprasegmental Categories. *Lund University, Depatment of Linguistics Working Papers*, **35**, 25–40.

Bruce, G. (1992). Comments. In J. Svartvik (Ed.), *Directions in corpus linguistics: Proceedings of the Nobel Symposium 82, Stockholm, August 4–8, 1991* (pp. 145–147). New York: Mouton de Gruyter.

Bruce, G., & Touati, P. (1990). On the analysis of prosody in spontaneous dialogue. *Lund University, Depatment of Linguistics Working Papers*, **36**, 37–55.

Burnard, L. (1991). What is SGML and how does it help? (Document No. TEI EDW 25). Text Encoding Initiative listserver (listserv@uicvm.bitnet).

Carroll, J. B., Davies, P., & Richman, B. (1971). *The American Heritage word frequency book*. Boston: Houghton Mifflin.

Chafe, W. (1992). The importance of corpus linguistics to understanding the nature of language. In J. Svartvik (Ed.), *Directions in corpus linguistics: Proceedings of the Nobel Symposium 82* (pp. 79–97). New York: Mouton de Gruyter.

Chafe, W., Du Bois, J. W., & Thompson, S. A. (1992). *Corpus of spoken American English*. Unpublished manuscript, Linguistics Department, University of California, Santa Barbara.

Church, K. W. (1991). [Review of J. Aarts & W. Meijs (Eds.), *Theory and practice in corpus linguistics*]. *Computational Linguistics*, **17**, 99–103.

Church, K. W., & Hanks, P. (1990). Word association norms, mutual information, and lexicography. *Computational Linguistics*, **16**, 22–29.

Church, K. W., & Liberman, M. (1991). A status report on the ACL/DCI. *Using corpora: Proceedings from the New OED Conference* (pp. 84–91) Waterloo, Ontario: The University of Waterloo Centre for the New OED and Text Research.

Coltheart, M. (1981). The MRC psycholinguistic database. *Quarterly Journal of Experimental Psychology*, **33A**, 497–505.

Dawson, J. L. (1977). Texts in machine-readable form and the University of Cambridge Literary and Linguistics Computing Centre. *CAMDAP*, **7**, 25–30.

de Haan, P. (1987). Exploring the linguistic database: Noun phrase complexity and language variation. In W. Meijs (Ed.), *Corpus linguistics and beyond*. Amsterdam: Rodopi.

Fawcett. R. P. (1980). Language development in children 6–12: Interim report. *Linguistics*, **18**, 953–958.

Fillmore, C. J. (1992). "Corpus linguistics" or "Computer-aided armchair linguistics." In J. Svartvik (Ed.), *Directions in corpus linguistics: Proceedings of the Nobel Symposium 82* (pp. 35–60). New York: Mouton de Gruyter.

Fisher, W. M., Doddington, G. R., & Goudie-Marshall, K. M. (1986). *Proceedings of the Speech Recognition Workshop* (Defense Advanced Research Projects Agency, Information Processing Techniques Office Report No. AD–A165 977).

Francis, W. N. (1980). A tagged corpus—Problems and prospects. In S. Greenbaum, G. Leech, & J. Svartvik (Eds.), *Studies in English linguistics for Randolph Quirk* (pp. 192–209). New York: Longman.

Francis, W. N. (1982). Problems of assembling and computerizing large corpora. In S. Johansson (Ed.), *Computer corpora in English language research* (pp. 7–24). Bergen: Norwegian Computing Centre for the Humanities.

Francis, W. N. (1992). Language corpora B. C. In J. Svartvik (Ed.), *Directions in corpus linguistics: Proceedings of the Nobel Symposium 82* (pp. 18–32). New York: Mouton de Gruyter.

Francis, W. N. & Kucera, H. (Eds.). (1979). *Manual of information to accompany a Standard Corpus of Present-Day Edited American English for use with digital computers* (rev. ed.). Providence, RI: Brown University, Department of Linguistics.

Francis, W. N. & Kucera, H. (1982). Frequency analysis of English usage: Lexicon and grammar. Boston: Houghton Mifflin.

Garside, R., Leech, G., & Sampson, G. (Eds.). (1987). *The computational analysis of English: A corpus-based approach*. New York: Longman.

Gavioli, L., & Mansfield, G. (1990). *The PIXI Corpora: Bookshop encounters in English and Italian*. Bologna, Italy: CLUEB.

Gellerstam, M. (Ed.). (1988). *Studies in computer-aided lexicology*. Stockholm: Almqvist & Wiksell International.

Gellerstam, M. (1992). Modern Swedish corpora. In J. Svartvik (Ed.), *Directions in corpus linguistics*. (pp. 149–163). New York: Mouton de Gruyter.

Greenbaum, S. (1988). A proposal for an international computerized corpus of English. *World Englishes*, **7**, 315.

Greenbaum, S. (1990). Standard English and the international corpus of English. *World Englishes*, **9**, 79–83.

Greenbaum, S. (1992). A new corpus of English: ICE. In J. Svartvik (Ed.), *Directions in corpus linguistics* (pp. 1761–179). New York: Mouton de Gruyter.

Halliday, M. A. K. (1992). Language as system and language as instance: The corpus as a theoretical construct. In J. Svartvik (Ed.), *Directions in corpus linguistics* (pp. 61–77). New York: Mouton de Gruyter.

Hayes, D. P. (1988). Speaking and writing: distinct patterns of word choice. *Journal of Memory and Language*, **27**, 572–585.

Hayes, D. P., & Ahrens, M. G. (1988). Vocabulary simplification for children: A special case of 'motherese'? *Journal of Child Language*, **15**, 395–410.

Hindle, D., & Rooth, M. (1991). Structural ambiguity and lexical relations. In *Proceedings of the 29th Annual Meeting of the Association for Computational Linguistics* (229–236).

Hockey, S. (1991). The ACH–ACL–ALLC Text Encoding Initiative: An overview (Document No. TEI J16). Text Encoding Initiative listserver (listserv@uicvm.bitnet).

Hughes, J. J. (1987). Bits, bytes and Biblical studies: A resource guide for the use of computers in Biblical and Classical studies. Grand Rapids, MI: Academie Books.

Ihalainen, O. (1987). The Helsinki Corpus of English Texts: Diachronic and dialectical—Report on work in progress, *ICAME Journal*, **11**, 58–60.

Johansson, S., Atwell, E., Garside, R., & Leech, G. (1986). *The tagged LOB corpus: Users' manual*. Bergen: Norwegian Computing Centre for the Humanities.

Johansson, S., Leech, G., & Goodluck, H. (1978). Manual of information to accompany the Lancaster–Oslo/Bergen corpus of British English for use with digital computers. Oslo: Department of English, University of Oslo.

Kjellmer, G. (1984). Some thoughts on collocational distinctiveness. In J. Aarts & W. Meijs (Eds.), *Corpus linguistics: Recent developments in the use of computer corpora in English language research* (pp. 163–171). Amsterdam: Rodopi.

Knowles, G., & Lawrence, L. (1987). Automatic intonation assignment. In R. Garside, G. Leech, & G. Sampson (Eds.), *The computational analysis of English: A corpus-based approach*. London: Longman.

Kucera, H. (1992). Brown corpus. In S. C. Shapiro (Ed.), *Encyclopedia of artificial intelligence* (Vol. 1, pp. 128–130). New York: John Wiley & Sons.

Kucera, H., & Francis, W. N. (1967). *Computational analysis of present-day American English*. Providence, RI: Brown University Press.

Kytö, M. (Ed.). (1991). *Manual to the Diachronic part of the Helsinki Corpus of English Texts: Coding conventions and lists of source texts*. Helsinki: University of Helsinki, Department of English. [Distributed by the Norwegian Computing Centre for the Humanities, Bergen].

Lamel, L. F., Kassel, R. H., & Seneff, S. (1986). Speech database development: Design and analysis of the acoustic-phonetic corpus. In *Proceedings of the DARPA Speech Recognition Workshop* (pp. 100–109).

Lancashire, I. (1991). [Review of H. van Halteren & T. van den Heuvel, *Linguistics exploration of syntactic databases: The use of the Nijmegen Linguistic DataBase program*]. *Computational Linguistics*, **17**, 457–461.

Lancashire, I., & McCarty, W. (Eds.). (1988). *Humanities computing yearbook 1988*. Oxford: Oxford University Press.

Leech, G. (1991). The state of the art in corpus linguistics. In K. Aijmer & B. Altenberg (Eds.), *English corpus linguistics: Studies in honour of Jan Svartvik* (pp. 8–29). London: Longman.

Leech, G. (1992). Corpora and theories of linguistic performance. In J. Svartvik (Ed.), *Directions in corpus linguistics: Proceedings of the Nobel Symposium 82* (pp. 105–122). New York: Mouton de Gruyter.

Leech, G., & Garside, R. (1991). Running a grammar factory: The production of syntactically analysed corpora or treebanks. In S. Johansson & A. B. Stenström (Eds.), *English computer corpora: Selected papers and research guide* (pp. 15–32). New York: Mouton de Gruyter.

Leech, G., & Svartvik, J. (1975). *A communicative grammar of English*. London: Longman.

Levelt, W. J. M., Mills, A., & Karmiloff, A. (1981). *Child language research in ESF countries: An inventory*. Strasbourg: ESF.

Liberman, M. (1989). Text on tap: The ACL/DCI. In *Proceedings of the DARPA Speech and Natural Language Workshop, Oct. 1989*. San Mateo, CA: Morgan Kaufman.

MacWhinney, B. (1991). *The CHILDES project: Tools for analyzing talk*. Hillsdale, NJ: Lawrence Erlbaum Associates.

MacWhinney, B., & Snow, C. (1985). The child language data exchange system. *Journal of Child Language, 12*, 271–296.

Maegaard, B., & Ruus, H. (1987). The compilation and use of a text corpus. In A. Cappelli, L. Cignoni, & C. Peters (Eds.), *Studies in honour of Roberto Busa SJ* (pp. 103–122). Pisa: Giardini.

Mergenthaler, E. (1985). Textbank systems: Computer science applied in the field of psychoanalysis. New York: Springer-Verlag.

Morris, J., & Hirst, G. (1991). Lexical cohesion computed by thesaural relations as an indicator of the structure of text. *Computational Linguistics, 17*, 21–48.

Oostdijk, N. A. (1988). Corpus for Studying Linguistic Variation. *ICAME Journal, 12*.

Perdue, C. (Ed.). (1984). *Second language acquisition by adult immigrants. A field manual*. Rowley, MA: Newbury House.

Perdue, C. (Ed.). (in press). *The crosslinguistic study of second languages*. Cambridge: Cambridge University Press.

Peters, P. H. (1987). Toward a corpus of Australian English. *ICAME Journal, 11*, 27–28.

Pierrehumbert, J. (1980). *The phonology and phonetics of English intonation*. Bloomington, IN: Indiana University Linguistics Club.

Pierrehumbert, J., & Hirschberg, J. (1990). The meaning of intonational contours in the interpretation of discourse. In P. Cohen, J. Morgan, & M. Pollack (Eds.), *Intentions in Communication*. Cambridge, MA: MIT Press.

Price, P. J., Fisher, W. M., Bernstein, J., & Pallet, D. S. (1988). The DARPA 1000-word resource management database for continuous speech recognition. In *Proceedings of the 1988 IEEE International Conference on Acoustics, Speech, and Signal Processing* (pp. 651–654).

Poplack, S. (1989). The care and handling of a mega-corpus: The Ottawa–Hull French Project. In R. W. Fasold & D. Schiffrin (Eds.), *Language change and variation* (pp. 411–444). Philadelphia: John Benjamins.

Quirk, R. (1974). *The linguist and the English language*. London: Longman.

Quirk, R. (1992). On corpus principles and design. In J. Svartvik (Ed.), *Directions in corpus linguistics* (pp. 457–469). New York: Mouton de Gruyter.

Quirk, R., Greenbaum, S., Leech, G., & Svartvik, J. (1972). *A grammar of contemporary English.* London: Longman.

Quirk, R., Greenbaum, S., Leech, G., & Svartvik, J. (1985). *A comprehensive grammar of the English language.* London: Longman.

Raben, J., & Gaunt, M. (forthcoming). Electronic scholars research guide.

Renouf, A. J. (1984). Corpus development at Birmingham University. In J. Aarts & W. Meijs (Eds.), *Corpus linguistics: Recent developments in the use of computer corpora in English language research.* Amsterdam: Rodopi.

Renouf, A. J. (1987). Corpus development. In J. M. Sinclair (Ed.), *Looking up: An account of the Cobuild Project in lexical computing.* London: Collins ELT.

Rissanen, M. (1992). The diachronic corpus as a window to the history of English. In J. Svartvik (Ed.), *Directions in corpus linguistics: Proceedings of the Nobel Symposium 82* (pp. 185–205). New York: Mouton de Gruyter.

Sampson, G. (1992). Probabilistic paesing. In J. Svartvik (Ed.), *Directions in corpus linguistics: Proceedings of the Nobel Symposium 82* (pp. 425–447). New York: Mouton de Gruyter.

Shastri, S. V. (1985). A computer corpus of present-day Indian English: A preliminary report. *ICAME Journal, 9,* 9–10.

Shastri, S. V. (1988). The Kolhapur Corpus of Indian English and work done on its basis so far. *ICAME Journal, 12,* 15–26.

Silverman, K., Beckman, M., Pitrelli, J., Ostendorf, M., Wightman, C., Price, P., Pierrehumbert, J., & Hirschberg, J. (1992, October). *TOBI: A standard for labeling English prosody.* Paper presented at the International Conference on Spoken Language Processing, Banff, Alberta, Canada.

Sinclair, J. M. (1982). Reflections on computer corpora in English language research. In S. Johansson (Ed.), *Computer corpora in English language research* (pp. 1–6). Bergen: Norwegian Computing Centre for the Humanities.

Sinclair, J. M. (Ed.). (1987). *Looking up: An account of the COBUILD project in lexical computing.* London: Collins ELT.

Sinclair, J. M. (1992). The automatic analysis of corpora. In J. Svartvik (Ed.), *Directions in corpus linguistics: Proceedings of the Nobel Symposium 82* (pp. 379–397). New York: Mouton de Gruyter.

Sinclair, J. M., & Kirby, D. M. (1990). Progress in English computational lexicography. *World Englishes, 9,* 21–36.

Sperberg-McQueen, C. M., & Burnard, L. (Eds.). (1992). *Guidelines for electronic text encoding and interchange* (Document No. TEI P2, Chapter 34). Text Encoding Initiative listserver (listserv@uicvm.bitnet).

Summers, D. (1991). Longman computerization initiatives, corpus building, semantic analysis and Prolog version of LDOCE by Cheng-ming Guo. *Proceedings of the International Workshop on Electronic Dictionaries* (Document No. EDR TR-031, pp. 141–152). Tokyo: Japan Electronic Dictionary Research Institute.

Svartvik, J. (Ed.). (1990). *The London–Lund Corpus of Spoken English: Description and research.* Lund, Sweden: Lund University Press.

Svartvik, J. (Ed.). (1992a). Corpus linguistics comes of age. *Directions in corpus linguistics: Proceedings of the Nobel Symposium 82* (pp. 7–13). New York: Mouton de Gruyter.

Svartvik, J. (Ed.). (1992b). *The London–Lund corpus of spoken English: Users' manual.* Lund, Sweden: Lund University, Department of English. [Distributed by the Norwegian Computing Centre for the Humanities, Bergen].

Svartvik, J., & Quirk, R. (Eds.). (1980). *A corpus of spoken English.* Lund, Sweden: Lund University Press.

Taylor, L., Leech, G., & Fligelstone, S. (1989). Lancaster preliminary survey of machine-readable language corpora. Lancaster, England: University of Lancaster, Linguistics Department. [available from the Humanist and NCCH fileservers, see text]

Taylor, L., Leech, G., & Fligelstone, S. (1991). A survey of English machine-readable corpora. In S. Johansson & A. B. Stenström (Eds.), *English computer corpora: Selected papers and research guide* (pp. 319–354). New York: Mouton de Gruyter.

Teubert, W. (1984). Setting up a lexicographical data-base for German. In R. R. K. Hartmann (Ed.), *LEXeter '83 Proceedings: Papers from the International Conference on Lexicography at Exeter* (pp. 425–429). Tübingen: Max Niemeyer.

van Halteren, H., & Oostdijk, N. (1988). Using an analyzed corpus as a linguistic database. In J. Roper (Ed.), *Computers in literary and linguistic computing: Proceedings of the XIIIth ALLC Conference (Norwich 1986).* Geneva: Slatkine.

van Halteren, H., & van den Heuvel, T. (1990). *Linguistic exploitation of syntactic databases.* Amsterdam: Rodopi.

Walker, D. E. (1987). Knowledge resource tools for accessing large text files. In A. Cappelli, L. Cignoni, & C. Peters (Eds.), *Studies in honour of Roberto Busa SJ* (pp. 279–300). Pisa: Giardini.

Walker, D. E. (1991). The ecology of language. *Proceedings of the International Workshop on Electronic Dictionarie* (Document No. EDR TR–031, pp. 10–22). Tokyo, Japan: Japan Electronic Dictionary Research Instititute.

Walker, D. E. (1992). Developing computational lexical resources. In E. F. Kittay & A. Lehrer (Eds). *Frames, fields, and contrasts: New essays in semantic and lexical organization.* Hillsdale, NJ: Lawrence Erlbaum Associates.

Walker, D. E., & Hockey, S. (1991). The Text Encoding Initiative. *Bulletin du CID.* Paris: Centre des Hautes Etudes Internationales d'Informatique Documentaire.

HUMANITIES COMPUTING BIBLIOGRAPHY (APRIL 1990)
SUSAN HOCKEY (HOCKEY@ZODIAC.BITNET)
(REPRODUCED WITH PERMISSION)

The following bibliography was distributed at a tutorial on Text Analysis Computing given by the CTI Centre for Literature and Linguistic Studies at the Conference on Computers and Teaching in the Humanities held in St. Andrews, Scotland in April 1990. The CTI Centre for Literature and Linguistic Studies is based at Oxford University. While some of these items date back over 10 years, they do cover all the basic techniques for text-based humanities computing, some of which are not so easy to find in more recent publications. All these items except the very latest, and of course many more, can be found in Ian Lancashire and Willard McCarty (Eds.), *Humanities Computing Yearbook*, Oxford University Press, 1989, which is an excellent starting point. The CTI promotes and supports the use of computers in teaching text-based subjects and is part of the Centre for Humanities Computing at Oxford, which supports several research projects in text analysis computing. The bibliography has been compiled over several years and is used in a course taught by Susan Hockey, the Director of the CTI Centre, at Oxford and in lectures and seminars given elsewhere by staff of the Centre. The CTI Centre has a mailing list, which can be contacted at CTITEXT@VAX.OX.AC.UK.

Books–Monographs

Butler, C. (1985). *Computers in linguistics.* New York: Blackwell.

Hockey, S. (1980). *A guide to computer applications in the humanities.* London: Duckworth.

Oakman, R. L. (1980). *Computer methods for literary research* (1st ed.). Columbia: University of South Carolina Press.

Oakman, R. L. (1984). *Computer methods for literary research* (rev. ed.). Athens: University of Georgia Press.

Rudall, B. H., & Corns, T. N. (1987). *Computers and literature: A practical guide.* Cambridge, MA: Tunbridge Wells; Kent: Abacus Press.

Books–Resources Guides

Hughes, J. J. (1987). *Bits, bytes and Biblical studies: A resource guide for the use of computers in Biblical and Classical studies.* Grand Rapids, MI: Academie Books.

Lancashire, I., & McCarty, W. (Eds.). (1988). *Humanities computing yearbook 1988.* Oxford: Oxford University Press.

Conference Proceedings

Ager, D. E., Knowles, F. E., & Smith, J. M. (Eds.). (1978). *Advances in computer-aided literary and linguistic research*. Birmingham, England: University of Aston, Department of Modern Languages. (ALLC, 1978)

Aitken, A. J., Bailey, R. W., & Hamilton-Smith, N. (Eds.). (1973). *The computer and literary studies*. Edinburgh: Edinburgh University Press. (Edinburgh conference, 1972)

Allen, R. F. (Ed.). (1986). *Data bases in the humanities and social sciences*. Osprey, FL: Paradigm.

Bailey, R. W. (Ed.). (1982). *Computing in the humanities: Papers from the Fifth International Conference on Computing in the Humanities*. Amsterdam: North Holland.

Burton, S. K., & Short, D. D. (Eds.). (1983). *Sixth International Conference on Computers and the Humanities*. Rockville, MD: Computer Science Press.

Cameron, K. C., Dodd, W. S., & Rahtz, S. P. Q. (Eds.). (1986). *Computers and modern language studies*. Chichester, England: Ellis Horwood; New York: Halsted.

Charpentier, C., & David, J. (Eds.). (1985). *La recherche française par ordinateur en langue et litterature*. Geneva: Slatkine.

Choueka, Y. (Ed.). (1990). *Computers in literary and linguistic research: Proceedings of the Fifteenth International ALLC Conference*. Geneva: Slatkine.

Cignoni, L., & Peters, C. (Eds.). (1983). *Computers in literary and linguistic research: Proceedings of the Seventh International Symposium of the Association for Literary and Linguistic Computing, Pisa 1982*. Pisa: Giardini.

Hamesse, J., & Zampolli, A. (Eds.). (1985). *Computers in literary and linguistic computing: Proceedings of the Eleventh International ALLC Conference*. Geneva: Slatkine.

Jones, A., & Churchhouse, R. F. (Eds.). (1977). *The computer in literary and linguistic studies: Proceedings of the Third International Symposium*. Cardiff: University of Wales Press. (ALLC, 1974)

Lusignan, S., & North, J. S. (Eds.). (1977). *Computing in the humanities: Proceedings of the Third International Conference on Computing in the Humanities*. Waterloo, Ontario: University of Waterloo Press.

Miall, D. S. (1990). *Humanities and the computer: New directions*. Oxford: Oxford University Press. (Conference on computers and teaching in the humanities, 1988)

Mitchell, J. L. (Ed.). (1974). *Computers in the humanities*. Edinburgh: Edinburgh University Press. (ICCH, 1973)

Patton, P. C., & Holoien, R. A. (Eds.). (1981). *Computing in the humanities*. Lexington, MA: Heath.

Raben, J., & Marks, G. (Eds.). (1980). *Databases in the humanities and social sciences*. Amsterdam: North Holland.

Rahtz, S. (Ed.). (1987). *Information technology in the humanities: Tools, techniques and applications*. Chichester: Ellis Horwood; New York: Halsted.

Roper, J. P. G. (Ed.). (1988). *Computers in literary and linguistic research: Proceedings of the Thirteenth International ALLC Conference*. Geneva: Slatkine.

Wisbey, R. A. (Ed.). (1971). *The computer in literary and linguistic research*. Cambridge: Cambridge University Press. (Cambridge conference, 1970)

Periodicals

Bulletin of the Association for Literary and Linguistic Computing ("ALLC Bulletin") (1973-1985). Three issues per year.

Computational Linguistics, formerly *American Journal of Computational Linguistics*. Now in volume 16 (1990). Quarterly published by ACL.

Computers and the Humanities (1966–). Has had several publishers. Now published by Kluwer. Four issues per year (six from 1989). Covers language, literature, history, archaeology, music, and education. Sponsored by ACH.

ICAME Journal, formerly *ICAME News*, International Computer Archive of Modern English, Norwegian Computing Centre for the Humanities, PO Box 53, Bergen, Norway.

Journal of the Association for Literary and Linguistic Computing ("ALLC Journal") (1980-1985). Was also published by the ALLC. Two issues per year.

Linguistica Computazionale, Giardini, Pisa.

Literary and Linguistic Computing (1986–). In 1986, the ALLC publications were merged into a single journal, Literary and Linguistic Computing, published by Oxford University Press. It covers all aspects of computer usage in literary and linguistic research.

Revue: Informatique et Statistique dans les Sciences Humaines.

Newsletters

Bits and Bytes Review (1986–). Bits and Bytes Computer Resources, 623 North Iowa Avenue, Whitefish, MT 59937, USA. Reviews of software, hardware, and new publications.

Computers in Literature (1990). Newsletter of the CTI Centre for Literature and Linguistic Studies, OUCS, 13 Banbury Road, Oxford, UK.

There are also a number of newsletters for specific subjects, some of which, for example, CALCULI (Classics) and CAMDAP (Medieval Studies), are now defunct but contain useful information. The Humanities Computing Newsletter, Office for Humanities Communication, Bath, UK, and Ontario Humanities Computing, obtainable from CCH, Toronto are two of the best general ones.

English for Language Research—Corpus Linguistics

Garside, R., Leech, G., & Sampson, G. (Eds.). (1987). *The computational analysis of English: A corpus-based approach.* New York: Longman.

Sinclair, J. M. (Ed.). (1987). *Looking up: An account of the COBUILD project in lexical computing.* London: Collins.

Stylistic Analysis

Burrows, J. F. (1987). *Computation into criticism: A study of Jane Austen's novels and an experiment in method.* Oxford: Oxford University Press.

Dolezel, L., & Bailey, R. W. (1969). *Statistics and style.* New York: Elsevier.

Ellegard, A. (1962). *Who was Junius?* Stockholm: Almqvist and Wiksell.

Kenny, A. (1978). *The Aristotelian ethics.* Oxford: Clarendon.

Kenny, A. (1982). *The computation of style: An introduction to statistics for students of literature and humanities.* New York: Pergamon.

Morton, A. Q. (1978). *Literary detection—How to prove authorship and fraud in literature and documents.* Epping, England: Bowker; New York: Scribner.

Morton, A. Q., & Winspear, A. D. (1971). *It's Greek to the computer.* Montreal: Harvest House.

Mosteller, F., & Wallace, D. L. (1964). *Inference and disputed authorship: The Federalist.* Reading, MA: Addison Wesley.

Muller, C. (1973). *Initiation aux méthodes de la statistique linguistique.* Paris: Hachette.

Author Index

Subject Index

Page numbers in standard type refer to Part I (Transcription) and Part III (Resources). Page numbers in italics refer to Part II (Coding).

A

Abandoned utterances, 65, see also Truncation

Accents; Stress, 24–25, 36, 43, 57–58, 78, 88, 99, 106–109, 116–118, 121, 128

Accents, if unpredictable, see Predictability and transcription

Activation states of ideas (active, semiactive, inactive), 33, 39–41, see also Given information

Aphasic speech, 126

Applause, 99, 114, see also Nonlexical events

Archives and repositories, see also Centers and associations

AIATSIS Aboriginal Studies, 280

Child Language Exchange System (CHILDES), 279

Gutenberg Project Archive, 280

International Computer Archive of Modern English (ICAME), 278

Oxford Text Archive (OTA), 278, 280

Articulation, 34, 128–129

marcato, 63, 69–70

see also Emphatic speech; Voice quality

B

Backchannel, 37, 50, 63, 77, 80, 116, 128, *231, 246,* see also Nonlexical vocalizations

Background information, 8, 12–19, 74, 81, 92, 111–112, 135, 140, see also Context

Booster, 25, 58, see also Emphatic speech

Breathing, 48, 64, 66–67, see also Nonlexical vocalizations

C

Catalogs and surveys of electronic data

Cambridge Literature and Linguistics Computing Centre, 282

Georgetown Catalog of Projects in Electronic Text, 281

Lancaster Survey, 280

Linguistic Society of America (LSA), 282

Oxford Text Archive (OTA), 280

of electronic publications, 280–282

of CD-ROM Projects, 282

of electronic dictionaries, 281

of electronic texts in philosophy, 281

Centers and associations, see also Archives and repositories

Association for Computers and the Humanities (ACH), 270

Association for Computational Linguistics (ACL), 271

Association for Literary and Linguistic Computing (ALLC), 271